MESSIAH
~ *made* ~
MANIFEST

◆ EXPLORING *the* BOOK OF MORMON ◆
as a TEMPLE

JON TERRENCE GORTON

CFI
An Imprint of Cedar Fort, Inc.
Springville, Utah

ISBN 13: 978-1-4621-1176-3

Published by CFI, an imprint of Cedar Fort, Inc.
2373 W. 700 S., Springville, UT 84663
Distributed by Cedar Fort, Inc., www.cedarfort.com

LIBRARY OF CONGRESS CATALOGING-IN-PUBLICATION DATA

Gorton, Jon Terrence, 1955- author.
Messiah made manifest : exploring the Book of Mormon as a temple / Jon Terrence Gorton.
  pages cm
Summary: A reader-focused exploration of how the Book of Mormon fulfills the two greatest roles of any temple: making the Messiah fully manifest and making the Abrahamic Covenants available.
ISBN 978-1-4621-1176-3
1. Mormon temples. 2. Book of Mormon—Criticism, interpretation, etc. 3. Church of Jesus Christ of Latter-day Saints—Doctrines. 4. Christian life—Mormon authors. I. Title.

BX8643.T4G67 2013
246'.95893—Doctrine & Covenants23

   2013021996

Cover design by Shawnda T. Craig
Cover design © 2013 Lyle Mortimer
Typeset by Emily S. Chambers

Printed in the United States of America

10 9 8 7 6 5 4 3 2 1

To Alice Gorton, my mom,
the first latter-day saint I ever met
and the clearest manifestation that God is love

ACKNOWLEDGMENTS

I wrote this book at the suggestion of my wife, Lisa, with my daughters Carli and Nikki as the projected audience. Those three served throughout as the constant muses for this project; what wouldn't sound right to them isn't part of this book. And a writer couldn't find a better standard.

The real subject of this book is gratitude, and as I look back on its completion, I also thank:

- My brother Bob, who led me to the tree, invited me to partake, and showed me what it means to be a fully committed disciple of Christ.

- Lyle Mortimer, who founded and steers CFI as an additional place for fledgling LDS authors to gather and share. Is there a more tangible act of faith than taking such huge risks on unknown, uncelebrated authors?

- All the dedicated professionals Lyle has brought to CFI, who have generously given their time and talents to assure this book's success, including Shersta Gatica, Justin Kelly, Catherine Christensen, Emily Chambers, Rebecca Greenwood, Shawnda Craig, Steve Acevedo, and Kelly Martinez.

And, going back a bit further—to the very foundations—I acknowledge all those nuns and priests at Our Lady of Lourdes Church and Grammar School, who in their own ways substituted for Father Lehi, inviting all-too-wandering sheep in white shirts with blue plaid ties to flee from Babylon, grip the iron rod, and find in Jesus Christ alone light, life, and truth.

CONTENTS

CONTENTS

PREFACE
Participating in the Book of Mormon Journey

President Ezra Taft Benson challenged "our Church writers, teachers, and leaders" to "let us know how [the Book of Mormon] leads us to Christ and answers our personal problems and those of the world." I could choose no better summary for the purpose and content of this book. President Benson also encouraged members to "tell us more Book of Mormon conversion stories that will strengthen our faith and prepare great missionaries."[1] When I was baptized, I committed to the Lord that I'd be ready and willing to bear witness of the restored gospel and of His guiding hand in my conversion; perhaps someone could benefit from the perspectives of a former New York Catholic altar boy turned LDS convert and then English professor—especially how crucial the Book of Mormon was in my coming to know and follow the Savior.

ACTIVATING YOUR OWN LIAHONA

Since I see the Book of Mormon as an epic adventure we embark upon each time we open its pages, I looked for ways to urge readers to step out upon their own odysseys. To encourage participation, I'll be asking a lot of questions, prompting you to search the Book of Mormon and words of other prophets. I invite you to write down your answers to each italicized question throughout the book—before you go on in your reading. Your own discoveries in response to these prompts will be exciting and instrumental in achieving the central goal of this book—knowing and following the Savior better as you personally survey the sacred hallways of the temple of Mormon. Please be sure to take along your own devices for activating the Liahona—which the Lord has placed beside your tent: pen and paper (or keyboard). These tools, along with the Book of Mormon, are shaped a bit differently than Lehi's ball and spindles but can serve much the same purpose.

THE SACRED AND THE SUBLIME IN THE BOOK OF MORMON

In focusing upon the Book of Mormon as an actual temple in which the most sacred events of eternity take place (especially, the full and plain manifestation of the Savior and His atoning mission), I know I am asking readers to stretch the normal boundaries of what a temple is and what it means to "enter" a temple. The best word available for the kind of experience the Lord offers as we open the gates of this scriptural temple is "sublime." A sublime experience by definition transcends rational and logical boundaries as it challenges, awakens, and inspires participants to escape the grasp of the routine, mundane, casual, or profane. An encounter with Nature often serves as the vehicle for such experiences (think of a visit to a raging water-fall, a vast cactus-filled desert landscape at twilight, or a seemingly primeval forest path), but great art, music, and writing may call upon the imagination as portals to the Sublime.

A sublime experience is a bit paradoxical: it humbles and sub-dues participants but then also exalts the soul, raising aspirations and bursting previous limitations. Ultimately, a sublime experience creates a sense of both duty and kinship to divinity—of both awe ("fear" in its original connotation) and worship. It is an experience that transports and transforms.

This kind of experience is described by William Wordsworth in the midst of his epic poem, *The Prelude*, as he and two companions ascend the highest peak of the British Isles, Mount Snowden, in Wales. Wordsworth's climb serves as a metaphor for the sublime encounters available as we enter and walk paths within the temple of Mormon—especially as our paths lead to God's very presence.

Our initial steps into the chambers of the temple of Mormon might start off somewhat unremarkably, but something marvelous and wonderful awaits us as we faithfully continue. "It was a close, warm, breezeless night," Wordsworth recalls, "with a dripping fog / Low-hung and thick that covered all the sky," and that soon "girt us round" as "we began to climb / The mountain-side." The ascent merges into a sort of "climbing routine" while "pensively we sank / Each into commerce with his private thoughts." But then, just as with our study, we may encounter something unanticipated—something our mortal minds would not even be *able* to anticipate: "At [his] feet the ground appeared to brighten, / And with a step or two seemed brighter still," when "instantly a light . . . / Fell like a flash." [2]

Unawares, Wordsworth has reached the summit, walks out of the surrounding fog, and beholds, with what seems like revelation, the bright moon-lit sky, the "silent sea" of mist beneath him, and the stream of mountains reaching into the Atlantic Ocean—all of which merged as one. As may happen in our Book of Mormon explorations, the encounter on the mountain serves to startle him into recognition of his true origins and potential, beyond mere mortal boundaries: the experience "raised" his "affections . . . from earth to heaven, from human to divine," providing an enhanced "consciousness of Whom [we] are" (114-6).

Such spiritual knowledge, the poet tells us, awakened within the "solemn temple" and sublime beauty of these "mountain solitudes," is accompanied by both restoration and power, particularly power to escape the world's hold upon us. Through that power, he—just as we, within the "solemn temple" of Mormon—can transcend the tendencies of

> Use and custom to bow down the soul
> Under a growing weight of vulgar sense,
> [That] substitute[s] a universe of death
> For that which moves with light and life informed,
> Actual, divine, and true . . .
> Hence, amid ills that vex and wrongs that crush
> Our hearts—that peace [w]hich passeth understanding
> . . . from this pure source
> Must come, or will by man be sought in vain. (14:124-129)

As spectacular as the results of this sublime manifestation of God's glory, it serves only as prelude to a still more powerful manifestation—that occurs when he takes the opportunity (as we do when we invite the Holy Ghost to guide our scriptural forays) to further reflect upon its meaning. Ultimately, such reflections lead to the font of all that exalts and transforms the soul: to love. This love may have been provoked by the sheer beauty of "the earth and all things that are upon the face of it . . . and its motions" (Alma 30:44; see also Doctrine & Covenants 88:41, 45–48), but finally leads to a deeper knowledge—or manifestation—of the creator, and thereby to the kind of love that we call worship, which never was better defined than here:

> *Love that breathes not without awe;*
> *Love that adores, but on the knees of prayer,*
> *By heaven inspired; that frees from chains the soul,*
> *Lifted, in union with the purest, best,*
> *Of earth-born passions, on the wings of praise*
> *Bearing a tribute to the Almighty's Throne. (14:181–7)*

Throughout the Book of Mormon, we hear prophets sing of such sublime peace and love—that follow from the manifestations of the Savior and His atoning gift to us—available within its pages. Such a manifestation empowers us to leave behind "a universe of death" and embrace "that which moves with light and life informed." "The remission of sins," writes Mormon to his son, "bringeth meekness, and lowliness of heart, and because of meekness and lowliness of heart cometh the visitation of the Holy Ghost, which Comforter filleth with hope and perfect love, which love endureth by diligence unto prayer, until the end shall come, when all the saints shall dwell with God" (Moroni 8:26).

As poetically described by Wordsworth, such knowledge and love of the Savior (in both senses of the word "of") empower us to rise above the most sordid and sorrowful worldly woes: "May not the things which I have written grieve thee," Mormon (and our Eternal Father, also) continues in another fatherly missive, after chronicling how completely both nations had severed themselves from any spiritual moorings, "to weigh thee down unto death."

But may Christ lift thee up,
and may his sufferings and death,
and the showing his body unto our fathers,
and his mercy and long-suffering,
and the hope of his glory and of eternal life,
rest in your mind forever. (Moroni 9:25)

It turns out that a very practical and concrete idea of the kind of sublime experience I am talking about—conveyed within the pages of the Book of Mormon—is readily available each time we walk into one of those sacred buildings erected throughout the world, the ones that bear nearly the same inscription upon their entrance as the Book of Mormon does upon its entrance: "Holiness to the Lord. The House of the Lord." [3]

Notes

1 "Flooding the Earth with the Book of Mormon, *Ensign*, November 1988.

2 *The Prelude*, 14:11–18, 35–49.

3 The equivalent "entrance inscription" of the temple of Mormon reads: "[Built] by way of commandment and also by the spirit of prophecy and of revelation . . . to show unto the remnant of the House of Israel what great things that the Lord has done . . . and that they may know the covenants of the Lord. . . . And also to the convincing of Jew and Gentile that JESUS is the CHRIST, the ETERNAL GOD, manifesting himself unto all nations."

I think the callings of various prophets contain these qualities of the sublime (see Moses 1:1–11; Isaiah 6:1–8; JS-H 1:11–17; Moses 6:26–36; 1 Nephi 1:5–15; Mosiah 4:1–3; 5:1–7).

"I will manifest myself," we learn
From his Word; beyond show or even reveal,
As divinity alone can seal
Upon us Truth, his light and life shall churn

Into our very souls, that we may discern
Silently somehow with thunderous peal,
Greater than carnal sight or sound, our real
Lord and Savior—as we simply turn

Over this book's leaf, entering again
The hallway of his holy house, full-drenched
And anointed in the Lamb's free-flowing blood
Streaming through its chambers, ingrained sins wrenched
From roots by love's torrent, the undammed flood
Of hosannas shouting anew: amen and amen.

INTRODUCTION

"And he did manifest himself unto them,
that they were redeemed by him." —Helaman 8:23

QUESTIONS TO CONTEMPLATE

- What are some of the important ways that you think the word "manifest" differs from such related words as "appear," "demonstrate," "perceive," "make apparent," "display," "declare," or "make evident"?

- Why might the Lord choose the word "manifest" to describe the kind of knowledge of the Savior available through these two locations in particular: 1) the scriptures and 2) the temple?

- How is the word "manifest" used in the New Testament? What might this teach us about its uses in the Book of Mormon?

"We ask thee, O Lord, to accept of this house . . . that the Son of Man might have a place to manifest himself to his people."
—Doctrine & Covenants 109:4–5

"And he testified that the things which he saw and heard, and also the things which he read in the book, manifested plainly of the coming of the Messiah, and also of the redemption of the world."
—1 Nephi 1:19

"And behold, whosoever believeth on my words [within the Book of Mormon], them will I visit with the manifestation of my Spirit; and they shall be born of me, even of water and of the Spirit."
—Doctrine & Covenants 5:16

"These last records . . . shall make known to all kindreds, tongues, and people, that the Lamb of God is the Son of the Eternal Father, and the Savior of the world; and that all men must come unto him, or they cannot be saved. . . . And it shall come to pass, that if the Gentiles shall hearken unto the Lamb of God in that day that he shall manifest himself unto them in word, and also in power, in very deed."
—*1 Nephi 13:40; 14:1*

"For behold, I have accepted this house, and my name shall be here; and I will manifest myself to my people in this house."
—*Doctrine & Covenants 110:7*[1]

You can see by these quotes above, and by the title of this book, that the word "manifest" will have a special place throughout. Why did the Lord choose this particular word to describe the kind of knowledge or appearances of Himself He makes available in two places above all: the holy temples and the Book of Mormon? What might the answer to this question teach us about the sacred role of the Book of Mormon?

Manifest is an interesting and powerful word—and not that easy to define. It has something to do with "make known," but adds an increased sense of clarity and vividness to the act of knowing: "distinctly perceived; hence, obvious to the understanding; apparent to the mind; easily apprehensible; plain; not obscure or hidden."[2] Something that is "manifest" is so clear as to be "unmistakable" and so obvious as to be "beyond doubt or question."[3] The word is formed by the Latin words for "hand" (*manus*) and "strike" (*fendere*) and therefore suggests knowledge that is "palpable" or as we might say, "striking." The Latin word *manifestus* literally meant "caught in the act." As a verb, the word "manifest" replaces words such as "show," "display," or "appear" in order to present a more precise and sophisticated notion of each of these actions.

NEW TESTAMENT USES OF "MANIFEST"

The word "manifest" as used in the New Testament Greek descends primarily from the Greek words *phaneroo*, "to put on display," and *emphanizo*, "to declare plainly." These New Testament equivalents of "manifest" are somehow more pronounced—and trustworthy—experiences than connoted through our English word "appear": "A person may 'appear' in a false guise or without a disclosure of what he truly is; to be manifested is to be revealed in one's true character (see 1 Peter 5:4; 1 John 1:1–5)."[4] *Phaneroo* is also similar to *apokalupsis* and *apokalupto*, which suggest the idea of "removing the veil from that which was veiled."[5] In the following uses of *phaneroo* in the New Testament, we notice the higher degree of knowledge available through this concept of "manifest" (note also how often this powerful kind of "manifestation" follows directly from the testimonies given through the apostles and the scriptures):

Romans 3:21: "But now the righteousness of God without [i.e., apart from] the Law has been manifested [phaneroo], being witnessed by the Law and the Prophets."

Romans 16:26: "But now is [the "gospel" or "the mystery" of the atoning mission of Jesus Christ] made manifest [phaneroo], and by the scriptures of the prophets, according to the commandment of the everlasting God, made known [phaneroo] to all nations for the obedience of faith."

Colossians 1:24–29: "Whereof I am made a minister, according to the dispensation of God which is given to me for you, to fulfill the word of God; Even the mystery which hath been hid from ages and from generations, but now is made manifest to his saints. . . . Whom we preach, warning every man, and teaching every man in all wisdom; that we may present every man perfect in Christ Jesus."[6]

"WHAT IS MANIFEST IS *VERY DISTINCTLY EVIDENT*"

One commentator explains the limitations of our English language to translate the full meaning and power of the word "manifest" as used in the scriptures:

The English word "appear" means primarily "to become visible;" the English word "manifest" primarily means "to be palpable," and hence a "manifesto," a proof, a public declaration. . . . The intention of John 3:21 or Ephesians 5:13 [where "manifest" is used] is *something deeper than mere appearance*, but we may never find a word in our language that will entirely rid it of some measure of ambiguity.[7]

The enhanced level of knowledge available in a "manifestation" is nicely relayed in this usage note, which places the act of being manifest three degrees beyond "clear," and more impressive and confirming than either "obvious" or "evident":

"What is clear can be seen readily; What is obvious lies directly in our way, and necessarily arrests our attention; What is evident is seen so clearly as to remove doubt; What is manifest is *very distinctly evident.*"[8]

Quite a word. We should pay special attention, I think, when the Lord uses such a power-packed word, especially when He uses that word to describe the kind of knowledge of the Savior made available through the Book of Mormon.

In this book, I invite readers to carefully examine what the Lord means when He tells us that the Book of Mormon's role is to make Jesus Christ, the Messiah, *manifest.* So palpable and striking is this manifestation that we may be said to enter the very house or dwelling of the Lord when we open this sacred book. There are many ways that the Lord makes a connection between the Book of Mormon and a temple. In this book, I will focus on just one: a sacred and supernal place where the Messiah is made fully *manifest* to us—so that we can come unto Him and embrace sacred covenants and blessings. Ultimately then, the path to salvation continues as we follow the Messiah made manifest into those physical temples where we may receive the saving ordinances of the gospel administered by those with keys and authority.

Notes

1 Further scriptural statements of the Book of Mormon's temple role of making the Messiah fully manifest to us: 2 Nephi 26:12–14, Doctrine & Covenants 19:26–27, Doctrine & Covenants 97:16, Moroni 10:4–5, Ether 2:12, the title page of the Book of Mormon.

2 1913 Webster Dictionary.

3 Dictionary.com.

4 Vines Expository Dictionary of the New Testament.

5 http://www.seekfind.net/Bible_Dictionary.

6 Additional New Testament uses of the word "manifest": John 17:6, Romans 1:19–20, Titus 1:2–3.

7 Charles Welch, *An Alphabetical Analysis of Terms and Texts*; emphasis added.

8 1913 Webster Dictionary; emphasis added.

Prayer
(After George Herbert)

Prayer: genie unjailed, Pegasus ridden,
Two mites' interest, compounded by seven,
Solomon's Ophir mine, now unhidden,
Disciple's periscope, peering to heaven;

Assault on Ego's fortress, repaired schism
Of head and heart, a thorn-adorned-crown;
Holy hues, refracted through spirit's prism,
Rest for the weary, head on Eden's down;

Soul's solo, aria on azure stage,
New-consumed shewbread, blazing menorah,
Alabaster spikenard, now sinner's aura,
Starry painting, on each eye's open page,
Angel stirring Bethesda's pool of grace
As we submerge, arising without a trace.

Part I

The Four Most Important Questions of Life

WHAT I HOPE YOU WILL GET OUT OF THIS PART

Just as is the case with the physical temples, important preparation precedes the glorious manifestations of the Lord: before seeking—and receiving—such a manifestation, we need to understand our place in Heavenly Father's plan, our divine origins and destiny, our need for a Savior, and the oppositions we must face and overcome as we turn to him. In other words, we need to understand *why* we must turn to the Savior, before learning *how* we turn to him. Therefore, in Part I of this book (just as in the Creation, Garden, and World rooms of the temple) we'll briefly focus on these foundational truths. Then we'll be better prepared to enter the "Celestial Room" or even the "Holy of Holies" in the temple of Mormon, where the Savior makes Himself fully manifest and His covenants fully available—which is the emphasis of Parts II and III. The next decision is ours—and eternity hangs in the balance. There could be no greater quest or more glorious adventure. And it all begins by opening a book.

QUESTIONS TO CONTEMPLATE

- Is there a particular spiritual experience above all that you wish you could have—that would cause you to become completely committed to following the Savior, putting aside any hesitations or doubts?

- In what ways does the world attempt to distract us from the living reality of our Heavenly Father and our Savior or else tempt us to completely deny such truths?

OPENING SCENARIOS FOR PART 1

How would you respond to each of these situations? (We'll have you return to these at the end of this section.)

Scenario #1

As David read once more the marvelous conversion story of Enos, he wondered why his prayers—as well as the prayers of his parents—had not yet made such a wonderful manifestation of the Savior's Atonement available to him. *Why not me,* he wondered?

Scenario #2

Jeff looked at the clock on his wall once more. It was a beautiful, clear summer morning. His backpack was all crammed with enough provisions for at least two days. He had his map all charted out for his mountain hike—to Avalanche Lake hidden high in the Adirondacks. Not many people know how to get there. But he was ready. He could almost taste the delicious cool water flowing from that secret spring he had discovered last year. He had just finished the Book of Enos and was reading through Mosiah 18. He glanced up again. Couldn't wait to put the Book of Enos to the test. He was ready to stay on his knees all day and night if he had to. He was so excited he couldn't wait any longer. He put his bookmark in the middle of a chapter, placed the book back on his nightstand, grabbed his compass, and dropped his pack in his vintage Ford pickup. *Now we'll see,* he said to himself.

THE FOUR QUESTIONS

There are four questions I would like you to consider. Your responses to these questions will have more effect upon your ability to know and follow the Savior—and therefore your welfare and happiness here and hereafter—than any other questions you could answer.

But then there is a problem. Not one of us is capable of answering any of these questions—on our own. Fortunately, we aren't left on our own. We can access a source of knowledge that goes beyond the limits of our mortal mind and senses. Those limits start with the things of the Spirit. "The things of God knoweth no man," The Apostle Paul explained, "but the Spirit of God."

> Now we have received, not the spirit of the world, but the spirit which is of God; that we might know the things that are freely given to us of God. Which things also we speak, not in the words which man's wisdom teacheth, but which the Holy Ghost teacheth; comparing spiritual things with spiritual. But the natural man receiveth not the things of the Spirit of God: for they are foolishness unto him: neither can he know them, because they are spiritually discerned. (1 Corinthians 2:11–15; see also Jacob 4:8; Alma 26:21; 36:5)

Yes, the Spirit of God works through our minds and senses—but magnifies them so that their mortal limits are exceeded. So, as I ask these questions, I invite you to seek the guidance of the Spirit as you look for answers. These promptings will come as you seek them. Often, as you exercise faith by putting your mind—and pen or keyboard—to work, you will have the exhilarating experience of feeling the Spirit guide and provide answers for you even as you are in the *process* of thinking and writing.

I'll warn you that two of the questions use a word that immediately adds enormous complexity to any question. The word is "why." When questions about spiritual principles begin with the word "why," the guidance of the Spirit is essential. Ready for the questions?

Question # 1: Does a person have to receive Jesus Christ to be saved (i.e., receive the gift of eternal life; be exalted in the Celestial Kingdom)? [Think . . . and listen . . . and follow your impressions.]

Question # 2: Why? [Think . . . and listen . . . and follow.]

Question # 3: Does a person have to receive the Book of Mormon to be saved (i.e., receive the gift of eternal life)? [Think . . . and listen . . . and follow.]

Question # 4: Why?

Grace

Is there a more beautiful word than grace?
Rain falling freely to refresh the earth,
The sun rising each day in a new birth
Of warmth and light, a mother's kiss to chase

Away defeat in this world's profane race;
Pure gifts, our acts of insufficient worth
To force or merit, presaged upon dearth
Alone. Above all these, came one to interlace

Both agony and love, from ev'ry pore
Let flow that bloody balm, and with head bowed
Beneath what scales of justice must allow
And with all that hell itself could plow
Into his soul, to Abba did implore:
"May these wounds their sins forever shroud."

SECTION ONE
Our Need for a Redeemer

OPENING SCENARIOS

(Respond to each of these scenarios right now, and then we'll return to these after we consider Questions 1 and 2—and give you a chance to respond once more.)

Scenario # 1

"It's actually quite liberating," Professor Sedgwick continued. "Once you get past this childish notion of some super-hero god coming to save you from some haunting spirit called the devil, you can finally learn to stand on your own two feet. You can get out of that comic strip that society or some church has created in your mind to keep you behaving like they want you to behave. You'll finally see through all that hocus-pocus and unlock your own hidden powers and potential that things like religions have stifled. Just watch the whole world open up to you for the first time in your life. Free at last."

Scenario # 2

"The human organism is astounding," the bearded speaker at the podium continued. "Adapted in every way to ensure that its genetic code will be transmitted. There's a gene for everything. Even a 'god gene.' That's right—a god gene. Something developed by nature over time that keeps societies from destroying each other. Genetically, nature has programmed us to posit some eternal being that rewards us with ecstasy in the next life if we just promote not only our own welfare, but the welfare of others—so that they can survive to transmit their genetic material also. Very tricky, nature, isn't it? It can even fool us into thinking we're being selfless or something called 'moral'—when we're actually just following some chemical and biological process preprogrammed inside our cells."

QUESTION # 1: DOES A PERSON HAVE TO RECEIVE JESUS CHRIST TO BE SAVED (I.E., TO RECEIVE ETERNAL LIFE)?

There is no more important question a person needs to successfully answer in this life. Likewise, there seems no greater goal in the world around us than to cause each of us to ignore or dismiss this question. We live inside a vast echo-chamber of voices constantly distracting our attention from such thoughts. And yet another—softer, stiller voice—somehow pierces the pandemonium, inviting each of us to fulfill a much nobler destiny, one that begins with an answer to this question.

The Spirit speaks to us in a variety of ways, but often simply brings a scripture to our minds. Did that happen to you? *If so, what scriptures can you think of that confirm this most critical of all eternal truths—that each of us relies completely upon Jesus Christ to be redeemed and must turn to Him for salvation?*

One of many scriptures that might come to mind in answer to that question is when the resurrected Savior speaks to the Nephites:

> Yea, verily I say unto you, if ye will come unto me ye shall have eternal life. Behold, mine arm of mercy is extended towards you, and whosoever will come, him will I receive, and blessed are those who come unto me.
>
> Behold, I am Jesus Christ the Son of God. I created the heavens and the earth, and all things that in them are. I was with the Father from the beginning. I am in the Father, and the Father in me; and in me hath the Father glorified his name. . . . And as many as have received me, to them have I given to become the sons of God; and even so will I to as many as shall believe on my name, for behold, by

me redemption cometh, and in me is the law of Moses fulfilled. (3 Nephi 9:14–15, 17)

The Spirit—and the scriptures—leave no room for doubt, equivocation, or qualification about this question:

> And moreover, I say unto you, that there shall be no other name given nor any other way nor means whereby salvation can come unto the children of men, only in and through the name of Christ, the Lord Omnipotent. (Mosiah 3:17–18; 4:2; see also Helaman 5:9; Alma 34:14; Doctrine & Covenants 76:22–24; Isaiah 43:11; John 3:17; 4:25–26; 14:6; Acts 4:12; 10:38–43; and so on.)

The still small voice of the Spirit thunders in our souls: *yes*, without question, we must receive Jesus Christ to be saved and exalted in the Kingdom of God.

QUESTION # 2: WHY?

We are naturally led to the next question: Why? *Why* must we receive Jesus Christ to be saved? This actually is quite a complex question—much more complex than might first appear. Your immediate response might be: "We must receive Jesus Christ because only he has the power to save us." But imagine asking the same question of someone who has never heard of Jesus Christ. "Saved from *what*?" might follow. She'd have to be aware of some *danger* she is in and that she is *personally incapable* of escaping from that danger on her own. She might also ask: "Who is Jesus Christ and why would he have this unique power?"

Yes, a lot of questions need answers before ever deciding to turn to Christ for salvation. "Just as a man does not really desire food until he is hungry," President Ezra Taft Benson teaches, "so he does not desire the salvation of Christ until he knows *why he needs Christ*."[1]

One of many powerful explanations of this vital doctrine comes early in the Book of Mormon. When Lehi taught his son Jacob about why we need to turn to Christ for redemption, he gave a cogent, inspired summary of the many things we need to understand. "The way is prepared," father Lehi taught, "from the fall of man, and salvation is free."

And men are instructed sufficiently that they know good from evil. And the law is given unto men. And by the law no flesh is justified; or, by the law men are cut off. Yea, by the temporal law they were cut off; and also, by the spiritual law they perish form that which is good, and become miserable forever.

Wherefore, redemption cometh in and through the Holy Messiah; for he is full of grace and truth. Behold, he offereth himself a sacrifice for sin, to answer the ends of the law, unto all those who have a broken heart and a contrite spirit; and unto none else can the ends of the law be answered. (2 Nephi 2:3–6)

"ISN'T RELIGION JUST A CRUTCH?"

It is perhaps not surprising that so many today feel no need to accept Christ as the Redeemer. The world (and the adversary) has convinced them they have no need to be redeemed; that there is no such thing as sin, a devil, or a battle between good and evil; no such thing as guilt or punishment; even no such thing as absolute truth or eternal verities. With such a free-floating philosophy of life, why even bother with the Savior's invitation to come unto Him to be saved?

Soon after I was baptized into the Lord's restored Church, I excitedly wrote home to a good friend to share the great news of the gospel—so that he too could receive these blessings. "Terry, don't you think that religion is just a crutch people use?" he wrote back.

How would you respond to such a question?

"Yes, the Savior's Atonement is definitely a crutch," I wrote. "A crutch that every one of us needs. Without His Atonement we would have no hope of rising above this world, of resurrecting from the dead, of returning to live again with our Heavenly Father."

My friend was using the word "crutch" in a pejorative sense—that we, in our weakness, look somewhere else for strength instead of relying upon ourselves. To rely upon Jesus Christ as a Redeemer to accomplish something for us that we were incapable of doing ourselves, seemed like a "cop-out" or a sign of surrender to him—and to many others in our world. "Turning to the Savior actually strengthens us," I wrote. "Only by relying upon him can we reach the potential each of us is destined to achieve—as eternal sons and daughters of God. What you call a 'crutch' is a *gift* that He offers us to help us overcome everything that keeps us from achieving that destiny. I am very thankful that Jesus Christ makes such a crutch available.

"Either all of this is true or it isn't," I continued. "If it's true, then it doesn't so much matter what words we use to describe it. But we need to live it." I then invited him to read the Book of Mormon in order to find out for himself.

THE KEY TO AN ABUNDANT LIFE

If you were to consider one quality, above all others, the presence or absence of which you can almost precisely measure in a person— even after just meeting that person briefly—what might that quality be? Likewise, what is one quality, the presence or absence of which determines the nobility or shallowness, the happiness or sorrow, the success or failure as parents, workers, and citizens than any other quality? Why?

I think that quality is gratitude. The key to living life abundantly is not admiring our own supposed self-sufficiency; it is conceding—and honoring—our debts to so many for so much; there is no more conspicuous or more pressing duty we owe each moment than gratitude.

Moses probably came away from his vision of the panoramic history of humanity (1:8) with such a recognition, instilling within him perhaps a prophet's most salient quality: gratitude—and an awareness of our complete dependence upon the hand of God. "Now for this cause," He tells us, "I know that man is nothing, which thing I never had supposed" (1:10).

Yet, nothing is so easy as taking gifts for granted. "If the stars should appear one night in a thousand years, how would men believe and adore; and preserve for many generations the remembrance of the city of God which had been shown!" Ralph Waldo Emerson wrote. "But every night come out these envoys of beauty, and light the universe with their admonishing smile."[2]

"I can't lend my brother-in-law any money," the comedian Henny Youngman quipped in this regard; "It gives him amnesia." How often do we forget our debts to the Lord after we have received

His gifts? When the rain was regular, the wicked paid no attention to Nephi's warnings or the Lord's commandments. But when "the earth was smitten that it was dry" and people "saw that they were about to perish by famine," they finally "began to remember the Lord their God; and they began to remember the words of Nephi." You can imagine how wonderful those first drops felt, as floods of gratitude dissolved self-centeredness: "And behold the people did rejoice and glorify God, and the whole face of the land was filled with rejoicing" (Helaman 11:6–7, 18).

Gratitude should be a choice we make every day, rather than after the cavalry arrives to save the day. In one of my favorite New Yorker cartoons, a bird perching on a branch explains to a camera-carrying birdwatcher: "I don't sing because I'm happy; I'm happy because I sing." Choosing to sing praises of gratitude can likewise edify everything within and around us.

OUR GREATEST DEBT: THE ATONEMENT & OUR GREATEST DUTY: RESPONDING TO SUCH LOVE

As a child, I was intrigued by the notion of growth. It fascinated me to think that I could rely upon some outside power to ensure that I would continue to mature as my parents and brothers had—to reach something called adulthood. I remember how grateful I felt for whatever power that guided such an amazing process. But there is a much more important growth that the Atonement makes available—one that goes beyond the physical growth I anticipated as a child. What an astounding, wonderful idea—that we can improve and amend our lives; not just adjust, but become a new person, a new soul.

This wonderful gift of the Atonement—as a second chance—was summed up nicely by my Catholic mother one day. A woman with a troubled past was lately developing a close relationship with a friend of ours that looked like it could lead to marriage. When her past kept coming up, my mother would mention more recent indications of a higher quality life. After a few more rounds of "tag" this way, my mother finally voiced the very essence of Christ's gift to us: "She doesn't have to *be now* what she once *was*."

"Why is Dickens's *Christmas Carol* so popular? Why is it ever new?" President Thomas S. Monson asks, and then goes on to share how this timeless tale portrays the significance of the atoning gift to us all.

> I personally feel it is inspired of God. It brings out the best within human nature. It gives hope. It motivates change. We can turn from the paths which would lead us down and, with a song in our hearts, follow a star and walk toward the light. We can quicken our step, bolster our courage, and bask in the sunlight of truth. We can hear more clearly the laughter of little children. We can dry the tear of the weeping. We can comfort the dying by sharing the promise of eternal life. If we lift one weary hand which hangs down, if we bring peace to one struggling soul, if we give as did the Master, we can—by showing the way—become a guiding star for some lost mariner.[3]

Can you think of an occasion when you celebrated the great opportunity you had to change, to grow, to become a better person than before—because of the Atonement? When?

QUESTIONS TO CONTEMPLATE

- Did I spend more time admiring my talents and accomplishments than honoring all those who made them possible? How will I adjust that tomorrow?

- What do I owe those who raised me from my infancy to adulthood? To my ancestors?

- What do I owe to this earth, for its rain clouds, rivers, lakes, aquifers, sunshine, trees, fruits, meadows, forests, wildlife, sights, sounds, smells, and beauty?

- What did I do today to apply the great opportunity the Atonement provides me—to grow, to change, to improve? What are some of the things I can do tomorrow to better activate this astounding gift of the Atonement in my life? How can I help my family members better appreciate and apply this wonderful gift of the Atonement in their lives?

- How might remembering my covenants (sacrament, temple, Book of Mormon) help me appreciate my great indebtedness and express gratitude for the Lord's Plan of Redemption?

- "Above all else, we should keep in mind that Life is a _____ "
- Why would you fill it in that way?

Notes

1 *Ensign*, May 1987; emphasis added.
2 *The Transcendentalist*, from Chap. I (Nature).
3 Thomas S. Monson, "May We So Live," *Ensign*, Aug. 2008, 2–7.

The River

As a child, I imagined Jordan's stream,
With cattails and grasses crowding the shore,
Heard water lapping and watched as one more
Waded into arms, beneath the soft gleam

And fluttering of wings, a new regime
Arising as a quiet piercing roar
Announced that His Begotten Son now wore
The crown, forlorn that I could only dream

Of being there. Yet in Bamberg flows
Another river, where long-necked swans nod
And a light somehow inside me grows;
As I balance a book's blue-bound covers,
I hear steps come ashore, a swan hovers
Above, and I towel-dry the feet of God.

The Tree of Life

We can barely see in the distance, near
The swaying leaves and branches, a lone
Figure, but we can hear, above the dron–
Ing murmurers and naysayers, his clear

Invitation, like a rolling tide
Drawing us as pages turn, past unknown
Precipitous paths, as he gathers his own,
Retrieving them from across a dark divide:

"Come unto me—take hold and come; Ignore
Those easy lies from the mansion's rim
Of pointing fingers. Come take, eat the flesh
From this tree, drink its nectar, I implore.
Enjoy its holy savor, shewbread fresh.
Come see, come touch, come feel, come feast—on Him."

SECTION TWO

The Links of Redemption

I've outlined below 37 different links of truth that each of us must understand and accept in order to choose to come unto Christ for salvation. I placed beside these links the false teachings the adversary and the world foist upon us as counterfeits or denials of these links. Each one of the 37 spiritual truths is a link in a chain of knowledge and faith that leads a person to recognize his or her need to come unto Jesus Christ. They are truths about ourselves, our situation, our Heavenly Father, and about our Savior. The adversary needs to break only one link in the entire chain to convince someone not to come to Christ.[1]

It may seem daunting at first to think that we have to keep all of these various links connected in our minds and hearts. The real answer is: *we* can't. Fortunately, we have access to a power that can *enable us* to accomplish such a task: the Spirit. The comprehension, acceptance, and interconnection of all these truths "into one great whole" is made possible only by the mediation of the Spirit and comprises what we know of as "faith in Jesus Christ." And there is no place anywhere where these truths are more clearly linked by the Spirit than in the Book of Mormon.

The adversary and the world will constantly argue against coming to Christ, so we can see why the Lord, through the scriptures and our leaders, constantly admonishes us to stay close to the Spirit, to the scriptures, to prayer, to the prophets, to the temple, and to our covenants—and away from Babylon—in order to keep this complex, interconnecting chain of faith intact and viable in our lives.

In the first column of the completed chart (found in the appendix), I'll include a list of those saving links of truths—as well as scriptural references that fortify these truths. In the second column, I include the associated lies the adversary promotes instead—along with scriptural references describing his tactics. You will find each of the adversary's arguments repeated in various philosophies of men today. We can see that the Lord has anticipated each of these modern variations of the adversary's strategies. As President Benson has taught, the Book of Mormon's purpose is not only to manifest Christ and help us come unto him, but also to manifest the methods of the anti-Christ so that we can avoid being deceived by them.[2]

YOUR PARTICIPATION: TRUTHS WE NEED TO KNOW

Before presenting the completed chart, I'll give you a chance to come up with your own answers. Later, perhaps the scriptures and suggestions offered may supplement your own efforts.

Step One: What Are Some Truths We Would Have to Believe about Ourselves, our Heavenly Father, Our Savior, and Our Situation in This Life in Order to Come unto Jesus Christ?

Go ahead and fill in as many things as you would like under each heading. After you fill in your list, go back and include scriptural references that support each item on your list.

Truths we would have to believe about ourselves and our situation in this life in order to come unto Jesus Christ
Truths we would have to believe about God the Father in order to come unto Jesus Christ

Truths we would have believe about Jesus Christ in order to come unto Him to be saved
Truths we would have to believe about the adversary (Satan, Lucifer, etc.)

Step Two: What Are Some of the Associated Untruths the Adversary and the World Would Have Us Believe about Ourselves and Our Situation in Life?

If you were to fill in the following sentence with one word, what would that word be? "Above all else, each day we should remember that life is a _____."

There are many possible answers to that question: life is a school, a test, an opportunity to grow and learn, to develop talents, to serve others; it is a marvel and a wonder, a daily miracle. But our ability to accomplish or enjoy any of those purposes could be compromised if we forget that, above all else, life is a battle between good and evil, Heavenly Father and the adversary, light and darkness, truth and deception, life and death, righteousness and sin. "The men and women, who desire to obtain seats in the celestial kingdom," President Brigham Young taught, "will find that they must battle with the enemy of all righteousness every day" (JD, 11:14–15). The Apostle Peter warns us to "be sober, be vigilant; because your adversary the devil, as a roaring lion, walketh about, seeking whom he may devour" (1 Peter 5:8). "Pray always," the Savior admonished His original disciples, the Nephites, and us today, "that ye may escape Satan . . . and those who do uphold his work" (see Doctrine & Covenants 10:5; see also Luke 21:36; Alma 13:28, 15:17, 34:39; 3 Nephi 18:18). Can you think of any other scripture that describes this battle?[3]

When the Lord calls a prophet, one of the first perspectives He seems to instill is the reality of the devil, as well as the stark contrast between Satan and Heavenly Father (for example, see Lehi in 1 Nephi 8; Moses 1:12–23; JS–H 1:15–16; Enoch in Moses 7:25–26; etc.). Besides demonstrating the tactics of the adversary, the Lord makes clear the adversary's ultimate impotence against the Lord's power as well as the adversary's ultimate destiny: defeat and dissolution (see Isaiah 14:12–15; Revelations 20:10).

ACCORDING TO MODERN PROPHETS: THE REALITY OF OUR BATTLE WITH SATAN

What do we learn from each of these modern prophets about the battle between good and evil?

- (Then) Elder Thomas S. Monson: "Today, we are encamped against the greatest array of sin, vice, and evil ever assembled before our eyes. Such formidable enemies may cause lesser hearts to shrink or shun the fight. But the battle plan whereby we fight to save the souls of [young women and] men is not our own. It was provided . . . by the inspiration and revelation of the Lord" (*Relief Society Magazine*, Apr. 1967, pp. 246–47).

- President Marion G. Romney on Satan's current tactic to have us deny His reality: "The general acceptance of Satan's declaration [in 2 Nephi 28:22], accounts in large measure for the decadence in our deteriorating society. . . . There is a personal devil, and we had better believe it. He and a countless host of followers, seen and unseen, are exercising a controlling influence upon men and their affairs in our world today" ("Satan—The Great Deceiver," *Ensign*, June 1971, 3).

- President James E. Faust on the reality, tactics, and limitations of Satan, and how to defeat him: "We will witness increasing evidence of Satan's power as the kingdom of God grows stronger. . . . It will be masked in greater sophistication and cunning, but it will also be more blatant. We will need greater spirituality to perceive all of the forms of evil and greater strength to resist it" ("The Forces That Will Save Us," *Ensign*, Jan. 2007, 4–9).

QUESTIONS TO CONTEMPLATE

- Was I sufficiently alert today to the fact that I was immersed in a battle between good and evil? What evidence was there?

- How will I better prepare, conduct, and protect myself tomorrow as the battle continues?

- What are some of the things I did for my family—with the knowledge that life is a battle between good and evil?

- How would a focus upon my covenants (sacrament, temple, Book of Mormon) help me as I engage in this battle?

- What do you think are some of the most effective tactics the adversary uses today—to try to keep us from turning to Christ? How do we combat these tactics?

NOTES

1 There is nothing sacrosanct or final about the number "37." It is just the number of links I happened to come up with. Each person who thinks about these things would probably formulate these links in an individual way and come up with various numbers of links.

2 *Ensign*, May 1975, p. 65.

3 Doctrine & Covenants 76:29:"Wherefore, he maketh war with the saints of God, and encompasseth them round about." See also Alma 13:28, 15:17, 34:39; 3 Nephi 18:18; Doctrine & Covenants 10:33, 38:13, 28, 5:33; Ephesians 6:12; Luke 22:31–32; I Thessalonians 5:5, 6; 2 Timothy 2:3, 4; etc.

The Hunter

How is it done, O Lord? My guilt all swept—
As in these mountain waters—clear away?
And joy—I thought no heart could so convey—
Now drench my soul? "Because your Savior wept

Such streams within a future garden's gate—
And then your faith in him unseen, unheard,
Built only on your father's words—has stirred
Your soul, and raised your voice to such great

Heights." Yeah, his words sunk deep and bade me kneel—
All day and night, and though not eyes nor ears
Beheld my Lord, a far more brilliant sight
Flashed through these leaves. One day, unseal
These plates, I pray, as he in such bright light
To all within such future groves appears.

SECTION THREE

Satanic Leitmotifs: Tactics of the Adversary
in Mass Culture and Education

"The devil's greatest trick is to persuade you that he doesn't exist!"
—Charles Baudelaire

DISTORTING THE DEVIL IN MASS CULTURE

Tactic # 1: Denial and Passivity

Therefore my people are gone into captivity, because they have no knowledge. . . . Therefore hell hath enlarged herself, and opened her mouth without measure. —Isaiah 5:13–14

The adversary has succeeded well in convincing many that he is just a figment of their imagination. "There is no devil," he whispers, even as he displays in increasingly graphic detail his perfidy and increasingly "rage[s] in the hearts of the children of men, and stir[s] them up to anger against that which is good" (2 Nephi 28:20). His denials come as his works gape wide at us: "And he saith unto them: I am no devil, for there is none" (2 Nephi 28:22). We know clearly from the scriptures why he uses such a strategy: "Others he will pacify, and lead them away unto carnal security" until he eventually leads "them away carefully down to hell" (2 Nephi 28:21; see also Alma 30:53).

The ultimate consequence of denying the reality of evil and of sin is to feel no need to turn to the Savior and partake of His atoning sacrifice—which cleanses us from our choices to submit to the persuasions of the adversary, who is ever at enmity with truth, light, and life and with all that God is, says, desires, and commands.

Tactic # 2: Obsession, Toleration, and Submission

For thou hast said in thine heart, I will ascend into heaven, I will exalt my throne above the stars of God: I will sit also upon the mount of the congregation, in the sides of the north: I will ascend above the heights of the clouds; I will be like the most High. Yet thou shalt be brought down to hell, to the sides of the pit. —Isaiah 14:13–15, 11–12

Conversely, our mass culture often serves as a "press agent" for Satan in both making him seem either all-powerful or in making his values seem so ubiquitous that many first tolerate and then simply accept them as inevitable and "natural." All this, of course, was prophesied. "Therefore, hell hath enlarged herself," we read, and today the world routinely "call[s] evil good, and good evil and put[s] darkness for light, and light for darkness" and "put[s] bitter for sweet, and sweet for bitter" (2 Nephi 15:14, 20).

We witness media dramatizing wickedness and satanic manifestations to the point that many obsess over him and dwell unhealthily upon his supposed power. This seems to follow from his overwhelming compulsion to be noticed, to look impressive or powerful, or, as he himself put it in his first recorded bellow: "Behold, here am *I*, send *me*. . . . Surely *I* will do it; wherefore, give *me* thine honor" (Moses 4:1). "*I* will ascend unto heaven," he bloviates. "*I* will exalt my throne above the stars of God; *I* will ascend above the heights of the clouds" (Isaiah 14:13–14).

One of the adversary's most potent tools is through what might be described by the advertising—or propaganda—field as "canvassing." You promote a ridiculous idea or lie forcefully enough until you break down such defensive bunkers as common sense or rationality.

Through such unhealthy obsessions, which we see in music, cinema, books, and so on, the adversary seems to convince many of these kinds of things:

- Everybody is like this—under the control of carnal and devilish impulses—so just "follow your vibes" and join the crowd.

- It's "natural," so how can it be wrong?

- You're weird and uptight if you show restraint or righteousness.

- Good is evil and evil is good.

CONSISTENT SATANIC LEITMOTIFS VIA SOME MODERN PHILOSOPHIES

The saying "there is nothing new under the sun" applies well to the efforts of the adversary to keep us from Christ through some modern philosophies and intellectual movements. The latest rein-carnations parade past us with new-fangled facades like Decon-structionism, Genetic or Biological Determinism, neo-Marxism, Pragmatism, Objectivism, etc., joining earlier entries such as Behav-iorism, secular Humanism, and Nihilism. These, in turn, follow in the paths of such ideologies as Materialism, Skepticism, Relativism, Astrology, Fatalism, Solipsism, Hedonism, and so on.

Some of these modern philosophies carry with them important truths. Several of them offer useful tools or lenses for describing aspects of our culture or society. While granting *some* truth to these modern philosophies, the essential question becomes: from whence does the great danger arise? As with Korihor, Sherem, and Nehor, the chief danger arises from the critical lies that accompany the occasional truths. The two most critical lies become the leitmotifs as each parades past us, singing different arrangements of the same basic tune: "Why bother with a redeemer?"

Leitmotif # 1:
The promotion of the idea that agency is an illusion

Just as the Book of Mormon anti-Christs, many adherents of modern philosophies extrapolate far beyond a few basic tenets, until this one, inevitable consequence subsumes any of their ini-tially acceptable truths: that these various impulses, influences, and forces completely obliterate our abilities to make self-critical, con-scious decisions independent of these forces. That is, not only are our actions *influenced* by these forces; they are in every case *determined* by them—since our hearts and minds are enslaved to them. Each of these philosophies thereby escorts us to the same prison cell—where we assent to the idea that freedom and agency are illusions (a key tactic of the adversary, of course; see Moses 4:3). And with that foundational lie as leverage, all other links of faith easily snap: because we cannot act freely, we also must accept that

- there are no such things as sin or guilt or punishment; nor their counterparts: virtue, forgiveness, or reward; and therefore:

- there is no extra-empirical or metaphysical source of either good or evil—which persuades us to freely choose between these alternatives; and therefore:

- there is no possibility of transcendence of our environment or of our ingrained self-delusion through such means as repentance, rebirth, or atonement; and therefore:

- there is no rhyme, reason, or role for a Redeemer

Purveyors of such philosophies don't announce their anti-theistic destinations—since any discussion of God has been relegated by them to an irrational nonentity. Yet, despite such silence, atheism crowds their seminar rooms as the proverbial elephant, which we're all not supposed to notice. "The trend of education throughout the world today is materialistic and mechanistic," President Joseph Fielding Smith teaches. "The swing is away from God. What the advocates of these doctrines are pleased to call 'modernism' and 'liberalism' eliminate faith in Jesus Christ as the Son of God."[1]

Father Lehi's inspired words to Jacob well describe the effects—and foolishness—of much modern philosophy:

> And if ye shall say there is no law, ye shall also say there is no sin. If ye shall say there is no sin, ye shall also say there is no righteousness. And if there be no righteousness there be no happiness. And if there be no righteousness nor happiness there be no punishment nor misery. And if these things are not there is no God. And if there is no God we are not, neither the earth; for there could have been no creation of things, neither to act nor to be acted upon; wherefore, all things must have vanished away. (2 Nephi 2:13)

Leitmotif # 2:
The insistence that all definitions of humanity exclude
anything beyond our physical selves and our mortal sphere

Besides their agency-less *destination*, these philosophies share a similar "naturalistic" error in their *presuppositions*: the insistence that the natural or material world circumscribes the whole of reality, and that virtually "all phenomena," from helium to humans, "can be explained in terms of natural causes and laws."[2] Extra-empirical, supernatural, "spiritual," or extra-physical reality are all out of the question in such a scenario; all human motivation and behavior is, they insist, determined solely by biology, heredity, and environment. Since consciousness itself is just a chemical reaction, the idea of a divine origin and destiny dissolves. "There is no aspect of man which is outside of nature, call that aspect what you will," insists Joseph L. Bau in his survey of philosophy. "You may talk of soul or spirit only on the condition that you mean thereby some aspect of man's natural behavior; but you may not describe the soul of man as immortal, for to do so would be to remove it outside of nature."[3] The philosophical category for such a stance is ontological reductionism, where the nature of "being" and existence is presumed and defined in exclusively naturalistic terms and processes.

NATURALISM: A CLOSED SYSTEM OF MATERIAL CAUSES AND EFFECTS

As with the postmodern philosophies discussed above, scientific "naturalism" can be a useful tool when properly defined and limited in its scope. For example, it is useful to have such a field as science to attempt to explain physical phenomena using exclusively empirical means (that is, employing *"methodological* naturalism," the scientific method or empirical rationalism, limiting explanations to what we can physically observe, test, replicate, and verify), ruling out or deliberately suspending for specific scientific purposes, supernatural causes, events, or forces, including such things as revelation, the miraculous, or the spiritual. We celebrate the contributions of such a field. In fact, the achievements of science provide wondrous demonstration of the divine potentials and capacities of humans.[4]

The problem arises when scientists and non-scientists decree such a method of inquiry as the *only* valid approach to ascertaining *all* knowledge about *all* existence—so that the once useful tool becomes a pernicious metaphysical philosophy of life (i.e., "*philosophical* or *metaphysical* naturalism," epistemological reductionism, or scientism, which defines the entire realm of existence as a closed system of material causes and effects—that cannot be influenced by anything from "outside"), turning humans into self-deluded lab specimens and morality into a hoax. Such a philosophy enthrones science or empiricism as the only reliable and final arbiter of meaning and truth and dictates that all questions about human life ultimately hinge on scientific or material analysis.[5]

"The absence of a scientific proof for God is more indicative of the limits of science than the lack of a deity," evolutionary biologist Robert J. Asher writes in *Evolution and Belief: Confessions of a Religious Paleontologist.*

> It is rational to believe that an entity beyond our comprehension was the agency by which something was derived from nothing at the beginning of time. . . . Although I acknowledge my belief to be non-scientific, it is entirely rational. Science is a subset of rationality; the former has a narrower scope than the latter. To ignore rationality when it does fall beyond the scientific enterprise would be an injustice to both reason and humanity.

NATURALISM USED AS A WEAPON AGAINST THE SPIRITUAL

Often today naturalism becomes an ideological weapon in an attempt to mock and suppress any moral or religious movement as an "attack on science," including, for example, efforts to promote abstinence before marriage and traditional definitions of marriage itself or to question the ethics of partial-birth abortions. "The primary problem is not to provide the public with the knowledge of how far it is to the nearest star and what genes are made of," contends Harvard geneticist Richard Lewontin. "Rather, the problem is to get them to reject irrational and supernatural explanations of the world, the demons that exist only in their imaginations, and to accept a social and intellectual apparatus, Science, as the only begetter of truth." Such an agenda follows from his philosophic, *not scientific*, presumptions. Such truths as the Atonement have no place in such extra-scientific metaphysics: "Every atom in your body came from a star that exploded and, the atoms in your left hand probably came from a different star than your right hand," Lawrence Krauss, a theoretical physicist and bestselling author, teaches. "You are all stardust . . . and the only way for them [i.e., "the carbon, nitrogen, oxygen, iron, all the things that matter for evolution and for life"] to get into your body is if those stars were kind enough to explode. So, forget Jesus; the stars died so that you could be here today."[6]

In a review of various books by proponents of such scientism, BYU English professor Steven Walker uses a couple of helpful metaphors to describe their confined point of view. Their pontificator-in-chief, Richard Dawkins's self-imposed limitations render him essentially "color–blind to theology. He focuses so intently on the black and white of material reality he cannot perceive the slightest tint of theological color."

> These scientists are superlatively good at their way of seeing; problem is, that way is better at deciding what cannot be than at discovering what is, and that is lethal when one tries to think theologically. Looking at the universe from this atheist view feels like cramping everything through a telescope or microscope—wonderfully focused on what can be seen, but drastically restricted by the frame.[7]

Brigham Young summarized well such a naturalistic attitude: "How difficult it is to teach the natural man," he taught, "who comprehends nothing more than that which he sees with the natural eye!"

> How hard it is for him to believe! How difficult would be the task to make the philosopher, who, for many years, has argued himself into the belief that his spirit is no more after his body sleeps in the grave, believe that his intelligence came from eternity, and is as eternal, in its nature, as the elements, or as the Gods. Such doctrine by him would be considered vanity and foolishness, it would be entirely beyond his comprehension. It is difficult, indeed, to remove an opinion or belief into which he has argued himself from the mind of the natural man. Talk to him about angels, heavens, God, immortality, and eternal lives, and it is like sounding brass, or a tinkling cymbal to his ears; it has no music to him; there is nothing in it that charms his senses, soothes his

feelings, attracts his attention, or engages his affections, in the least; to him it is all vanity (*JD*, 1:2).[8]

QUESTIONS TO CONTEMPLATE

- Have I done, thought, or said anything today that would indicate I am buying into the world's notion that I am simply a passive victim of such things as materialism, historical forces, passions, subconscious drives, societal circumstances, biology, chemistry, the positions of the stars at my birth, or Tarot cards?

- How have my words and actions taught my family that they are eternal spirits of a living God, whose spirits are temporarily clothed in a mortal body?

- How would a focus upon covenants (sacrament, temple, Book of Mormon) help me (and my family) better know and truly feel our essence as divine, spiritual beings—clothed in mortality?

- What critical aspect of the nature of men and women do you think might be the single most hidden aspect of their natures—as far as the world's knowledge and beliefs?

- Why and how would a correct understanding of this aspect of the nature of men and women help us avoid the confusions and distortions that the world attempts to foist upon us about our true nature?

NOTES

1 *The Progress of Man*, p. 379.

2 *The American Heritage Dictionary of the English Language*, Fourth Edition, 2000, Houghton Mifflin.

3 *Men and Movements in American Philosophy* (New York: Prentice-Hall, Inc., 1953), p. 315.

4 Leaving aside, for a moment, our belief that even the contributions of self-proclaimed atheistic scientists have relied upon inspiration from God, we Latter-day Saints celebrate the natural world as a blessing from God and as a witness and window to the very existence of God. (See Psalm 19:1: "The heavens declare the glory of God; and the firmament sheweth his handiwork"; Alma 30:44: "All things denote there is a God; yea, even the earth... and its

motion, yea, and also all the planets which move in their regular form do witness that there is a Supreme Creator"; Doctrine & Covenants 88:47: "Behold,
all these are kingdoms, and any man who hath seen any or the least of these
hath seen God moving in his majesty and power"; Moses 6:63: "And behold,
all things have their likeness, and all things are created and made to bear
record of me..." See also: Romans 1:20.) At the same time, it would be wrong
to categorize LDS as ashamed of or antagonistic to the "natural" bodies that
frame our eternal spirits. On the contrary, LDS above all others—whether
religious or secular—celebrate and revere the gift of a physical body. We alone
believe God has such a physical body (exalted and perfected) and that one of
our main purposes and blessings of our coming to this earth was to receive
such a body—as a step to godhood. We do believe, however, that one of our
greatest challenges and opportunities in this life is to learn to properly harness our bodily appetites and passions—so that the needs of our Spirit, not
our mortal bodies, direct our actions and priorities in life. Under the direction
of our Spirit, the human body can be a sublime source of joy and progress
toward developing divine character. "The spirit and the body are the soul of
man . . . and spirit and element, inseparably connected, receive a fulness of joy"
(Doctrine & Covenants 88:15, 93:33; see also 138:17).

5 "The scope of science is the world of nature: the reality that is observed,
directly or indirectly, *by our senses*," says geneticist and molecular biologist
Francisco J. Ayala. "Science advances *explanations about the natural world*,
explanations that are accepted or rejected by observation and experiment.
Outside the world of nature, however, science has no authority, no statements to
make, no business whatsoever taking one position or another. Science has
nothing decisive to say about values, whether economic, aesthetic or moral;
nothing to say about the meaning of life or its purpose" (in *The Guardian*, 28
May 2010, emphasis added; article found online here: http://www.guardian.
co.uk/science/blog/2010/may/28/religion-science-richard-dawkins).

6 From an address given in 2009: "A Universe From Nothing."

7 "The God Delusion: Selling the Soul of Science for a Pot of Message," in
BYU Studies 47:1, byustudies.byu.edu.

8 "One great reason why men have stumbled so frequently in many of their
researches after philosophical truth is that they have sought them with their
own wisdom, and gloried in their own intelligence, and have not sought unto
God for that wisdom that fills and governs the universe and regulates all
things. That is one great difficulty with the philosophers of the world, as it now
exists, that man claims to himself to be the inventor of everything he discovers.
Any new law and principle which he happens to discover he claims to himself
instead of giving glory to God" (John Taylor, *The Gospel Kingdom*, 47).

Alma the Younger

While in the very deepest, dark abyss,
Beyond the farthest reach of hope enjailed,
All sides round by judgment's lance assailed,
I craved a crypt more dark and deep than this—

To be always interred in nothingness;
When words I'd heard my father speak unveiled
Feint thoughts of one upon a pole impaled,
Whose pains my pains somehow could turn to bliss.

"Oh, Jesus, send such balm to me," I cried
And felt him blast the cover from my tomb,
Bathing me in music from the skies
And joy—exquisite as was once my doom.
This metal serpent raised can now provide
Within its brazen folds the same surprise.

SECTION FOUR

"What Is Man, That Thou Art Mindful of Him?"

"For thou hast made him a little lower than the angels,
and hast crowned him with glory and honour.
Thou madest him to have dominion over the works of thy hands;
thou hast put all things under his feet." —Psalm 8:4–6

Indeed: Who am I? This is perhaps the ultimate question we each pose and which directs how we live our lives. "What is man, that thou art mindful of him?" the Psalmist asks, "and the son of man, that thou visitest him?"

Shakespeare's Hamlet is amazed at both man's potential—as revealed in scripture and sometimes demonstrated by noble souls—as well as the profanity much more often displayed in Elsinore:

"What a piece of work is a man, how noble in reason, / how infinite in faculties, in form and moving how / express and admirable, in action how like an angel, / in apprehension how like a god! the beauty of the / world, the paragon of animals—and yet, to me, / what is this quintessence of dust?" (Act 2, Scene ii).

"What is the meaning of life?" Hamlet is always asking. Isn't there more to life than serving our passions?—which is what he mostly observes round about him.

"What is a man, / If his chief good and market of his time / Be but to sleep and feed? a beast, no more. / Sure, he that made us with such large discourse, / *Looking before and after*, gave us not / That capability and god-like reason / To fust in us unused" (Act 4, Scene iv).

"LOOKING BEFORE AND AFTER"

Perhaps Hamlet has hit upon a key to defining ourselves:

"Looking before and after." The great error of the following supposition flows from the false notion that our existence begins with our births here on earth: "Man is the result of purposeless and natural processes," Harvard paleontologist George Gaylord Simpson insists, "that did not have him in mind."[1] In bright contrast, a modern prophet, President Howard W. Hunter, declares:

> Part of our reassurance about the free, noble, and progressing spirit of man comes from the glorious realization that we all existed and had our identities, and our agency, long before we came to this world. To some that will be a new thought, but the Bible teaches clearly just such an eternal view of life, a life stretching back before this world was and stretching forward into the eternities ahead.[2]

What difference does it make to you when you consider that you lived before you came to earth? How does that knowledge affect the way you live your life now? Why?

I remember how liberating—and motivating—it was for me when I first learned from my recently converted brother that I had existed before I came to this earth, as a spirit child of God. It was such an ennobling idea: that there was a part of me, the *most essential part* of me, that transcended—and preceded—my mortal weaknesses and nature; and that my destiny was to find a way to stay true to such divinity within me. Glorious windows, doors, and paths seemed immediately to open before me—especially the path and possibility of returning to be with the Father for eternity, through the gift of the Atonement. That innate recollection of a noble sphere before earth and an anticipation of an even nobler destiny touch each person somehow.

Likewise, my brother—pointing to three orbs at the end of a bright, colorful Plan of Salvation chart on the wall of his barracks room in Bad Kreuznach—shared another astounding idea that never before had occurred to me: the ultimate destiny awaiting those who faithfully follow the Savior is to "be *exalted* in the Celestial Kingdom," meaning we could progress to become the same kind of being our Heavenly Father is. That, my brother told me, is the true definition of "eternal life": becoming one with God. Becoming *as* God. "After all," Bobby asked, "Wouldn't a father want to make it possible for his children to become like him?" One of the purposes in coming to earth, my brother then told me, was to take upon us a physical body—because in the premortal existence we saw that God had such a body and knew that a fulness of happiness required a physical body like his. And so Our Heavenly Father instituted a plan for us to enter this phase called mortality—where our Spirits would be clothed in this body and be tested to see how we would respond to this godly attribute. Talking about "raising your sights"! I was amazed. Scriptures from the New Testament I had skimmed past—or didn't accept in their glorious literality—now took on new meaning for me: "We are the offspring of God" (Acts 17:28–29); "Our Father, which art in Heaven" (Matthew 6:9); "Be ye therefore perfect, even as your Father, which is in heaven is perfect" (Matthew 5:48). In just a few minutes, my true—and divine—identity, origin, and destiny appeared before me in ways I had never conceived. I would never be the same.

QUESTIONS TO CONTEMPLATE

- How have my thoughts and actions today flowed from my firm convictions that I lived with God before I came to this earth?

- What have I said or done today that would impress such truths upon my family?

- What are some ways today that the adversary or the world attempted to have me denigrate or debase the gift of a physical body—and how did I resist such attempts?

- How would a focus upon covenants (sacrament, temple, Book of Mormon) help me better understand and apply these truths in my own life and also teach them to my family?

- How much influence do you think our culture exercises upon our (and our children's) moral values? Why? How? What can we do to stem such influences? How would you fill in these blanks: "Nothing is more important for me this day than g_____ ing and k_____ing the _____ ."

NOTES

1 *The Meaning of Evolution: A Study of the History of Life and of Its Significance for Man*, rev. ed. (New Haven, CT: Yale University Press, 1967), 345.

2 "The Golden Thread of Choice," *Ensign*, November 1989.

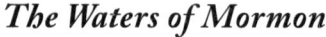

The Waters of Mormon

"Taste," he said, handing the golden chalice
To an older man, seated on layers of slate
Overhanging a pool close by cascade-
ing falls, passing this remnant of a palace

To his friend. "Our legends sang these streams'
Refreshments," Jacob said. "Though such stories
Of Mormon's fountains left these glories
Unexplored." "But now," said Alma, "Such dreams

Our constant quenchings." Watching the sun haste
Above pines, like flames upon piled kindling,
He retrieved and unraveled a parchment scroll,
With words surpassing even the dawn's roll-
ing conflagration, replenishing dwindling
Hopes, the mists whispering as he read: "Taste."

SECTION FIVE

A Comma Instead of a Period

So, despite any worthwhile truths they have to offer, many modern and naturalistic philosophies are woefully astray—in the same way we would all go astray if we put a period at the end of this phrase from King Benjamin: "For the natural man is an enemy to God [and completely bounded by natural, material processes, which he of himself cannot transcend], and has been from the fall of Adam, and will be, forever and ever[.]" Fortunately, we are all saved from that fate through a comma and a subordinating conjunction (and, of course, by the truths that accompany such grammar): "For the natural man is an enemy to God, and has been from the fall of Adam, and will be, forever and ever, *unless* he yields to the enticings of the Holy Spirit, and putteth off the natural man and becometh a saint through the Atonement of Christ the Lord." (Mosiah 3:19). That is, without the guidance of the Spirit of Christ, we become subject to such carnal forces as greed, materialism, pride, heredity, environment, and unrestrained passions. In essence, the comma—which makes possible the guidance of the Spirit—allows us to "act" rather than simply being "acted upon" by natural or carnal forces.[1]

Can you think of any scriptures that teach this truth: that we remain in bondage until we turn to God?[2]

Unlike King Benjamin (who was relaying the words of an angel), naturalistic and materialist-based philosophies *do* put a period after that initial phrase. Skepticism and Cynicism remain their dominant features—because that really is all that is ultimately available to "natural man." Paraphrasing Paul: If this life (that is, the life of mortality and the flesh) is all there is, we are of all men most miserable (1 Corinthians 15:19).

Jacob well summarizes the promises and problems of much of modern philosophies when he describes "the vainness, and the frailties, and the foolishness of men!"

> When they are learned they think they are wise, and they hearken not unto the counsel of God, for they set it aside, supposing they know of themselves, wherefore, their wisdom is foolishness and it profiteth them not. And they shall perish. But to be learned is good if they hearken unto the counsels of God. (2 Nephi 9:28–29; see also Doctrine & Covenants 1:16, 93:39, 84:49, 1:15–16, 82:5, 38:11, 33:4, 35:7 for more recent warnings)

ACCORDING TO MODERN PROPHETS: THE INCREASING INFLUENCE OF EVIL IN OUR SOCIETY

How do each of the following modern prophets teach you to beware of Satan's influences today?

- President Thomas S. Monson on the waves of wickedness today: "We often find ourselves swimming against the current, and sometimes it seems as though the current could carry us away. . . . My brothers and sisters, He has prepared us. If we heed His words and live the commandments, we will survive this time of permissiveness and wickedness— a time which can be compared with the waves and the winds and the floods [encountered by the Jaredites] that can destroy" (*Ensign*, Nov. 2009, 109–10).

- "We are here in this wicked world, a world shrouded in darkness, principally led, directed, governed, and controlled, from first to last, by the power of our common foe—him who was opposed to Jesus Christ and to His kingdom" President Brigham Young warns us (*JD* 3:223).

- President Spencer W. Kimball on how evil seems to engulf our society: *Ensign*, May 1979, 4; "The False Gods We

Worship," *Ensign*, June 1976, 3; and "Fortify Your Homes against Evil," *Ensign*, Nov. 1978, 5.

- President Gordon B. Hinckley on guarding the home against evil: "Walking in the Light of the Lord," *Ensign* (Nov. 1998), pp. 97–100.

- Elder David R. Stone on how the island of Zion is under siege by the waves of Babylon, which determines and molds many of our values and priorities: *Ensign*, May 2006, pp. 90–92.

WHERE DO WE TURN?

As King Benjamin notes (above), each person remains a "natural man," and therefore a citizen of Babylon, "*unless* he yields to the enticings of the Holy Spirit. . . ." And this great escape option cannot be celebrated too much: through the Holy Ghost we can *always* rise above, transcend, and triumph over any forces, predilections, powers, people, influences, habits, temptations, deceptions, entrancements, or carnalities that anyone or anything could ever throw at us. "If God be for us [and His Holy Spirit with us], who can be against us?" (Romans 8:31).

The gift of the Holy Ghost, Joseph Smith taught, is what finally separates the Lord's church and kingdom from all other organizations.[3] "Teach the people that they must labor and so live as to obtain the Holy Spirit," a long-departed Brigham Young returned to teach a principle he learned from the Prophet Joseph. "Without the spirit of God you are in danger of walking in the dark."[4]

Over the years, as a home teacher, I have given a short quiz to those I visited by having them fill in the blanks from the following sentence on a three by five index card: "Nothing is more important for me to do this day than g_____ing and k_____ing the H_____G _____." Give it a try yourself. Our discussion would lead to these answers ("getting," "keeping," and the "Holy Ghost,"), after which I invited them to tape the card to their bathroom mirror—so that they could be reminded of their first and most important priority for each day.

In the end, every source of knowledge—other than that relayed through the Spirit of Jesus Christ—is ultimately unreliable and open to deception (Mosiah 23:14; see also 1 John 2:15). However, knowledge from the Spirit is unimpeachable and eternally reliable (see Jacob 13:13; Doctrine & Covenants 93:30).

Fortunately, a "fruit" of our faithful study of the Book of Mormon is the power to "get the Holy Ghost," the spirit and presence of the Lord, to enrich and sanctify our lives—and separate us from Babylon (1 Nephi 11:17–19; 2 Nephi 32:4, 31:17–21; etc.): "Learn of me, and listen to my words; walk in the meekness of my Spirit, and you shall have peace in me" (Doctrine & Covenants 19:23; see also John 14:26, 16:33). In our day, the Lord describes those who will have the ability and power to "abide the day" as "they that are wise and have received the truth, and have taken the Holy Spirit for their guide" (Doctrine & Covenants 45:57).

"We do not need to become as puppets in the hands of the culture of the place and time," Elder David Stone enjoins us. "We can be courageous and can walk in the Lord's paths and follow His footsteps. And if we do, we will be called Zion, and we will be the people of the Lord." Zion is the place where the Lord was able to dwell among His people. Surely temples are such places, and surely the Book of Mormon is such a place. Elder Stone's closing description of Zion well describes all three of these places: "We seek [Zion, and temples, and the Book of Mormon] because [they are] the habitation[s] of our Lord, who is Jesus Christ, our Savior and Redeemer. In [them] and from [them], His luminous and incandescent light will shine forth, and He will rule forever."[5]

YOUR PARTICIPATION:
UNTRUTHS (LIES) WE NEED TO RESIST

With all of these things in mind, consider now the kinds of persuasions the adversary and the world use—through whispers and less subtle means—to subvert or compromise each essential "link of truth." This time use the right column in the table below to consider an associated untruth that the adversary attempts to replace for each truth you wrote in the left column. It would also be valuable, after writing your list, to consider scriptures that support each of your responses.

Associated Untruths the Adversary and the World Would Have Us Believe about Ourselves, Our Situation, Our Heavenly Father, Jesus Christ, and the Adversary

Truths we would have to believe about ourselves and our situation in this life in order to come unto Christ	Associated *untruths* the adversary and the world would have us believe about ourselves and our situation in life
Truths we would have to believe about God the Father in order to come unto Christ	Associated untruths the adversary and the world would have us believe about God the Father
Truths we would have to believe about Christ in order to come unto Him to be saved	Associated untruths the adversary and the world would have us believe about Jesus Christ
Truths we would have to know and believe about the adversary (Satan, Lucifer, etc.)	Associated untruths the adversary and the world attempt to make us believe about the adversary

QUESTIONS TO CONTEMPLATE

- When did I earnestly and diligently seek the Holy Ghost today so that I would not be bound and controlled by materialistic and naturalistic impulses?

- What will I do tomorrow so that I will not feel bound and controlled by materialistic and naturalistic impulses?

- What are some things I did today that encouraged my family to seek and follow the Holy Ghost so that they could escape the materialistic influences around them?

- How would a focus upon covenants (sacrament, temple, Book of Mormon) help me (and my family) better escape these materialistic impulses and be guided by the Spirit?

- What do you think is the best way to preserve these links to the Savior? Why?

Take a minute to look at this diagram to see some links of faith to the Savior. The adversary only needs break one of these links of faith to keep us from turning to the Savior for our Salvation.

Some Links of Faith of the Savior

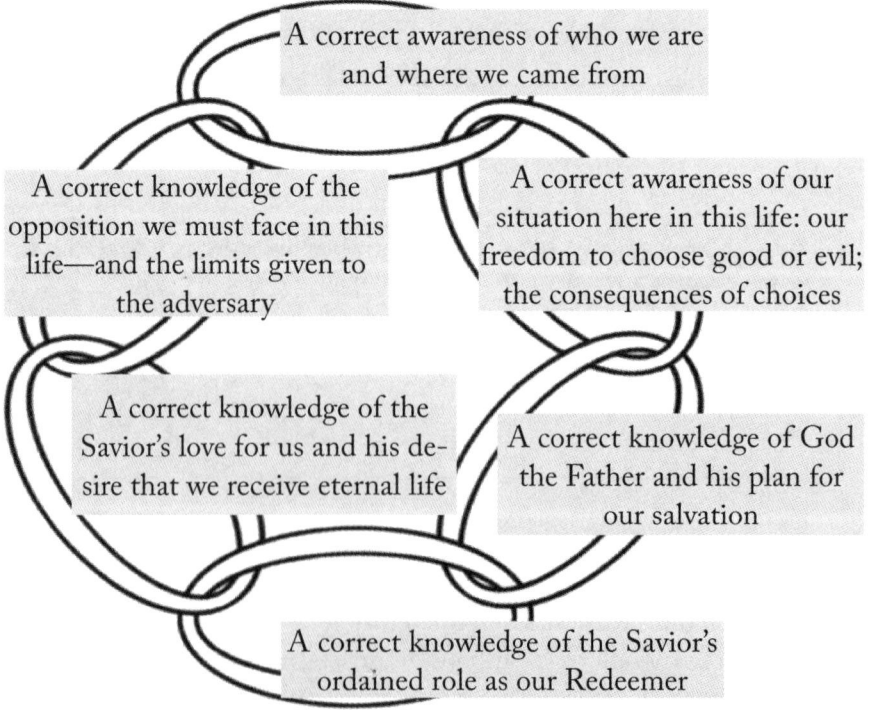

A correct awareness of who we are and where we came from

A correct knowledge of the opposition we must face in this life—and the limits given to the adversary

A correct awareness of our situation here in this life: our freedom to choose good or evil; the consequences of choices

A correct knowledge of the Savior's love for us and his desire that we receive eternal life

A correct knowledge of God the Father and his plan for our salvation

A correct knowledge of the Savior's ordained role as our Redeemer

Notes

1 In fact, this angelic messenger makes clear the most defining aspect of all aspects of humanity—including fallen humanity: that even fallen, "natural" men are divine to the core and therefore retain within them the opportunity to freely act, to make moral choices (how else could anyone—even natural men—be considered "disobedient" or "rebellious" if they had no choice in the matter?), and to make for themselves the most essential choice of time and eternity; they of themselves may choose to "yield" to the enticings of the Holy Ghost, and then having accessed and embraced a greater power than their own, through the grace of Christ, they may rise above and transcend all other carnal, fallen, and naturalistic forces, bondages, predilections, habits, inclinations, and impulses. (Interestingly, and paradoxically, such transcendence of naturalistic bonds occurs when we "submit" ourselves instead completely and unreservedly to "all things" demanded by the Lord; i.e. when we voluntarily place ourselves in "bondage" to the will of God. Such an opportunity for transcendence is first sparked and guided by the flickering whispers of the Light of Christ and then ignited into the full flames of renewal and rebirth as we find and then fully receive and embrace Him (and His covenants) whose abode we enter as we open the Book of Mormon.

2 Did any of these come to mind? JS–H 1:15–17; 2 Nephi 2:28–29; Mosiah 16:5; Alma 12:11, 26:21, 41:11, 42:10; Doctrine & Covenants 84:49, 57; Romans 3:10.

3 *History of the Church* 4:42.

4 Quoted in President Kimball's *Faith Precedes the Miracle*, p. 25.

5 *Ensign*, May 2006, p. 92.

Were You There

Facing the House of God in an open tent,
Your eyes rapt upon a new-built tower
And witness borne with overwhelming power
Of a Son descending to circumvent

Our penalties and pains, with such torment
Of body and soul that blood will shower
From every pore—and in that eternal hour
Redeem with himself the debt our sins spent;

Would we, as they, then fall upon the ground
And cry aloud for the atoning blood
Of such a Christ to purify our hearts?
Let's open wide our tents and let that flood
Yet flow out from this temple's sacred parts—
With no less power to cleanse and to astound.

SECTION SIX

The 37 Links of Redemption Completed

Spend some time looking over chart 1.6.1 on page 298 in the appendix B at the back of the book. These are the 37 links with scriptural citations, along with the lies used by the adversary to try to break each of these links of redemption.

HOW THE BOOK OF MORMON HELPS TO MAINTAIN THE "LINKS OF FAITH" AND COMBAT THOSE WHO WOULD BREAK THOSE LINKS: THE PROMISES OF MODERN PROPHETS

When we consider how vital it is to have an understanding of so many things in order to truly recognize our danger and truly recognize Jesus Christ as our only hope for salvation from these dangers, and when we likewise consider the false ideas constantly planted by the adversary to try to keep us from the Savior, then we have an idea of the crucial role of the Book of Mormon—because nowhere else is each of these links so clear and accessible. "The Book of Mormon exposes the enemies of Christ," President Benson taught. "It fortifies the humble followers of Christ against the evil designs, strategies, and doctrines of the devil in our day."[1]

Consider each of these warnings and promises about how the Book of Mormon empowers you to follow the Savior and overcome the false ideas and temptations that sever those ties with the Savior—as given by modern prophets.

YOUR PARTICIPATION

Take some time to look up and then write down each blessing or power promised by modern prophets below—and decide whether or not you want that power in your life.

And then prayerfully decide—and write down—what you will do to ensure you receive such blessings.

The blessing or power promised by modern prophets—that will come to you through the Book of Mormon
Why I want or need that power in my life
What I will do to help ensure that I receive these blessings

ACCORDING TO MODERN PROPHETS: THE POWER OF THE BOOK OF MORMON IN OUR LIVES

From the Prophet Joseph Smith

- The Book of Mormon keystone and greatest way to get near to God (*History of the Church*, 4:461; *Teachings of the Prophet Joseph Smith*, sel. Joseph Fielding Smith, Salt Lake City: Deseret Book, 1938, p. 39).

From President Ezra Taft Benson

- Book of Mormon provides spiritual and intellectual unity, without which we place our souls in jeopardy; it testifies of Christ and reveals His enemies (*Ensign*, May 1975, p.65).

- Book of Mormon leads us to fruit of life, and gives us power to resist temptations and thwart the work of Satan ("The Power of the Word," *Ensign*, May 1986, p. 80).

- Book of Mormon combats those who reject the divinity of the Savior, His perfect life, and His resurrection; and provides the most complete explanation of the Atonement: (*Ensign*, November 1986, p. 6).

- Book of Mormon exposes the enemies of Christ and fortifies us against false educational and philosophical ideas: ("The Book of Mormon is the Word of God," *Ensign*, Jan. 1988, p. 3).

- Our families risk being corrupted by worldly trends and teachings unless we use the Book of Mormon to combat these falsehoods: (*Ensign*, Jan. 1988, p. 4).

From Elder Marion G. Romney

- We need to study the Book of Mormon in order to resist evil and deception, escape the lusts of the flesh, avoid the evils of the world, and be drawn to the things of the Spirit; reverence, mutual respect, love, faith, peace, and joy will increase in our homes ("The Book of Mormon," *Ensign*, May 1980, 65).

From President Gordon B. Hinckley

- Added measure of the Lord's Spirit, increased testimony, and strengthened resolution to keep the commandments will follow from prayerful reading of the Book of Mormon ("The Power of the Book of Mormon," *Ensign*, June 1988, p. 6.).

From the Book of Mormon

- We rejoice that the Lord knew the tactics the adversary would employ in these latter days to hide or pervert these plain and precious truths; and that the Lord restored them to us. "After the Gentiles do stumble exceedingly, because of the most plain and precious parts of the gospel of the Lamb which have been kept back," the Lord says, "I will be merciful unto the Gentiles in that day, insomuch that I will bring forth unto them, in mine own power, much of my gospel, which shall be plain and precious" (1 Nephi 13:35). As the angel said to Nephi, these latter-day records "shall establish the truth of the first . . . and shall make known the plain and precious things which have been taken away from them; and shall make known to all kindreds, tongues, and people, that the Lamb of God is the Son of the Eternal Father, and the Savior of the world; and that all men must come unto him, or they cannot be saved" (1 Nephi 13:40). [See also Doctrine & Covenants 3:19–20; 20:17–37].

- "The words which I have written in weakness will be made strong unto them; for it persuadeth them to do good . . . and it speaketh of Jesus, and persuadeth them to believe in him, and to endure to the end, which is life eternal. . . . And it speaketh harshly against sin, according to the plainness of the truth; wherefore, no man will be angry at the words which I have written save he shall be of the spirit of the devil. . . . If ye shall believe in Christ ye will believe in these words, for they are the words of Christ, and he hath given them unto me; and they teach all men that they should do good" (2 Nephi 33:4–5, 10).

- "[The rod of iron] was the word of God; and whoso would hearken unto the word of God, and would hold fast unto it, they would never perish; neither could the temptations and the fiery darts of the adversary overpower them unto blindness, to lead them away to destruction" (1 Nephi 15:24).

- "Yea, we see that whosoever will may lay hold upon the word of God, which is quick and powerful, which shall divide asunder all the cunning and the snares and the wiles of the devil, and lead the man of Christ in a strait and narrow course across that everlasting gulf of misery which is prepared to engulf the wicked" (Helaman 3:29).

QUESTION TO CONTEMPLATE

- How will you make sure you keep intact the "37 links" of truths that help you turn to the Savior?
- Which one of those 37 links do you especially need to "polish" right now? How will you do that?
- How would a focus upon sacred covenants you have made (sacrament, temple, Book of Mormon) help you keep these links intact?
- What do you think is the most essential purpose of the Book of Mormon?
- How does the Book of Mormon fulfill that purpose?

RETURN TO OPENING SCENARIOS FOR QUESTIONS 1 & 2

How might you now respond to these scenarios?

Scenario # 1

"It's actually quite liberating," Professor Sedgwick continued. "Once you get past this childish notion of some super-hero god or something coming to save you from some haunting spirit called the devil, you can finally learn to stand on your own two feet. You can get out of that comic strip that society or some church has created in your mind to keep you behaving like they want you to behave. You'll finally see through all that hocus-pocus and unlock your own hidden powers and potential that things like religions have stifled.

Just watch the whole world open up to you for the first time in your life. Free at last."[2]

Scenario # 2

"The human organism is astounding," the bearded speaker at the podium continued. "Adapted in every way to ensure that its genetic code will be transmitted. There's a gene for everything. Even a 'god gene.' That's right—a god gene. Something developed by nature over time that keeps societies from destroying each other. Genetically, nature has programmed us to posit some eternal being that rewards us with ecstasy in the next life if we just promote not only our own welfare, but the welfare of others—so that they can survive to transmit their genetic material also. Very tricky, nature, isn't it? It can even fool us into thinking we're being selfless or something called 'moral'—when we're actually just following some chemical and biological process preprogrammed inside our cells."[3]

NOTES

1 *The Teachings of Ezra Taft Benson*, Salt Lake City: Bookcraft, 1988, p. 56.

2 Scenario 1: These are typical tactics of the anti-Christs, which resurge with many modern philosophies: they want believers to feel foolish, weak, and immature for relying upon the power and atoning mission of Jesus Christ to be released from the penalties of sin and disobedience. And they want us to deny the reality of evil and of Satan. While in reality, such faith is not a sign of weakness, but of strength and commitment to truth. These false teachers also want us to believe that we place ourselves in bondage when we accept such truths—when such truths actually free us.

3 Scenario 2: An example of how the world and the adversary will attempt to persuade us that we are simply mindless slaves to such forces as biology, chemistry, and genetic determinism and that we have no hope to transcend such forces acting upon us. An example of the fulfillment of Isaiah's and Book of Mormon prophecies that in the latter days, many will call evil good and good evil and how "their wisdom will be foolishness." In reality, although we are influenced by various social, cultural, emotional, chemical, and genetic forces, as literal sons and daughters of God, and through the grace and atoning power of Christ's intercession

for us, we can be free from all such forces and take upon us the Spirit, name, and mind of Christ Himself. We can be reborn through His divine love.

Emmaus

This Jesus, who to you such sorrow brought
—as if ye knew Him well—should his life not free
You from such grief? Is there no victory,
No joy nor peace in all the deeds he wrought?

Him we held a mighty prophet, thought
By him all Israel would at last be free;
But Rome has nailed our hopes unto a tree;
And redemption? Just an idle tale. *Ought*

He not have suffered so, by what ye read
In that ye call his Word; should ye not believe
That from the grave and sin all could be free
At last—when he from every pore did bleed
To cleanse all men? And then new life conceive
Out of the tomb? Here—open up and see.

SECTION SEVEN

How and Why Is the Book of Mormon the Manifestation of the Messiah? A Scriptural Adventure and an Analogy

"Earth's crammed with heaven,
And every common bush afire with God:
But only he who sees takes off his shoes"
—Elizabeth Barrett Browning

OPENING SCENARIOS

We'll have you return and respond to these at the end of this section.

Scenario #1

"Look at the experience Alma had," Jim said to himself after reading Alma 36 once more and having the same question in his mind each time. "Visited by an angel, seeing and hearing choirs of angels praising God on His throne. And what did he do to rate such an experience? He was actually in rebellion against the Church. Just like Paul in the New Testament. Why should they be allowed such experiences—and not the rest of us? I'd be able to stand and bear witness anywhere too if I had those experiences."

Scenario #2

When speaking to various people about my decision to be baptized into the Church of Jesus Christ of Latter-day Saints, I explain to them the importance of my testimony of the Book of Mormon in my conversion. A question then frequently follows from many of these people. "Where are those plates now?" they ask. When I tell them that Joseph Smith gave them back to an angel, some respond with a wry smile. "How convenient," they say. How would you respond to such a reaction and to such questions?

QUESTION # 3: DOES A PERSON HAVE TO RECEIVE THE BOOK OF MORMON TO BE SAVED?

I'd like to probe this question a little further by adding a fill-in-the-blank section. I'll quote a couple of verses from the scriptures, leaving two blanks. You fill in the blanks with what you think is the best word. It is the same, single word for each blank. As you fill in these blanks, please remember what we read from the scriptures as we answered our first question: "Does a person have to receive Jesus Christ to be saved?" (See 3 Nephi 9: 14–17.). Ready? "Those who receive _____ in faith, and work righteousness, shall receive a crown of eternal life; But those who harden their hearts in unbelief, and reject _____, it shall turn to their own condemnation."

So, what word goes in the blank? In the past, some have suggested "Christ," or "Him," referring to the Savior. All great answers, since we are aware that only in and through Jesus Christ we can be saved and receive eternal life. But interestingly, the word that goes in the blanks is "it." So what could "it" possibly refer to?

I just quoted from Doctrine & Covenants section 20, verses 14 and 15. The pronoun "it" has as its antecedent "the Book of Mormon," which is introduced in verse 8. So let's read the verses again, based on what we just learned: "Those who receive the Book of Mormon in faith, and work righteousness, shall receive a crown of eternal life; But those who harden their hearts in unbelief, and reject the Book of Mormon, it shall turn to their own condemnation."

Isn't that astounding to think about? Our eternal salvation depends upon whether or not we receive the Book of Mormon? (see also Doctrine & Covenants 84:52–57; 3:16–20).

> Perhaps there is nothing that testifies more clearly of the importance of this modern book of scripture than what the Lord Himself has said about it. By His own mouth He has borne witness (1) that it is true (Doctrine & Covenants 17:6), (2) that it contains the truth and

His words (Doctrine & Covenants 19:26), (3) that it was translated by power from on high (Doctrine & Covenants 20:8), (4) that it contains the fulness of the gospel of Jesus Christ (Doctrine & Covenants 20:9, Doctrine & Covenants 42:12), (5) that it was given by inspiration and confirmed by the ministering of angels (Doctrine & Covenants 20:10), (6) that it gives evidence that the holy scriptures are true (Doctrine & Covenants 20:11), and (7) that those who receive it in faith shall receive eternal life (Doctrine & Covenants 20:14).[1]

But how could that be, you may ask. It is only by receiving *Christ* that we can be saved. That leads us to our final question.

QUESTION # 4: WHY?

Why does a person have to receive the Book of Mormon to be saved? Certainly, the Book of Mormon helps us to keep intact those links of faith to the Savior and to reap all of those powerful blessings detailed by modern prophets. But, just as was the case with question #2 above, the answer is a little more complicated than it may seem at first. When we decide to accept or reject the Book of Mormon, we literally decide to accept or reject the Savior. Put another way, the way the Book of Mormon writers often put it: the Book of Mormon is the very *manifestation* of the Messiah in His fulness—perhaps the greatest and fullest manifestation available to any of us. As such, the Book of Mormon fulfills the most glorious role of all temples—helping us find and follow the Savior. To help make this astounding idea clearer, let me share with you a scriptural adventure I had about twenty years ago.

When I study the scriptures, I keep a pen and paper handy (or lately, keyboard and computer file). That is one way of showing the Lord that I anticipate that he'll give me valuable ideas as I read; by having the pen and paper nearby I exercise some faith (as the Lord teaches in Doctrine & Covenants 8:1, 10). The "paper" I often use are a set of large index cards: I punch a hole in the upper corner and hook them together with a metal ring. I noticed that sometimes prophets in the Book of Mormon recorded on their plates ideas that followed from their study of some book of scripture—such as Jacob and Nephi did in 2 Nephi 9 and 25, after reading from Isaiah, or as current prophets did after reading in the New Testament (see

Doctrine & Covenants 76 and 138). And I thought that I should likewise be prepared to receive instruction from the Lord as part of my scripture study.

Another way I used the pen and paper followed from my studies as an English major about an ancient Greek concept called "rhetoric." What the ancient Greeks meant by *rhetoric* is still not clear to us, but it was some method of finding and organizing ideas and expanding these ideas into larger talks and essays. The more I read about rhetoric, the more convinced I became that it was, in a sense, an *act of faith* in the power of language: writers exercised this faith by simply putting their pens to paper and letting a somewhat hazy thought or truth inside them *become better articulated* through the attempt to clothe that idea or feeling in the garb of *words*. And then as they struggled to articulate these ideas, thoughts would flow more clearly and smoothly, until what was once a nascent idea grew into a substantial and expanded truth. I added my own definition of this process of rhetoric: "Rhetoric is a means of discovering truth, in which truths are discovered, evaluated, and substantiated through the *process of attempting to verbally articulate some nascent idea*. Metaphorically, rhetoric is the vessel that takes us on the voyages of insight and discovery, and words are the winds in our sails."

The thought dawned on me that perhaps the best way to study the scriptures was to employ a kind of *spiritual rhetoric*. Imagine the power of such a tool of discovery when it is combined with the Holy Ghost—as we seek to discover *spiritual* truths. I think Elder Marion G. Romney described such a process when he said he knew when he'd spoken under the influence of the Spirit because "I learned something that I did not know."[2] I wondered if that may have been part of what the Lord was trying to teach Oliver Cowdery—and us—in sections 8 and 9 of the Doctrine & Covenants. "You must study it out in your mind. . . . I will tell you in your mind and in your heart . . . Therefore, ask in faith. . . . Ask that you may know the mysteries of God, and that you may . . . receive knowledge from those ancient records. . . . You shall feel that it is right. . . . Therefore, you cannot write that which is sacred save it be given you of me."

And so I would begin a new study of a chapter from the Book of Mormon by opening my "plates" and putting the chapter title at the top of the card. Then I would simply follow the directions the Lord gave to Brother Oliver. Sometimes wonderful ideas would flow as the Spirit seemed to guide my pen. Other times, I would get what seemed like a "stupor of thought" (or "writer's block," perhaps), and realize I needed to go another direction. Occasionally, I would just write somewhat ordinary–seeming ideas down for several study sessions and then discover after a week or so how all of these ideas fit together marvelously. I was hooked.

READING FROM 2 NEPHI 5

All of this leads to an experience I had many years ago while reading chapter five from the Second Book of Nephi. I began as usual by asking the Lord to guide my thoughts as I read. I just read and looked for any impressions that I might want to expand in writing or investigate further through footnotes and the Topical Guide. When I finished reading and annotating, the chapter hadn't impressed me more than usual—except for the fact that Nephi had built a temple in the wilderness. So I just began with that idea as I put my pen to my card: "That's interesting—a temple in the wilderness. Quite an undertaking. I wonder where else in the Book of Mormon we read about temples." That thought led me to cross reference other places in the Book of Mormon where temples were mentioned. As I studied about them, I noted something very interesting about temples in this Nephite record: "Whenever a temple is mentioned or a prophet speaks at a temple, the greatest manifestations of the Savior and His mission occur." I wrote about King Benjamin's great sermon from the temple at Zarahemla, about Abinadi's testimony before King Noah and his court. And I noted that before there was a temple available, the Lord took Nephi "to a high mountain" (one of the Lord's substitutes for a temple) for his great manifestation of the Savior we read about in 1 Nephi 11–15, just as the brother of Jared received his great manifestation after ascending to "the top of a high mount" in Ether 3:1. It seemed reasonable to me also that right after Nephi records the building of the first Nephite temple, that the great manifestations of the Savior given by Jacob (2 Nephi 6–10) and by Nephi (2 Nephi 11–33) would have occurred in this temple. And when the Savior appeared to the Nephites in 3 Nephi 11, it was at the temple of Bountiful. Things were suddenly getting very interesting and exciting as I continued to write.

I then wrote down on my card a simple question—which resulted in a not-so-simple answer: "What is the primary purpose of a temple?" I ended up in Doctrine & Covenants 109:5, where I read that the purpose of building the Kirtland Temple was "that the Son of Man might have a *place to manifest himself to his people*." I then thought back to all those places in the Book of Mormon where the greatest manifestations of the Savior and His mission occurred—*at temples*. And I wrote about how fascinating that was, and what message the Lord seemed to be making about the Book of Mormon by having us see that these great manifestations of the Savior and the Atonement in this book *occurred in temples*—a place that, we are later taught, is explicitly consecrated to make the Savior manifest.

Further cross-referencing led to another fascinating connection. I noticed that when Nephi and other Book of Mormon prophets described the plates, they preferred a particular word: "sacred" (see: 1 Nephi 19:5–6; see also Jacob 1:4, 8; Alma 37:2, 14, 10, 47; 63:1, 11, 13; 3 Nephi 1:2; 4 Nephi 1:48; Mormon 1:3; 6:6). We most often associate the word *sacred* with what goes on inside our temples. I looked up its meaning in various dictionaries ("holy," "consecrated," "dedicated or set apart for the worship of deity," and one I really liked: "the word sacred is generally conceived spatially, as referring to the area around a temple"), but an even greater understanding of how the Book of Mormon prophets used "sacred" came when I looked up the etymology of the word that is its *opposite*. The word "profane" has very simple and straightforward Latin roots: to be profane is to be *outside* (Latin *pro-*, before, outside) the *temple* (Latin *fānum*, temple). So, if the opposite of sacred means "to be outside the temple," then that which is sacred lies *within* or *inside* a *temple*. Using this definition of sacred, we learn Nephi only includes within the Book of Mormon that which is found within a temple—or only that which makes the Son of God manifest.

And then, one of the personally (I emphasize *personally*—since this process simply allows us to receive ideas for ourselves) most sacred sentences I have ever written came out like this: "Not only is the Book of Mormon all *about* temples as the place where the greatest manifestations of the Messiah occur; but the Book of Mormon *is* a temple—perhaps one of the greatest temples of these latter-days, and the temple where the Savior makes Himself most clearly and powerfully manifest to each of us. Yes, the Book of Mormon *is a temple.*"

That all resulted in a lot more cards being filled—in fact, about twenty years' worth of cards. Later in this book, we'll further consider how the Book of Mormon fulfills this temple role, and how the Lord has always used the scriptures as a primary means of making Himself manifest. But for now, I'd like to use a little analogy to describe how the Book of Mormon is a temple in which the Savior manifests Himself.

HOW AND WHY IS THE BOOK OF MORMON THE MANIFESTATION OF THE MESSIAH? AN ANALOGY

"Moreover he said unto me, Son of man, eat that you find; eat this scroll, and go speak unto the house of Israel. So I opened my mouth, and he caused me to eat that scroll. And he said unto me, Son of man, feed your belly, and fill your stomach with this scroll that I give you. Then did I eat it; and it was in my mouth as honey for sweetness." —Ezekiel 3:1–3

Part 1

Start by writing down the letters B R E A D on a piece of paper.

What do you think of when you see these letters? Write down the thoughts this word brings to your mind.

It's truly amazing that these various lines, curves, and shapes could form a word and then an image in each of our minds—something a bit different in each of our minds. Perhaps a kitchen at home where a hot loaf of homemade bread comes steaming out of the oven. Perhaps cinnamon bread or rolls or muffins. Perhaps the weekly sacrament covenant we make. Perhaps a bit of all these things.

Now write down these letters on a piece of paper:
J E S U S   C H R I S T
What do you think of when you see these words?
Write down any thoughts these words bring to your mind.

Again, it is amazing that these letters forming these words could evoke such powerful images, feelings, and thoughts from us. Like the hymn, "Jesus, the Very Thought of Thee," just seeing this sacred name may evoke feelings of awe, gratitude, humility, hope, and love. These words may cause you to think of the Savior at His birth, or His death, or His resurrection; teaching the Sermon on the Mount or revealing His messianic mission to the woman at the well; chastising the scribes and Pharisees or healing the blind and leprous. All wonderful manifestations of the Savior and His atoning mission. And when we read from the Book of Mormon, all of these great and marvelous manifestations may become available to us.

Part II

But as powerful as these manifestations of both bread and the Savior that arise from these words are, we may ask ourselves if a *more* powerful and immediate manifestation is available. In other words, is there a greater manifestation of the Messiah available for readers of the Book of Mormon?

Imagine now a picture of bread. Just as you may more clearly envision the bread now than when you simply saw the letters and word, perhaps when reading the Book of Mormon, we may also have a clearer, more powerful manifestation of the Savior as we continue to read from its pages, so that we seem to get past the mere letters and words, and almost see Him upon the pages, and even feel His presence and Spirit as we study the book.

But, the questions continue: Is there yet a still more powerful manifestation of the Savior available? More powerful than even seeing Him and feeling you are in His presence? How could it get better than that?

Part III

I'd like to now invite you to go find a fresh loaf of bread and take a slice from it. Now you are not just envisioning the bread, but actually touching it. Is there any more powerful manifestation of bread available than even this? You now know where this is leading. Go ahead and taste from the slice of bread. Might we receive as full a manifestation of the Savior as we "partake" of the Book of Mormon?

Can you see that when we say the Book of Mormon is the manifestation of the Messiah, that such a manifestation can be much more powerful than you might at first suppose? Perhaps this is one of the things the Lord means when He said that the Book of Mormon contains the "fulness of the gospel." "Except ye eat of my flesh, and drink of my blood," the Savior taught, "Ye cannot enter the Kingdom of God." "Feast upon the words of Christ," Nephi admonishes us. "Take, eat, this is my body," the Lord teaches. "I am the bread of life. . . . Whoso eateth my flesh, and drinketh my blood, hath eternal life; and I will raise him up at the last day. For my flesh is meat indeed, and my blood is drink indeed. He that eateth my flesh, and drinketh my blood, dwelleth in me, and I in him" (John 6:35, 54–56).

QUESTIONS TO CONTEMPLATE

- What could such a phrase mean—that the Book of Mormon is an actual temple, where, as in other temples, the Messiah is made fully manifest to us?

- How would you respond if you were present on the day the Lord multiplied the loaves and fishes and then turned to you and others and said what He did in John 6:35? Why?

- Shouldn't we expect that the Lord would make available to us today the opportunity to have as close a relationship—and as clear a manifestation—of the Savior as those we read about in the Old and New Testaments?

- Wouldn't it be sad if such a powerful manifestation of the Savior was available through the Book of Mormon, but we stopped at an earlier knowledge of the Savior, thinking that was all that was available from simple words on a page?

- What does this have to do with the covenants we make (sacrament, temple, Book of Mormon)?

- What do you think is the most insatiable and deepest of all human longings? Why?

NOTES

1 President Ezra Taft Benson, *Ensign*, November 1986, pg. 4.

2 Quoted by Elder Theodore Tuttle in "Teaching the Word to the Rising Generation," address delivered 10 July 1970 at BYU summer school; also found in *Duties and Blessings of the Priesthood: Basic Manual for Priesthood Holders, Part A*, p. 132.

The Ship of Rhetoric

Your sacred quest begins, with sails all taut—
Ly puffed, and ports-of-call well beyond earth's
Narrow climes. Anticipate sudden births
Of truth from mysterious fathoms, caught

In nets of words as semantic streams brush
You along inspiration's paths, splashing
Waves of insight that come crashing
Upon your ship's plunging bow with a gush

Of revelation from uncharted seas,
While you steer by faith through a starless night,
Squalls nor doldrums leaving you astray,
As the Spirit hovers, imploring you please:
Follow these flickerings to the light of day,
As you put pen to paper and simply write.

SECTION EIGHT
The Most Insatiable of All Human Longings

After I left the army, I attended my local ward in Utica, New York, and would meet regularly with a small group of young adults in the area. One evening, after a social, we held an impromptu testimony meeting. After a few testimonies, a young woman named Maureen got up. She had never been baptized but would socialize with us regularly—just not at Church. I'll never forget her words. "I know I'm not a member of your church. But I thought I'd get up and say something. You guys are probably wondering why I keep hanging out with you. I'll tell you why. It's because you are all so different from anyone else I've met. And I keep trying to figure out what makes you so different. And I just figured it out, so I thought I'd tell you: you're happy. Truly happy. In ways I've never seen in any other people. Now I don't know what it is that makes you so happy, but I do have some advice for you: whatever it is that makes you happy: keep it, nurture it, and share it." I don't know if I've gotten any better advice from anyone. I don't know where Maureen is now, but I've got to hope—and figure—that she has discovered what it was, and is following her own advice right now.

How would you respond to Maureen? What do you think it is, above all else, that makes Latter-day Saints truly happy?

And how would you answer this question: Well, what is it that above all other things has the greatest potential to make any person most truly happy?

I'd suggest this as one possible response to Maureen: the greatest happiness possible for a person in this life is *being in the presence of*

God and being committed to doing whatever it takes to remain in His presence. (There is, I think, only one other thing that can bring a similar kind of happiness—and that is helping to bring others into the presence of God.) By being in His presence, we feel one with Him, we have His very Spirit in us, we replace our will with His, we feel His love and then become extensions of His love for others. What else could possibly bring as much happiness?

I think people somehow intrinsically recognize that need and always feel something is lacking until that need is fulfilled. And I am confident that our Heavenly Father is anxious above all else to invite us into His presence.

THE POWER OF THE WORD

"In a thousand words I can have the Lord's Prayer, the 23rd Psalm, the Hippocratic Oath, a sonnet by Shakespeare, the Preamble to the Constitution, Lincoln's Gettysburg Address and almost all of the Boy Scout Oath. Now exactly what picture were you planning to trade for all that?"
—Roy H. Williams

It is interesting, isn't it, how often the prophets in the scriptures strive to convince those around them of the power of *the word* and we should accept that the Lord exercises and manifests His power primarily through the word?

Can you think of anywhere in the scriptures where the prophets attempt to persuade others to rely upon and recognize the Lord's power through "the word"?[1]

We early showed how Nephi's sharpest rebukes to his brethren followed their unwillingness to seek personal revelation (see 1 Nephi 15:8–10), which Nephi knew alone could free them from the snares of the adversary. Obviously related is his sharp exhortation for them to accept that the Lord works through "the word": "And ye also know that by the power of his almighty word he can cause the earth that it shall pass away; yea, and ye know that by his word he can cause the rough places to be made smooth, and the smooth places shall be broken up. O then, why is it, that ye can be so hard in your hearts?" (1 Nephi 17:46).

Nephi also teaches us to look for power in the word: "And it came to pass that according to his word he did destroy them; and according to his word he did lead them; and according to his word he did all things for them; and there was not any thing done save it were by his word" (1 Nephi 17:31; see also Mormon 9:17).

It seems counterintuitive to suppose that "mere" words really can be a more powerful "manifestation" of something than actually seeing with our physical eyes. Yet, how many of us have walked out of a movie thinking *the book was a lot better*? Why is that, do you suppose? Part of the reason is that no producer, director, casting agent, cinematographer, or sound engineer can ever outdo our own mind's abilities.

But how about the experience of reading a book compared with an actual visitation that we can experience "first-hand"? We have seen in the first chapter of Nephi that the most powerful manifestation of the Savior Lehi experienced in his "first vision" occurred from reading from a book (more on this in the next section).

One of those in history who most respected the power of "the word" was Desiderius Erasmus, the great Renaissance humanist and contemporary of Martin Luther, from whose translations of the Bible Luther in turn gave the world a German version.

"If the footprints of Christ are anywhere shown to us we kneel down and adore," Erasmus wrote. "Why do we not rather venerate the living and breathing picture of him in these books [of the New Testament]?"

> If the vesture of Christ be exhibited, where will we not go to kiss it? Yet were his whole wardrobe exhibited, nothing could exhibit Christ more vividly and truly than these Evangelical writings. Statues of wood and stone we decorate with gold and gems for the love of Christ. They only profess to give us the form of his body; these books present us with a living image of his most holy mind. Were we to have seen him with our own eyes, we should not have so intimate a knowledge as they give of Christ, speaking, healing, dying, and rising again, as it were in our actual presence.[2]

THE FULNESS OF THE EVERLASTING GOSPEL

We've already seen how the word "manifest" indicates a much more vivid and powerful sense of knowing than other words in our language. There is perhaps another simple word worth our consideration that may help us distinguish the kind of knowledge available in a "manifestation" over and beyond other forms of knowledge. That word is "fulness." This leads us to consider a very important phrase the Lord uses to describe what is contained in the Book of Mormon.

When the angel Moroni first told Joseph about a "book deposited, written upon gold plates," how did he describe the book (see JS–H 1:34; see also Doctrine & Covenants 20:8–9; 14:10)?

What do you think Moroni meant when he said "that the fulness of the everlasting gospel was contained in it"?

The gospel is the "Good News" that Jesus is the Christ and that we can come unto Him and be saved (John 17:3; 3 Nephi 27:13; Doctrine & Covenants 76:40–42; see also Bible Dictionary: "Gospel," p. 682); *so, could something contain the "fulness of the gospel" if it didn't manifest Christ fully? Why?*

And likewise, if something contained and made available a full manifestation of Christ available so that we can come to Him and be saved, wouldn't it contain the fulness of the gospel (John 5:39)? Why?

In the following scriptures from the Book of Mormon, *what great blessing does the Lord associate with receiving the "fulness of the gospel":* 1 Nephi 10:14; 15:13–14; 3 Nephi 20:30–31?

"After the Gentiles had received the fulness of the Gospel, the natural branches of the olive-tree . . . should be grafted in, or come to _____" (1 Nephi 10:14).

". . . after the Messiah shall be manifested in the body unto the children of men, then shall the fulness of the gospel of the Messiah come unto the Gentiles . . . And at that day . . . they shall come the knowledge of their _ _____" (1 Nephi 15:13–14).

"When the fulness of my Gospel shall be preached unto them . . . they shall believe in _____, that I am _____" (3 Nephi 20:30–31).

ACCORDING TO MODERN PROPHETS: THE "FULNESS OF THE GOSPEL"

How do the following words (below) of Presidents Ezra Taft Benson,

Joseph Fielding Smith, Gordon B. Hinckley, and Elder Russell M. Nelson help us understand the meaning of these Book of Mormon scriptures, and teach us one way that the Book of Mormon can be said to contain "the fulness of the gospel"?

- President Ezra Taft Benson on how The Book of Mormon's testimony of the Savior is "clear, undiluted and full of power": "The Book of Mormon—Keystone of Our Religion," *Ensign*, November 1986, 5–6.

- President Gordon B. Hinckley on how the Book of Mormon adds a tangible confirmation and testimonial to the First Vision witness of the reality of Christ: *Ensign*, November, 2002, 5.

- Elder Russell M. Nelson on how the "fulness of the gospel . . . connotes a fuller comprehension of the Atonement": "A Testimony of the Book of Mormon," *Ensign*, Nov. 1999, 69.

How do these following scriptures help us better understand this principle taught by these modern prophets?

"Then [the rich man] said, I pray thee therefore, father, that thou wouldest send him to my father's house: For I have five brethren; that he may testify unto them, lest they also come into this place of torment. Abraham saith unto him, They have Moses and the prophets; let them hear them. And he said, Nay, father Abraham: but if one went unto them from the dead, they will repent. And he said unto him, If they hear not Moses and the prophets, neither will they be persuaded, though one rose from the dead." (Luke 16: 27–31)

"For he that believed not John concerning me, cannot believe me. . . . And except ye repent, the preaching of John shall condemn you in the day of judgment." (JST Matthew 21:32–34)

So what? What difference should this knowledge make in our lives? The following questions I have to regularly ask myself as I consider the principles about the Book of Mormon we have just discussed.

THE BIG QUESTION

What kind of experience would you hope to have so that you, with your whole heart and soul, would become totally committed to following the Savior at all times and at all places?

What If I Had Lived Then?

As we look back across twenty centuries to the New Testament times, *do you ever think to yourself: if only I had lived when the Savior was physically on the earth; if only I had walked with Him as He taught the Sermon on the Mount, as He multiplied the loaves and fishes, as He gave sight to the blind and healed the lepers; if only I had lived then, I would live each moment of my life in complete and total dedication to the gospel and to following the Savior?*

And aren't we all amazed as we read the New Testament account of the Savior—of His teachings, His miracles, of the power of His own testimony and of the scriptures that so clearly testified of Him—that so many of those who witnessed these things did not embrace Him with all their hearts as their Savior? Although many witnessed these things with their own eyes and ears, relatively few became His faithful disciples.

And as we continue to look back across those centuries and see people making these choices, in our heart of hearts isn't there a hard question we each ask of ourselves: had *I* lived at that time, would *I* have recognized the Savior, and would I have followed Him with all my heart?

WHAT KIND OF MESSIAH AM I LOOKING FOR?

"That they may believe the gospel, and look not for a Messiah to come who has already come."—Doctrine & Covenants 19:27

What was it that blinded so many of the people of that day to the reality of the Savior's mission as the promised Messiah?

A few leaders at that time seemed fearful that Jesus would take away from them some power and prestige and therefore sought His death. Others seemed aware that Jesus was indeed everything He testified He was, and everything His works and teachings demonstrated He was—the very Son of God, the Christ, the Redeemer—and such knowledge seemed to only increase their hatred of Him and their insistence that He should die.

What kept so many others from accepting Him as their Savior and becoming His devoted disciples? What kind of a Messiah were they mistakenly anticipating?

It seems that for many, Jesus didn't meet their expectations of what the Messiah was supposed to be. Perhaps they wanted a warrior Messiah to free them from Roman tyranny; or a Messiah that they felt would interpret the Mosaic Law as strictly and mercilessly as they did; or a Messiah that spent less time with sinners and common "riff-raff"; or a Messiah that didn't make their lives harder by insisting they forgive enemies, respect their marriage covenants, purify their thoughts, serve others, feed the poor, clothe the naked, forget themselves, be born again, and become as little children. Perhaps, ultimately, the Messiah they could not accept was a Messiah upon whom they find themselves totally and completely dependent for both temporal and spiritual salvation. They, like others, reject a Messiah who teaches that "unless ye eat of my flesh and drink of my blood" ye cannot be saved.

We are glad to have the New Testament and to learn from the awful errors of those who decided the Savior wasn't the kind of Messiah they were looking for.

And yet, the tough questions continue—really tough questions.

Such as: Are there some of us today, even while Christ has restored the fulness of His gospel to the earth, who in one sense or another, like some of the Jews of Christ's day, are still waiting for the right Messiah to show up? That is, do we sometimes insist that a true testimony and manifestation of the Savior must involve more than what we receive from our study of the Book of Mormon? Do we place a higher value upon knowledge obtained via our physical eyes and ears than from spiritual sight and sound? And when we do so, is the Lord speaking to us in Doctrine & Covenants 84:54–57? I think those scenarios presented at the beginning of this section may fit here.

Returning to the initial question: *What kind of experience would we hope to have so that we, with our whole heart and soul, would become totally committed to following the Savior at all times and at all places? That is, to accepting Him as the true Messiah?*

Do we ever say to ourselves, in our heart of hearts: "Boy, if I ever had a chance to visit and talk with the Savior face-to-face, to be in His physical presence for just a moment—that would certainly put a zip into my dedication and commitment"? No more half-steppin' after that! What do you think I am really saying when I say such a thing?

When I say such things to myself, is it possible I am really saying, "I'm still waiting for the Messiah to show up"? "I'm waiting for the kind of Messiah to show up that meets my personal expectations." At such times, should I include myself in that group of whom the Lord speaks in Doctrine & Covenants 19:27? Why? Have I been underestimating the power of the word in my life? How? Why?

QUESTIONS TO CONTEMPLATE

- Have I striven today to do whatever it takes to actually be in the Lord's presence? How?

- What were some things today that took me in or out of His presence?

- What will I do tomorrow to feel myself more often in His presence?

- Is there any way today I showed my faith that the Lord can fully reveal Himself through words?

- How have I shown or taught my children that I have such faith—in the scriptures?

- What does this have to do with the covenants we make (sacrament, temple, Book of Mormon)?

- What do you think is the most powerful manifestation of the Savior available? Why?

NOTES

1 Throughout the Book of Mormon we are reminded of the power of "the word": 2 Nephi 31:20; 2 Nephi 32:3; "Alma 5:7; 36:26; 32:41; 32:42; 32:40; Helaman 3:29–30; Ether 4:9. We find such testimonies of the power of God's word in all of scripture: Hebrews 4:12; Doctrine & Covenants 6:2; 11:2; 12:2; 14:2; 33:1; 84:45

2 Stubbs, Charles William, *Cambridge and Its Story* (Cambridge: Galloway and Porter, 1903), 171.

Abrahamic Covenant

How shall the seed of Abraham the whole
World bless with eternal life? In the Word
Gathered by the priesthood: where we first heard
Of a Savior, then watched him take the toll

Of our sins, invite us each to enroll
In his debt-free plan of salvation, spurred
By a love without bounds, which we preferred
To the world's profanations of the soul.

In return, in ways that natural man
Cannot conceive, we enter the presence
Of the Lord, every bit as real as when
In the full light and glory of a noon
Day sun Joseph could directly commune
With the Great I AM: his very essence.

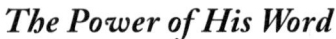

The Power of His Word

When I'm slipping, it lends an iron grip,
Or doldrummed, its Spirit sends a breeze;
A flaming torch, when on strange paths I trip
And stumble, then guides me to my knees;
When I've fallen, gracefully spreads its wings,
Alighting in Gethsemane, beside vermilion springs.

Would then I sing, the Bible is my Psalter,
Or dance, join angels in its holy reel;
And worship, unfolds at once an altar,
Whereon I place myself, His soul to seal;
And worship more, reveals the Father's will
For others of His children—then sends me to fulfill.

And thinking of the Lord's Judean days
Wishing I had walked upon that stage,
I unlatch the gospel gate and gaze
At His visage now extending from the page,
His words more clear than once I could conceive:
"I'll manifest myself in full—just open and believe."

SECTION NINE

The Most Powerful Manifestation: What Could Be More Powerful than a Physical Appearance of the Savior?

"Whom having not seen, ye love;
in whom, though now ye see him not, yet believing,
ye rejoice with joy unspeakable and full of glory:
Receiving the end of your faith, even the salvation of your souls."
—1 Peter 1:8–9

What if the most powerful manifestation of the Messiah—more powerful than even the physical presence of the Savior—was readily available, and we were putting that manifestation on hold, still waiting for our personal idea of what a *really* powerful manifestation should be?

But what could be more powerful than the physical presence of the Savior?

If you had to make a choice between a physical manifestation of the Savior ("in the flesh," as the Book of Mormon writers distinguish it) and a spiritual manifestation of the Savior ("in word, and in power"), which would you prefer? Why?

ACCORDING TO MODERN PROPHETS: THE GREATEST MANIFESTATION OF CHRIST

How does this idea fit with these words of these modern prophets?

- President Heber J. Grant: "Many men say: 'If I could only see an angel, if I could only hear an angel proclaim something, that would cause me to be faithful all the days of my life!' It had no effect upon these men that were not serving the Lord, and it would have no effect today" (*Conference Reports,* Apr. 1924, p. 159).

- President Joseph F. Smith: "When I as a boy first started out in the ministry, I would frequently go out and ask the Lord to show me some marvelous thing, in order that I might receive a testimony. But the Lord withheld marvels from me, and showed me the truth, line upon line, precept upon precept, here a little and there a little, *until he made me to know the truth from the crown of my head to the soles of my feet,* and until doubt and fear had been absolutely purged from me. He did not have to send an angel from the heavens to do this, nor did he have to speak with the trump of an archangel. By the whisperings of the still small voice of the Spirit of the living God, he gave to me the testimony I possess" (*Gospel Doctrine,* p. 7, emphasis added).

- President Joseph Fielding Smith: "When a man has the manifestation from the Holy Ghost, it leaves an indelible impression on his soul, one that is not easily erased. It is Spirit speaking to spirit, and it comes with convincing force. A manifestation of an angel, or even the Son of God Himself, would impress the eye and mind, and eventually become dimmed, but the impressions of the Holy Ghost sink deeper into the soul and are more difficult to erase" (*Answers to Gospel Questions,* 2:151; see also *Seek Ye Earnestly,* pp. 213–4; *Doctrines of Salvation,* 1:48).

- President Harold B. Lee: "The most important testimony does not come by sight, but by the inner witness. Christ may be nearer than we have knowledge. 'I am in your midst, but you do not see me.' The Holy Ghost bears the sure witness. 'Mine eyes are upon you. The day cometh when ye shall know that I am.'" (Address to meeting of Provo Temple workers, 9 July 1972, Historical Department Archives, The Church of Jesus Christ of Latter-day Saints, 10. Quoted in *Teachings of Presidents of the Church: Harold B. Lee,* "Chapter 19: Take Time to Be Holy," 175.)

How does all this fit with these words of the Savior: "Therefore blessed are ye if ye shall believe in me and be baptized, *after that ye have seen me* and know that I am. And again, *more* blessed are they who shall believe in your words because that ye shall testify that ye have seen me, and that ye know that I am" (3 Nephi 12:1–2); "Thomas, because thou hast seen me, thou hast believed: blessed are they that have not seen, and yet have believed" (John 20:28–29); "For had ye believed Moses, ye would have believed me: For he wrote of me. But if ye believed not his writings, how shall ye believe my words" (John 5:46–47); "He that will not believe my words will not believe me—that I am" (Ether 4:12)?

How does all this fit with these words of the Savior to Alma? "Blessed are thou, Alma, and blessed are they who were baptized in the waters of Mormon. Thou art blessed because of thy exceeding faith *in the words alone* of my servant Abinadi [which we also have available today in the Book of Mormon]. And blessed are they because of their exceeding faith *in the words alone, which thou hast spoken unto them*" (Mosiah 26:15–16).

Along these lines, what kind of a witness did so many anti-Christs (and anti-prophets) insist upon, and what objection did so many of them register when attacking the Lord's prophets, such as Abinadi, Amulek and Alma, and so on? (See: Jacob 7:13; Alma 30:43; 32:17; Matthew 12:39; Alma 21:5.)[1]

Can you think of those in the Book of Mormon who received wonderful manifestations of the Savior and His Atonement—after demonstrating faith in the words alone of the Lord's messengers? (See Alma 18:23; 19:9–10; 22:7; 15:9; Enos 1:8, 3–4; 1 Nephi 10:17.)

IS THE LORD ALSO SPEAKING TO ME?

With all of these things in mind, in what way might I, if I look beyond or undervalue the full manifestation of the Messiah provided in the Book of Mormon, be included with those the Lord names in these verses:

"And again, I command thee that thou shalt not covet thine own property, but impart freely to the printing of the Book of Mormon, which contains the truth and the word of God—Which is my word to the gentile, that soon it may go to the Jew, of whom the Laman-ites are a remnant, that they may believe the gospel, *and look not for a*

Messiah to come who has already come" (Doctrine & Covenants 19:26–27; emphasis added; see also 2 Nephi 25:16, 18; 2 Nephi 28:16; 1 Nephi 19:6–7; 2 Nephi 33:2; Jacob 4:14).

What word does Nephi use to describe the kind of knowledge and testimony of Christ available to us in the Book of Mormon?

Because of this, under what responsibility does that place each of us who read the manifestation available in the Book of Mormon (see 2 Nephi 25:28; 33:10–11)?²

Such a full and clear manifestation of the Savior is also available to us. Our encounter with the Savior may be as immediate and supernal as others who walked and talked with Him in Jerusalem or at the temple in Bountiful—or who visited Bethlehem and the empty tomb on Easter morning.

What does the Apostle Peter teach us about the relative power and efficacy of the manifestation of the Savior available through the scriptures (such as the Book of Mormon, in our case) compared to the other manifestations available—and which he personally experienced—through either physical sight or hearing (2 Peter 1:16–19)?

Notice that in this epistle Peter is certifying the "power and coming of the Lord, Jesus Christ" to the saints, that they may be assured that "we have not followed cunningly devised fables" but have unimpeachable knowledge of these truths (2 Peter 1:16). And upon what is such unimpeachable knowledge based? Interestingly, he first mentions that he and the other apostles were both *"eyewitnesses* of [Christ's] majesty" and clearly *heard* the "voice [of God the Father] . . . which came from heaven to declare "This is my beloved Son" (2 Peter 1:16–18). But then, Peter adds another source of his witness of these truths, one upon which both he and the Saints can *with even greater confidence rely*, and finds a wonderfully apt metaphor to express the increased power of this witness: "We have also a *more sure word* of prophecy, whereunto ye do well to take heed, as unto a light that shineth in a dark place, until the day dawn, and the day star arise in your hearts" (2 Peter 1:19).³

How does Alma the Younger teach us this lesson?

Did Alma ever receive any powerful physical manifestations of the power of God (see Mosiah 27:11)? How?⁴

After having been visited by an angel, upon what experiences does

Alma later draw when he bears his testimony to the people of Zarahemla (see Alma 5:46–47)?[25]

How does Jacob teach us the same lesson?

Did Jacob ever receive a physical manifestation of the Savior? That is, did the Savior ever physically appear to him (see 2 Nephi 11:3)?

Yet, in the latter part of his life, when confronted with an anti-Christ, what does Jacob say is the foundation of his testimony of the Atonement of Christ (see Jacob 7:12)?[26]

How does Jacob's recording of the last words of Sherem teach a similar lesson—about the relative power of the manifestation of Christ available through the scriptures (Jacob 7:19)? Why did Sherem fear he had committed "unpardonable sin"? What kind of knowledge would have to be available to someone to commit such a sin?

Where does Sherem say such knowledge is to be found?[27]

In what way can we, through the scriptures, "see" Christ (Doctrine & Covenants 67:10; see also Doctrine & Covenants 50:45; 88:68; 97:15–16; 110:7)?[28] How do you know that Jesus is the Christ?

A "REAL-LIFE" PARABLE OF GALILEE / GERMANY

The following is a "real-life" parable that I told to my saintly Catholic mother after I joined the restored Church in order to help her understand my decision. I should preface by saying that my mom is easily the most Christlike person I have ever met. I will relate the story as I told it to her.

"When I was very young and went to Mass or when we read from the Bible at home, I used to think how wonderful it would have been if I had lived when Jesus lived. I had sort of a regular daydream that I lived at that time, and one evening I was late getting home. It was twilight, so I took a shortcut by the shores of the lake Galilee. As I hurried along the shore, it was getting dark enough so that from a distance I could see the fluttering orange flames of a fire pit someone had built—probably to fry some fish for a late dinner, I guessed.

"As I got closer, I could see a group of men gathered around the fire. I decided to quietly wade a bit out into the low-lapping waves of the lake to avoid the men. As I had nearly gotten past them, I looked over to the group and saw that one member was looking toward me.

I thought to break into a run, but it was perfectly clear to me that I was in no danger. In what seemed hardly any time at all, this person calmly walked down to the shore where I was and introduced himself. 'Terry, I am Jesus Christ, and those men by the fire are some of my disciples. I have been sent by Our Heavenly Father to come save you all from any mistakes you make, and bring all of you back to Him to be happy together forever. Would you like to also be my disciple?'

"I knew instantly that every word He spoke was true. I couldn't be happier. I answered 'yes,' and then ran home to tell you and Dad and Timmy and Bobby and Billy that Jesus Christ was on the earth and we could all become His disciples. You were all happy at the news too, and we all went to meet Him together and become His disciples.

"Well, Mom, when I went to Germany, this dream became a reality. I found out that the Savior returned to bring back His original Church. And He personally invited me to join His Church and become His disciple. And so I rushed to tell you and Dad and the whole family about Him and His Church. Just like in the dream."

SO WHAT? WHAT DIFFERENCE DOES ALL THIS MAKE?

Imagine if you and I were to recognize that the greatest and most powerful manifestation of the reality and mission of the Savior, much more powerful and vivid than even the physical presence of the Savior, is available to each and every one of us—every time we open that sacred record known as the Book of Mormon? Imagine if you and I were to fully accept the power and reality of that manifestation to such an extent that for us it would be at least as powerful as if we personally met the Savior in the flesh as did Peter, James, John, and their families, and heard the Savior announce His mission as the promised Messiah, watched Him heal the blind, raise the dead, and walk on water; or as Thomas and the Nephites at Bountiful, if we physically placed our hands in the wounds of the risen Savior? Can we even imagine that simply reading from a book could supply for us as powerful a manifestation as available to those who physically walked and talked with the Savior? If the answer is "no," then why not? If the answer is "yes," then we have a chance to be part of those of whom the Savior said: "blessed are they that have not seen, and yet have believed" (John 20:29). Or to be among those of whom the Lord later spoke: "More blessed are they who shall believe in your words. . . . Yea, blessed are they who shall believe in your words, and come down into the depths of humility. . . ." (3 Nephi 12:2; see also Mosiah 26:15–16).

RETURN TO OPENING SCENARIOS FOR QUESTIONS 3 & 4

With what you have learned in this book from the scriptures and from modern prophets and apostles, go back to the opening scenario(s) and respond to that challenge.

First Scenario

"Look at the experience Alma had," Jim said to himself after reading Alma 36 once more and having the same question in his mind each time. "Visited by an angel, seeing and hearing choirs of angels praising God on His throne. And what did he do to rate such an experience? He was actually in rebellion against the Church. Just like Paul in the New Testament. Why should they be allowed such experiences—and not the rest of us? I'd be able to stand and bear witness anywhere too if I had those experiences."[9]

Second Scenario

When speaking to various people about my decision to be baptized into the Church of Jesus Christ of Latter-day Saints, I explain to them the importance of my testimony of the Book of Mormon in my conversion. A question then frequently follows from many of these people. "Where are those plates now," they ask. When I tell them that Joseph Smith gave them back to an angel, some respond with a wry smile. "How convenient," they say. How would you respond to such a reaction and to such questions?

Here is my response to this second scenario, in the form of a dialogue:

"Whatever happened to those gold plates? Can we see them today?"

"Joseph Smith returned the plates to an angel in 1829," I say. "No one has seen them since then."

"That was convenient. So no plates. Doesn't that bother you?"

"It doesn't bother me at all that I can't see the plates—because seeing the plates would have very little impact on my commitment to the Church. It would have had very little impact on my decision to join the Church."

"You mean because you didn't need that much tangible evidence?"

"No, because I needed *more* tangible evidence before I joined the Church. Seeing and touching the plates would not have been nearly *enough* evidence for me. All those things that you think are important and conclusive evidences would not have been sufficient for me. If I did see the plates and touched them, even if an angel descended from heaven in a cloud of light with the plates and allowed me to hold them, and declared that Joseph Smith was a true prophet and Jesus Christ had restored His original Church to the earth through the prophet Joseph Smith—based on that experience I would not now be a Mormon—or a member of the Church of Jesus Christ of Latter-day Saints. I needed a *lot more evidence* before ever allowing myself to be baptized, and before I ever made a decision to dedicate my entire life to the principles of this church."

Let me ask you: Do you always feel you can trust your eyes? Have you ever been sure you saw something and later been amazed at how mistaken you were? Has that ever happened with something you were sure you heard? Or touched?

I lived in Germany for almost three years. One time I was taking a train between two towns that weren't far from each other. When I reached a halfway station, I had to wait over an hour for my next transfer. But the train I was in wouldn't be leaving for over an hour and a half. So I decided to take a little nap where I was then sitting. I would have plenty of time to get to my next train. The only problem was that the train I was in was an express train to Frankfort—much, much farther and out of the way from my destination. So I just had to be sure to wake up in time.

Well, I must have been a lot more tired than I realized, because I immediately went into a deep sleep—and suddenly awoke to the sound of a moving train. As I looked out the window I could obviously see that the train I was in was moving. I was in deep trouble—I thought. But then something very weird happened. As clear as all the signs indicated to me that the train I sat in was moving—both by what I heard and saw—I was mistaken. My train was actually standing still. It was the train on the track right next to mine that was moving and making all that noise. I had only been asleep for less than a half hour.

Before I ever allowed myself to be baptized, and before I ever dedicated my life to doing everything this church asked of me—I had to rely on knowledge and evidence that I could trust more than what had been available to me up to my life at that time. I had to be *surer* than that. There could be no possibility of being deceived—and so my eyes, my ears, even my mind in and of itself would not be sufficient. I needed more.

What more tangible evidence is available?

Well, if the Book of Mormon really is true, then there is a person named Jesus Christ who can make Himself manifest to us in ways that leave absolutely no room for doubt. That was the kind of evidence I was looking for, the kind I prayed for, and the kind I was given. I know the Book of Mormon is true—not because I've seen the plates it was written on—but because the person about whom the plates bear witness, Jesus Christ, made Himself and His mission of redemption clearly manifest to me—in a way that leaves no room for doubt or deception. I needed Jesus Christ Himself to make the truth manifest to me. Not the plates. Not an angel. But the Savior Himself—in His fulness.

REVIEW FOR QUESTIONS 3 & 4:

- In what location throughout the Book of Mormon do the most powerful manifestations of the Savior and His atoning mission occur? Why do you think this is so? What point could the Lord be making by having us find such a connection? What is the purpose of a temple (see Doctrine & Covenants 109:5)?

- In what way does the Book of Mormon fulfill its role of making the Messiah manifest to us and help us to come unto him?

- In what way does the Book of Mormon "contain the fulness of the everlasting gospel"?

- In what way are we now in a similar situation as those who lived during Christ's earthly ministry who were looking for the Messiah, but who were in danger of "not seeing" the Messiah clearly manifested to them?

- How can we be sure that we also don't undervalue or under appreciate the glorious and sacred manifestation of the Messiah that is now available to each of us?

- What difference do these ideas make in your life?

- Can you think of any places in the Book of Mormon where the Lord demonstrates to us this sacred role of the Book of Mormon—to make the Messiah fully manifest? Where?

NOTES

1 Sherem, Korihor, and the Amalakites insisted on a physical "sign," and Alma warned the poor Zoramites against seeking such physical or carnal manifestations.

2 We will be eternally judged by how faithfully we receive and follow these words.

3 The JST reads: "We have therefore a more sure knowledge of the word of prophecy, to which word of prophecy ye do well to take heed."

4 Alma saw and heard an angel.

5 "How do you suppose I know of [the] surety" of the truths of the gospel, Alma asks the people of Zarahemla. And then, instead of bringing up the angelic visit, Alma says that "they are made known unto me by the Holy Spirit of God. Behold, I have fasted and prayed many days that I might know these things of myself. And now I do know of myself they are true; for the Lord God hath made them manifest unto me by his Holy Spirit. . . . And moreover, I say unto you that it has been revealed unto me, that the words which have been spoken by our fathers are true . . . which is also by the manifestation of the Spirit of God."

6 After testifying that he has physically "heard and seen," he adds that "it also has been made manifest unto me by the power of the Holy Ghost; wherefore, I know if there should be no atonement made all mankind must be lost."

7 The "unpardonable sin" follows from denying the Savior after receiving the greatest possible witness—or manifestation—of him. Sherem fears he has committed such a sin because he both denied the Christ and said he believed the scriptures, which "truly testify of him."

8 We may "see" Christ and "know . . . I AM" with our spiritual, "not with the carnal neither natural mind." We see and know Him as the Christ only when He serves as the Christ or the Savior to us personally, that is, when we exercise faith in His words unto redemption and rebirth. Such "knowledge" of "I am" is always a spiritual process and is ultimately based on the faith we exercise in the testimonies of Him we find in the scriptures.

9 Amazingly, as we read from the Book of Mormon, we have access to the same words and power that Alma the Younger accessed when he received such an astounding manifestation of the Savior—the words of His father, Alma the Elder. So we too have been visited by an angel (those prophets within the Book of Mormon, who are now angelic messengers from God relaying with equal power His words to us) and now can choose to act upon such a marvelous and wonderful manifestation—just as Alma the Younger did.

Lehi's First Vision

How could he in greater glory appear
Than within a blazing pillar of fire?
All doubts incinerated on that pyre,
And truth then branded on both eye and ear.

Or as the hidden halls of heaven premier
Music streaming from celestial lyres,
Accompanying numberless choirs
Of angels, praising their Redeemer near

His throne; then he descends, splashing a sea
Of light upon you. How could you possibly
In light and glory more sublime now greet
Him, who that very throne and choirs did flee
To be crowned and reign in Gethsemane?
Behold! And put those shoes from off thy feet.

SECTION TEN

Self-Referentiality in the Book of Mormon

Earlier, I shared an experience that occurred while reading and studying 2 Nephi 5 that led me to see the Book of Mormon in a whole new light—an extremely *sacred* light. In that sacred light, it seemed clear that the Book of Mormon fulfills one of the most wonderful roles of a temple—the *role of making the Messiah manifest to us* so that we can come unto Him, receive covenants, take upon ourselves His name and Spirit, and continue to follow Him and bring others to Him. In the power and fulness of that manifestation, I suggested, the Book of Mormon not only fulfills the role of a temple, but actually and literally *becomes* a great latter-day temple for us. When we open the Book of Mormon, we enter the temple of Mormon.

Some other questions may now arise, such as: If the Book of Mormon fulfills such a marvelous role (of making the Messiah fully and completely manifest), how else might the Lord make that role of the Book of Mormon clear to us? In what other ways might the Book of Mormon itself teach us this principle—that the most powerful way we come to know and receive the redeeming grace of the Savior is through the Book of Mormon?

It turns out that the Book of Mormon talks about this sacred role of the Book of Mormon throughout its pages.

The literary name for the concept of a book referring to itself within its pages is "Self-Referentiality" or "meta-reference." In this section of the book, I'd like to invite readers to explore some examples of how the Book of Mormon announces its role—both explicitly and implicitly—as a powerful means the Lord has provided to make the Messiah manifest and the covenants available.

These chapters in the Book of Mormon will be very familiar to you. What I hope is to help you appreciate them in a way that may not always be immediately apparent—as a way that the Lord points us to the central message of the Book of Mormon and its role as the manifestation of the Messiah.

OPENING SCENARIOS: HOW WOULD YOU RESPOND TO EACH OF THESE SITUATIONS?

We'll have you return to these at the end of this section.

A Dialogue of Faith in the Book of Mormon

Have you noticed the following dialogue pattern throughout the Book of Mormon?

Q. "Do you believe in *these words*" (from one or another Book of Mormon prophet)?

A. Yes, I believe *these words*.

Response: Blessed are you for you believe *in Jesus Christ*.
What would such a dialogue teach us?

The Experience of Nephi

Fill in the blanks:

Q. And the Spirit said unto me: Behold, what desireth thou?

A. And I said: I desireth to behold the things which my father saw.

Q. And the Spirit said unto me: _____ thou that __ _____saw the tree of which he hath spoken?

A. And I said: Yea, thou knowest that *I believe ____the ___ of _* _____.

Response:

And when I had spoken these words, the Spirit cried with a loud voice, saying: . . . blessed are thou, Nephi, because *thou _____in the _____*; wherefore, thou shalt behold the things which thou hast desired (1 Nephi 11:2–6).

What do we learn about the power and purpose of the Book of Mormon from that dialogue above between Nephi and the "Spirit" (1 Nephi 11:2–6)?

The Experience of Zeezrom

Fill in the blanks:

Q. "Believest thou in the __of _____unto salvation?

A. "Yea, I believe all the ____which _____has ____."

Q. And Alma said: If thou believest in the _____of ___ thou canst be healed.

A. And he said: Yea, I believe according to _____."

Response:

And then Alma cried unto the Lord, saying: O Lord our God, have mercy on this man, and heal him according to his _____ which is in _____" (Alma 15: 6–10).

What do we learn about the power and purpose of the Book of Mormon (which includes the words of Alma) from the dialogue above between Alma and Zeezrom (Alma 15:6–10)?

The Experience of Helaman

Fill in the blanks:

And it came to pass . . . that Alma came unto his son Helaman and said unto him:

Q. Believest thou the _____which _____spake unto thee concerning those records which have been kept?

A. And Helaman said unto him: Yea, I believe [in _____].

Q. And Alma said unto him again: Believest thou in _____ _____, who shall come?

A. And he said: Yea, I believe all the words which _____hast spoken. (Alma 45:2–5).

What do we learn about the power and purpose of the Book of Mormon (which includes the words of Alma) from that dialogue above between Alma and his son, Helaman (Alma 42:2–5)?

The Experience of Mahonri

And he answered: . . . Lord, show thyself unto me.

Q. And the Lord said unto him: Believest *thou the words* which I shall speak?

A. And he answered: Yea, Lord, I know that thou speakest the truth, for thou art a God of truth, and canst not lie.

Q. And when he had said words, behold, the Lord showed himself unto him (Ether 3:10–13).

Nephi Again:

"and when that day shall come that they shall believe in _____
. . . and look not forward any more for another _____
then, at that time . . . it must needs be expedient that they should believe____" (2 Nephi 25:16).

HOW IS THAT PURPOSE SHOWN IN THE FOLLOWING CHAPTERS OF THE BOOK OF MORMON?

The Book of Mormon invites us readers to better understand and see it as a great latter-day temple—a place where the Messiah is made fully manifest.

Let's now consider several key chapters in the Book of Mormon, chapters that are very familiar to you. But in considering these chapters, I'll ask some questions about some things that happen in those chapters that may help us consider these events in a different light.

1 NEPHI 1 "AND ALSO THE THINGS WHICH HE READ IN THE BOOK, MANIFESTED PLAINLY OF THE COMING OF A MESSIAH, AND ALSO THE REDEMPTION OF THE WORLD"

Preliminary Questions

We begin with the testimony of a prophet (Nephi), who became a prophet as he faithfully and prayerfully responded to the exhortations and testimonies of another prophet (Lehi, his father), who became a prophet as he faithfully and prayerfully responded to the exhortations and testimonies of other prophets sent by the Lord to Jerusalem (1 Nephi 1:4). Remembering that, "in a general sense a prophet is anyone who has a testimony of Jesus Christ" (see: LDS Bible Dictionary; Revelations 19:10; Numbers 11:25–29: "Would God that all God's people were prophets"), what opportunity, even responsibility, seems now available to us—based on this pattern given to us in this opening chapter of the Book of Mormon, and as we now "enter" that pattern?[1]

How can we, likewise, receive a testimony—or manifestation—of Jesus Christ? Is such a testimony, or manifestation, of the Messiah—as obtained by these prophets we are now reading about—available to us? How?

Where would we go to obtain such a manifestation as they received? What would it take for us to receive such a manifestation? Might it be more available to us than we think? Wouldn't that be exciting if it was? Once we obtain such a manifestation, what responsibility would we then have?

Are you prepared to take on such a responsibility? Why or why not? Does it seem like too heavy a burden? Do you think the Lord would give you the power—or grace—to shoulder such responsibility at the same time He gave you the testimony? How? What would it take for you to "tap into" that source of power of grace?

It turns out that this entire book may have as one of its most sacred purposes leading you to both that testimony and to that grace ("But behold, I, Nephi will show unto you that the tender mercies of the Lord are over all those whom he hath chosen, because of their faith, to make them mighty even to the power of deliverance" [1:19]). *Would you like to be led there? How can you show that you would? How did those other prophets we are reading about show that they would (see also 1 Nephi 2:16; 10:17)?* As you will hear often in this record: "Come" (1 Nephi 8:15–16).

Questions about Lehi's "First Vision"

Let's say the Lord wanted to make it clear to you and me that the most powerful way to receive a manifestation of the Messiah occurs through reading *a book* (not just any book, but a very special book). *And what if the Lord wanted to make that clear right from the beginning of the Book of Mormon? How would He do that?*

One way He could do that is by showing us a vision in which someone (in this case, Lehi) receives his most powerful manifestation of the Messiah *by reading a book* during that vision? Now that may seem like a strange vision for someone to have. And such a vision may even seem counterintuitive to all of our expectations about how we best understand things. After all, don't we learn things best by experiencing them *directly*, as opposed to *reading* about them? Let's see what happens as we look at Lehi's "first vision."

In response to his prayers, Lehi receives various manifestations from the Lord, including what might be called Lehi's "first vision" (1:6–13). *Is there anything about that vision that strikes you as particularly interesting, surprising, or unexpected—as far as the way the Lord makes things manifest to Lehi?*

What is the main difference between what Lehi learns and experiences in the first half of his vision (1:8–10) versus what he learns and experiences in the second half of the vision (1:11–13)?

In the first half of the vision, does he know who all of the people are whom he sees?[2]

What clues does he give us as to their probable identity?[3] Why do you think he isn't more definite as to their identity?[4]

Turning now to the second half of Lehi's vision, at what point in Lehi's vision was the manifestation so powerful that he "was filled with the Spirit" (1:12)?[5] According to this verse, what caused him to be "filled with the Spirit"?[6] How does that relate to what you are doing right now? What does that teach you?[7] Why do you think the Lord proceeded this way in this vision?[8]

What does Lehi now know and proclaim about the "Lord God Almighty" (see especially 1:14)? What specific qualities of the Lord does Lehi now declare?[9] And, instead of hearing "angels in the attitude of singing and praising their God," who now assumes that very role himself, and who now personally sings to and praises "his God" (1:15)?

What do you think made possible such great enhancement in Lehi's knowledge, understanding, and appreciation of the Lord?

Besides the things "he saw and heard," what do we learn "manifested plainly" to Lehi "of the coming of a Messiah, and also the redemption of the world" (1:19)?[10]

How do you suppose that you and I could receive the same plain manifestation? What does Nephi promise us that his words—that he is now compiling—will do for us (1:20)?[11]

What does all this teach you about the opportunity that is now available to you as you read from a book that the Lord has placed in your hands and "bade [you] that [you] should read"?[12]

What does all this teach you about the Book of Mormon as the manifestation of the Messiah for you right now?

Lehi's First Manifestations

At first blush, it would hard to imagine that any experience could be more powerful than the very first manifestation Lehi receives after his mighty prayer—when he "saw and heard much," including "a pillar of fire" which "dwelt upon a rock before him." Indeed, the power of this manifestation was so great that it caused Lehi to "quake and tremble exceedingly" and left him so exhausted that when he returned home he "cast himself upon his bed, being overcome with the Spirit and the things which he had seen" (1:6–7).

But Lehi then immediately experiences several increasingly *more powerful and sublime manifestations* from the Lord and of the Lord when he is "carried away in a vision" (1:8). Each one of these next manifestations seem to be the very limit of what we might expect someone might be privileged to experience in this life—until we go to the next experience, when those presumed limits are again transcended.

For example, in the first part of Lehi's vision "he saw the heavens open, and he thought he saw God sitting upon His throne, surrounded with numerous concourses of angels in the attitude of singing and praising their God" (1:8). He then goes on to also see "one descending out of the midst of heaven" whose "luster was above that of the sun at noon-day" followed by "twelve others" whose "brightness did exceed that of the stars in the firmament" (1:9–10).

The Second Part of the Vision: A Manifestation of the Messiah

Wonderful and marvelous manifestations. And yet, something else is about to occur in this vision which will cause Lehi to be "*filled* with the spirit of the Lord" and also cause "his soul [to] rejoice, and his *whole* heart [to be] filled" and to exclaim these words of the Lord's redeeming power: "Thy power and goodness and mercy are over all the inhabitants of the earth; and because thou art merciful, thou wilt not suffer those who come unto thee that they shall perish!" (1:12, 14, 15).

What happened in the vision that elicited such reactions from Lehi? Something very interesting: a personage in the vision had given "unto him a book, and bade him that he should read. And it came to pass that *as he read*, he was filled with the Spirit of the Lord" (1:11, 12) and when he "had read and seen many great and marvelous things, he did exclaim many things unto the Lord" (1:14). In fact, instead of seeing and hearing others surrounding a heavenly throne "singing and praising their God," Lehi himself assumes this very role—all of which took place after reading.

We learn that through his reading of the book Lehi received a plain manifestation of the Messiah and that his reading became the foundation of his testimony of the mission of Savior as he went forth to prophecy among the people: "he testified that the things which he saw and heard, and also the *things which he read in the book, manifested plainly of the coming of the Messiah*, and also the redemption of the world" (1:19; emphasis added).

Patterns of Redemption

It is interesting how this whole chapter chiastically converges upon two kinds of manifestations—both experienced by Lehi in his "first vision." The first part of the vision (see verses 8–10 below) concerns what might be called "physical manifestations" of the Messiah, while the second part of the vision concerns manifestations received *while reading a book*.

1: Here is a book (or record) for you to read that will make manifest the goodness and mysteries of God

3: And I testify of the truth of what I will make manifest about the Messiah in this book (or record)

8–10: As Lehi prays, he is overcome with the Spirit and then sees in vision what appears to be the Father, the Savior, and the Twelve, as well as hears angels in the attitude of singing and praising their God—all wonderful manifestations of the Lord

11–14: But a still more powerful reaction occurs to Lehi, and a greater manifestation of the Messiah occurs to him, as he is given a book, invited to read, and then reads from the book. As he read he was filled with the Spirit of the Lord, and now instead of seeing visions of the Lord, he has personal knowledge of the Lord's power, mercy, and redemption; and now instead of hearing angels singing and praising the

Lord for these things, Lehi himself does the singing and praising—i.e., he becomes the "angel" in the "presence" of the Lord's throne.

16–18: We are now introduced to apostles of the Lord who are keeping another record and testimony of the Savior—Lehi and Nephi—who are in the attitude of praising their God, and who will also give us a book and invite us to read.

19: Lehi testified that the things he read in the book manifested plainly of the Messiah and redemption

20: Through this book (or record) I am writing, I will make manifest to you the tender mercies of God, and how His power of redemption can be manifest to you

OUR OPPORTUNITY AND RESPONSIBILITY

And now, after making it clear to us through Lehi's experiences how a manifestation of the Messiah can follow from reading a book, the Lord seems to invite *us* to have the same experience as Lehi by reading the book he has now placed in *our* hands—the Book of Mormon. Notice how in the closing verse of this first chapter, Lehi's vision of reading a book and our current reading of a book are unified as Nephi invites us to continue reading *the book we have started*, testifying that the same manifestations of the Messiah will *thereby be available to us*: "But behold, I, Nephi, will show unto you [through this book you are reading] that the tender mercies of the Lord are over all those whom he hath chosen, because of their faith, to make them mighty even unto the power of deliverance" (1:20).

Something else the Lord makes clear in this opening chapter—that He has called Lehi to be His prophet and spokesman, and that, from this point on, we will be held accountable for how we either accept or reject His words, which will be found in the subsequent pages of the book we now have in our hands. In other words, we have become the current moment's equivalent to those 600 BC inhabitants of Jerusalem (in verses 4 and 18) to whom the Lord now calls to repentance and whose reactions to Lehi's words and testimony determine our relationship with the Lord as well as the power of His manifestation to us.

1 NEPHI 8: "COME UNTO ME"

Preliminary Questions

What was it that likely preceded and provoked this great vision of Lehi that is recorded in this chapter? How might this vision have been provoked in some way by the events recorded in chapter five, where Nephi and his brothers retrieved the brass plates and Lehi "did search them from the beginning" (1 Nephi 5:10, 17)?[13]

How might this vision have been provoked in some way by Lehi's impressions of the writings of Joseph of Egypt, where he learns of his relationship to Joseph, "who was preserved by the hand of the Lord, that he might preserve his father, and all his household from perishing with famine" (1 Nephi 5:14)?[14]

While Nephi and his brothers returned to the land of Jerusalem to retrieve Ishmael and his family, what activity do you suppose occupied much of Lehi's time (1 Nephi 5:20–22)? How do you think this activity might have "planted the seeds" that led to his great vision of the tree of life?[15]

Finally, how might this vision also have been provoked by the activity of Lehi's family—gathering seeds and fruit from area trees and grain (1 Nephi 8:1)?

In what ways does this dream of Lehi parallel his first vision (see 1 Nephi 1)? How is Lehi's reaction to reading the book in the earlier vision (1 Nephi 1:14–15, 18) similar to his reactions to tasting of the fruit of the tree of life in this later dream (8:11–12, 15)? In what condition did Lehi first find himself in his dream (8:4)? What might that condition represent? What was Lehi's reaction to his condition (8:8)? How does his reaction show us what the first step for each of us is as we seek redemption? What are some of the qualities of the fruit of the tree?[16]

Whom does Lehi resemble as he stands by the tree? How? What especially suggests that resemblance (8:15, 16)? Are there any particular words that Lehi uses—and repeats four times in four verses—that are meant to clearly echo the Lord's role (8:15–18)? How and why would following these words of Lehi also fulfill the Lord's invitation?[17]

Nephi later teaches that "the tree of life was a representation of the love of God" (1 Nephi 11:25, 21–23). What is the great manifestation of that love (John 3:16)? How does the Book of Mormon enable us to taste of that love?[18] Where in the scriptures do we find a correspondence between tasting the love of the Savior and tasting the word of the Savior?[19]

Perhaps then the vision of the tree of life represents, in some way, the different reactions people have to the Book of Mormon, that serves as the instrument in our day for making the Messiah—and His love—fully manifest to us (see Alma 37:43–47; 34:6; see also the Lord's parable of the sower and the seed where the Lord emphasizes different reactions of those who hear the word). Every possible reaction to the Book of Mormon—and therefore to the Messiah—are contained within this vision: from ignoring, rejecting, or disparaging them on one hand to accepting them to various degrees on the other. Even the various reasons we accept or reject the Book of Mormon—and therefore the Messiah—are contained within the vision—and parallel those reasons for accepting or rejecting the word given in the Savior's parable of the seed: the temptations of the adversary; the cares, riches, and pleasures of this life; fears of and submission to the persuasions of men; those who receive the word with joy; but then afterward become ashamed of the word.

The Manifestation

What determines which group we will become part of? What are some of the things we must we do to help ourselves become the particular group in the vision we would prefer to belong to?[20]

How are we as able to see and taste the very same fruit Lehi saw and tasted as we now read from this book? How is the fruit of the tree every bit as sweet to us and capable of filling us with joy as the fruit in the dream was for Lehi?

Why must we hearken to the invitation of Lehi (and his posterity) in this book we are now reading if we want to partake of the fruit and be in the presence of the Lord (8:36–37)?

What might be a possible, though unmentioned, contrasting building to the "large and spacious building"? Is there another building that we may choose to enter instead of this large and spacious building?[21]

How are the qualities of those entering that other building in contrast to the qualities of those entering the large and spacious building?[22]

What is the ultimate consequence of those who do not "come unto" Lehi (8:36)?[23] *Therefore, what is the ultimate consequence of those who do "come unto" Lehi?*[24]

Therefore, we also "come unto" Lehi (as a stand-in for the Lord) when we receive the Book of Mormon—which contains Lehi's words and testimonies of the Savior and is thereby the manifestation of the Messiah (see 8:37). And so this vision also becomes a fulfillment of Lehi's first vision (in 1 Nephi 1) for those in our day. That is, we now are given a book by one of the Lord's servants, invited to partake of the book, and may taste of the love of the Savior as we so partake.

THE EXPERIENCE OF ENOS: THE BOOK OF MORMON AS THE MANIFESTATION OF THE MESSIAH AND THE KEY TO FINDING THE FAITH THAT BRINGS US TO A KNOWLEDGE OF THE MESSIAH

When you think of the Book of Enos, what doctrinal principal or lesson first comes to mind? The Book of Enos is a wonderful example of the power of a mighty prayer of faith. Certainly, Enos exercises great faith when he cries unto the Lord "all the day long" and then "when the night came" did still "raise [his] voice high that it reached the heavens" (Enos 1:4). In the next verse, we see the result of such wonderful faith: he receives a manifestation of the Messiah, who addresses him by name, telling him "Enos, thy sins are forgiven thee, and thou shalt be blessed" (1:5) "because of thy faith in Christ, whom thou hast never before heard nor seen" and who has not yet "manifest[ed] himself in the flesh" (1:8).

The Wellspring of Faith

A great lesson for us all, but let's consider another lesson we may garner from the experience of Enos. To get to that lesson, we need to ask this question: where did that great faith of Enos come from? *What was it that made it possible for Enos to exercise the kind of faith that made such a prayer possible; what made it possible for Enos to "wrestle . . . before God" with such faith and persistence (1:2)?*

We would all benefit enormously if we could find the answer to that question, wouldn't we? To find the answer, let's go to the verse immediately preceding his description of his prayer. According to that verse (Enos 1:3), what appears to be the motivating event that provoked his great prayer of faith?

Enos tells us that in the midst of his hunting trip he found him-self reflecting upon something, which "sunk deep into his heart." Upon what was he reflecting?

It was the words of Jacob (some of which we now have as part of the Book of Mormon) that provoked his prayer of faith: "The words which I had often heard my father speak concerning eternal life, and the joy of the saints," he tells us, "sunk deep into my heart" (Enos 1:3). So, Jacob, as he has been out hunting in the forests, probably misses his dad and thinks about what his dad has taught him. Per-haps Enos also had read from some of the sacred plates presented to him by his dying father (Jacob 7:27).

What was the result of such reflection and pondering upon these words of his father, Jacob (Enos 1:4–6)?[25]

What made such an experience (or manifestation of the Lord) possible, according to the Lord? (Enos 1:7–8)?[26] *Where did that kind of faith come from?*[27] *Where, according to these same verses, did that faith not come from?*[28] *What does this tell us about how we, likewise, may generate within us that same kind of faith? Are the words of Enos' father available for us to likewise ponder and allow "to sink deep into [our] heart"? What does this tell us about the role the Book of Mormon can have in our lives?*

The Power of the Plates

Clearly, Enos tells us that the words and testimonies of Jacob about the Savior empowered his prayer of faith and consequent visi-tation (or manifestation) from the Savior. So, the Book of Enos con-tains a powerful message about how the Book of Mormon nurtures in us the kind of faith that makes the Messiah manifest—so that we then can turn to Him in mighty prayer and receive His atoning gift.

And then, the rest of the Book of Enos further demonstrates the critical role that the Book of Mormon will continue to play in our efforts to find and receive the Savior.

What indication do we have as we continue reading this chapter that Enos is well aware that those plates given to him by his father are the key to finding and receiving the Savior? After having such a wonderful manifestation of the Savior, what does he now want for others (Enos 1:9, 11)?

According to what we read in this chapter, what does Enos clearly recognize will be the key that will enable others—both the Nephites and Lamanites (and us)—to have the same wonderful experience that he just had (see Enos 1:13, 16)?

In what way did Enos's request echo the prayers of other prophets (see Enos 1:18)?

Since Enos wants others to have the same experience he just had, he pleads with the Lord that the "record of my people, the Nephites" might "be brought forth at some future day unto the Lamanites, that perhaps, they might be brought forth unto salvation" (Enos 1:13).

What lesson, do you think, that the Lord might be teaching us through this experience of Enos? How does this experience teach us about the role of the Book of Mormon as the manifestation of the Messiah—such that we can exercise sufficient faith in Him to have the same kind of experience as that of Enos?

How do these words and experiences of Enos bring to mind the words the resurrected Savior said to His disciples: "blessed are ye if ye shall believe in me . . . after that ye have seen me and know that I am," but "more blessed are they who shall believe in your words because ye shall testify that ye have seen me, and know that I am" (3 Nephi 12:1–2; see also Mosiah 26:15–16; John 20:28–29).

Certainly, the Book of Enos is a great testimony of the power of prayer. But there is another lesson the Lord seems to make available through the experience of Enos that merits our attention as well: The Book of Enos gives us all a clear message and prompting of where we may go to develop and exercise the very same faith that he did: to the plates. The Book of Enos teaches us about the power of a persistent prayer; but it also teaches us about the power of persistent faith in the full manifestation of the Messiah available within the pages of the Book of Mormon.

THE EXPERIENCE OF ALMA THE YOUNGER

Let's now move from the experience of Enos to the experience of Alma the Younger to see what this book may teach us about the sacred role of the Book of Mormon in helping generate within us the kind of faith in Jesus Christ that leads us to come unto Him and receive His atoning blessings—or, in other words, help us to receive a manifestation of the Messiah.

What great transformation occurred in the life of Alma the Younger (see Alma 36)? What made such a transformation possible?

There are various possible answers to the last question. You may have answered that such a transformation occurred because of two things that happened to him, each of which was necessary for the great spiritual transformation or rebirth within him: 1) his mind at some point in his spiritual pains "caught hold upon" the wonderful truth about "the coming of one Jesus Christ, a Son of God, to atone for the sins of the world" (Alma 36:18, 17); and 2) he then "cried within [his] heart," to that person, Jesus Christ: "O Jesus, thou Son of God, have mercy on me" (Alma 36:18).

Another way that we may answer that same question ("what made such a transformation possible"), perhaps, is to say: *he exercised faith in Jesus Christ.* And we would all agree that, yes, Alma was able to be "born of God" because he exercised great faith in the atoning blood of Jesus Christ. But knowing that, there is still a very critical question that we have yet to consider, a very crucial part of Alma's transformation and rebirth that we would do well to investigate further. We would all benefit immensely by searching in Alma's account for the answer to this question: *What was it that generated within Alma that kind of great faith in Jesus Christ?*

It turns out that the answer to this question about Alma's experience is the same as the answer we found when we studied the experience of Enos. We will find that Alma's mighty faith arose from the same wellspring as the faith exercised by Enos. *What was the wellspring or ultimate source that gave Alma the kind of faith in Jesus Christ that led to his great transformation (see Alma 36:17)?*

In the midst of his guilt and pains, as he was "harrowed up to the greatest degree and racked with all [his] sins," what was it that brought to his mind and heart that great faith in Jesus Christ that enabled him to call upon the Savior? Whose words did he recall?[29]

How was Alma's experience similar to the experience of Enos?[30]

Is there anywhere we can now go to find some of those same words and witness of Jesus Christ that generated such great faith in Alma the Younger? Where?[31]

Is there any reason we should not expect that the words of Alma's father (a Book of Mormon prophet and author) could have the same effect on us that it had on Alma the Younger?[32]

What lesson, do you think, the Lord might be teaching us through this experience of Alma? How does this experience teach us about the role of the Book of Mormon—such that we can exercise sufficient faith in Him to have the same kind of experience as that of Alma the Younger?

Surely, the Lord has a lesson to teach us through the experience of Alma the Younger, the very same lesson taught through the experience of Enos, and the same lesson He taught Lehi: when we open the Book of Mormon, we open to a temple of the Lord, a sacred place where "the Son of Man might . . . manifest himself to his people" (Doctrine & Covenants 109:5).

Interestingly, and amazingly, as though Alma (and the Lord) wanted to make sure that his son, Helaman (as well as we) understood the sacred role of the plates in his—and our—redemption, what charge does Alma immediately give to Helaman after relating his conversion story (see Alma 37:1–2)?[33] In what ways does Alma's description of the role of the scriptures echo the words we have just read from Enos (try substituting in your mind the "Book of Mormon" whenever Alma talks about "The Brass Plates"; see Alma 37:4–10, 14, 17–19)?[34]

THE EXPERIENCE OF ALMA THE ELDER

Let's say that the Lord was helping us to understand the role of the Book of Mormon as the Manifestation of the Messiah—or the means He provides for us to exercise the kind of faith in the Savior so that we can come unto Him and seek His mercy and redeeming love? Would it help if the Lord plainly said right in the middle of the Book of Mormon: "This book you are now reading, the Book of Mormon, is the means I have provided for you in these latter days to come to a full knowledge of your Redeemer"?

Is it possible that He has been that plain already?

The Lord is very careful with names of places and people: Shalom, Jerusalem, Immanuel, Abraham, Sariah—Sarah, Joseph.

After Alma (the Elder) accepted the words of Abinadi, "repented of all his sins," and taught these words to others, to what location did those people who believed his words flee (Mosiah 18:4)?[35]

What are some of the things that made this location particularly attractive to Alma and his followers (see Mosiah 18:5)?[236] What are some of the specific things that were taught in this location (Mosiah 18:7–10)?[237]

What specific blessings did the people who gathered here receive (Mosiah 18:8–10, 13, 16)?[238] What was the specific name of the pool of waters, fed by "a fountain [i.e., spring or waterfall] of pure water" into which the people were immersed so that they could become part of the "fold of God" and receive covenants of salvation as well as having "his Spirit more abundantly upon [them] (Mosiah 18:8, 5)?[239]

What do we learn was the name of the location where all of these great blessings were made available (Mosiah 18:30)? What was the location where these people "came to a knowledge of their Redeemer" or received a full manifestation of him? Is there some message the Lord has for us in the following verse? What message might that be?

"And now it came to pass that all of this was done in Mormon, yea, by the waters of Mormon, in the forest that was near the waters of Mormon; yea, the place of Mormon, the waters Mormon, the forest of Mormon, how beautiful are they to the eyes of them who there came to the knowledge of their Redeemer" (Mosiah 18:30).

THE EXPERIENCE IN ZARAHEMLA

What affect did the words of King Benjamin have upon the people of Zarahemla (see Mosiah 4:1–3; 5:1–5)?[240]

If we had attended King Benjamin's speech, with our families gathered at the temple, don't we expect that we, like all others gathered to hear his words, would have had a similar reaction and experience (Mosiah 6:2)?

But were all of those gathered to the temple that day able to hear the words of King Benjamin? What arrangements did he make for those who could not hear his voice (see Mosiah 2:8)?[241]

Do you suppose that the Lord made sure that the people who were on the outside edges, reading His words, were able to enjoy the same kind of spiritual power and transformation as those closer to the sound of his voice? Why?

Would you expect that those who "only" read the words of King Benjamin—as his words were distributed to those beyond the reach of his voice—were included with those who responded to his words in Mosiah 4:1–3 and 5:1–4 (see Mosiah 6:1–3)?[242]

Don't we, as we now read and ponder these very same words that King Benjamin spoke to his people, have the very same opportunity available to us as the people on the outer edges of that gathering had then? Is there any reason the Lord would not or could not make the same experience and power available to us right now? Why?

What message do you suppose the Lord might be relaying to us by making us aware of these two different ways that Benjamin's people received his words?[43]

What point might the Lord be making to us about the role and power of the Book of Mormon to make the Messiah and His Atonement fully manifest and available to us as we plant our tents facing the temple of Mormon and open our hearts and minds and spirits to the words on those pages?

Besides the great manifestation we may now receive, of what other blessing may we likewise partake—even as those in King Benjamin's day (see Mosiah 5:5–8, 11, 15)?[44] How does this also help us understand the blessings and power that is available to us through the Book of Mormon— and how it fulfills two of its goals from the title page?[45]

What an amazing lesson the Lord teaches us through this celestial sermon of King Benjamin—and through the simple truth that those who read His great words of life and light, on the outer edges of the gathering, received a manifestation of the atoning love of the Savior as fully and completely as those who physically heard those words. How could the Lord possibly make clearer to us the sacred power and potential this scriptural temple known as the Book of Mormon holds for us right now? How could He possibly make clearer to us that the Book of Mormon is the great latter-day manifestation of the Messiah and by "entering" this book we enter the most sacred corridors and precincts of knowledge and redemption?

THE EXPERIENCE OF THE BROTHER OF JARED

We all stand amazed at the power of the Lord's manifestation to the brother of Jared. What was it that made that particular manifestation so powerful and unique?[46] What would it take for us to have a similar experience as the brother of Jared?[47]

What does Moroni tell us he has placed upon the plates (Ether 4:4)?[48] And what does the Lord tell us will also be available to us—as we receive this record (Ether 4:7)?[49] Therefore, what kind of experience should we expect to find available through our study of the Book of Mormon?[50]

How does the Lord tell us such an experience will become available to us (Ether 4:11)?[51] What risk do we take if we esteem lightly the opportunity that the Lord now presents to us—through these words (Ether 4:8)?[52] How do we avoid that risk and those consequences?[53]

In what way can we, through our reading of the Book of Ether (and of the Book of Mormon in general), see, as the Brother of Jared did, "the finger of the Lord"?[54] How can we likewise as we read from the Book of Mormon "see" the Lord (Ether 4:13)?[55] How can we likewise as we read from the Book of Mormon be brought back into His presence?[56]

QUESTIONS TO CONTEMPLATE

- What did the Lord teach us about our relationship with the Book of Mormon through each of the seven experiences above?

- What if you were in their situation? How would you hope you reacted?

- In what way are we in their situations today? What does the Lord expect of us?

- What does all this have to do with those covenants we make (sacrament, temple, Book of Mormon)?

- Are you prepared to actually enter and explore the precincts of one of the holiest places in all this world? What are some of the ways we can prepare ourselves for such a journey of sacred discovery?

RETURN TO OPENING SCENARIOS FOR PART 1

Based on what you've learned in part 1, how would you now respond to the following scenarios:

As David read once more the wonderful conversion stories of Enos and Alma the Younger, he wondered why his prayers—as well as the prayers of his parents—had not yet made such a wonderful manifestation of the Savior's Atonement available to him. *Why not me,* he wondered?

Jeff looked at the clock on his wall once more. It was a beautiful, clear summer morning. His backpack was all crammed with enough provisions for at least two days. He had his map all charted out for his mountain hike—to Avalanche Lake hidden high in the Adirondacks. Not many people know how to get there. But he was ready. He could almost taste the delicious cool water flowing from that secret spring he had discovered last year. He had just finished the Book of Enos and was reading through Mosiah 18. He glanced up again. Couldn't wait to put the Book of Enos to the test. He was ready to stay on his knees all day and night if he had to. He was so excited he couldn't wait any longer. He put his bookmark in the middle of a chapter, placed the book back on his nightstand, grabbed his compass, and dropped his pack in his vintage Ford pickup. *Now we'll see*, he said to himself.[57]

NOTES

1 In the sense that "a testimony of Jesus is the Spirit of prophecy," we, too, become prophets (with a small "p") just as Lehi and Nephi became prophets, and then as such we too can share our testimonies of Jesus with others.

2 No, he says he "*thought* he saw God" and describes the others generically ("he saw One" and "and he also saw twelve others.")

3 The "luster" of the "One" that was "above that of the sun at noon-day" implies the Savior; the number 12 as well as their "brightness" implies that he saw the Apostles.

4 Perhaps the Lord is teaching us that a physical manifestation is not as definite as that supplied by the scriptures—which Lehi is about to receive.

5 *After* reading from the book he was given.

6 Reading from the book.

7 I also have been given a book to read by the Lord and now have the very same opportunity Lehi had—as I read, with potentially the very same results: being "filled with the Spirit of the Lord" and testifying of truth.

8 To show us today that the greatest witness we can have is also through reading a book; and therefore to have high expectations as we read.

9 Lehi proclaims that he now knows how "great and marvelous" the works of God are, and that God's power and goodness and mercy are over all the inhabitants of the earth, all of which followed from Lehi's reading of the book.

10 "The things which he read in the book."

11 We will also receive a personal manifestation—like Lehi did—of the tender mercies of the Lord over all who exercise faith, which begins with our faith in the power of the words we are now reading.

12 The very same opportunity avails us now as we read from a book as did Lehi when he read from a book.

13 Lehi's diligent searching of the Brass Plates would have made him keenly aware of the need to rely upon the Lord, His prophets, and the scriptures as they seek salvation, and to forsake the voices of the world and the adversary—all of which are emphasized in the vision of the tree of life. His reading also "filled him with the Spirit" as well as the gift of prophecy.

14 Certainly Lehi must see parallels between his current situation and his ancestor's. Preserving his household—both physically and spiritually—has been Lehi's object since his first vision in 1 Nephi 1. And he has now seen his son, Nephi, mistreated by his elder brothers as was Joseph.

15 We can suppose that Lehi continued his diligently searching of the Brass Plates during this time—which enabled the Spirit of the Lord to inspire him—and make the atoning mission of the Messiah clear.

16 As earlier, Lehi finds himself in a Babylon-like wilderness, seeks mercy from the Lord, and partakes of fruit that brings him the same kind of joy he experienced as he "partook" of the message of the book. All of these suggest our own conditions as we are reading about Lehi's vision: we are currently in a lost and fallen state—which becomes more apparent as we now read from the Book of Mormon. We too have the chance to turn to the Lord for mercy, and are likewise led—as we continue reading from the book—to the fruits of tree that is "most sweet, above all" and "whose fruit was desirable" to make us, too, happy."

17 Lehi resembles the Lord as he invites all to "come unto me" and partake of the fruits of salvation. When we "come unto" Lehi by our reading and acceptance of his words within the Book of Mormon, we, like Nephi, thereby come unto the Savior (see 1 Nephi 2:16; 10:17).

18 The Savior and His atoning sacrifice on our behalf are the great manifestations of God's love. Therefore, as we faithfully read from the Book of Mormon we move along the path to tasting that love; and when we "receive" the truth of the Book, we partake fully of that love.

19 See Isaiah 55:1–3; Mosiah 4:11; 2 Nephi 31:20; Alma 32:28; 36:26; Hebrews 6:4–5. "As ye have come to the knowledge of the glory of God . . . and have tasted of his love" (Mosiah 4:11); "Wherefore ye must press forward with . . . a love of God . . . feasting upon the word

of Christ" (2 Nephi 31:20); "Ho, every one that thirsteth, come ye to the waters, and he that hath no money; come ye, buy, and eat; yea, come, buy wine and milk without money and without price . . . hearken diligently unto me, and eat ye that which is good" (Isaiah 55:1–3).

20 The most important key to reaching the tree and partaking of the fruit: "heeding" the words of Lehi (and other prophets in the Book of Mormon), instead of those who are mocking them (1 Nephi 8:15, 33–34; see also Doctrine & Covenants 84:52–57).

21 The temples of the Lord.

22 In the temples, we enter the Lord's presence, become committed to the Lord and His kingdom, as well as bringing others to taste of His love.

23 They are "cast off from the presence of the Lord."

24 They come into the presence of the Lord.

25 As a result of such pondering upon the words of his father, Jacob, Enos was able to exercise the kind of faith in Christ that caused his soul to hunger, and enabled Him to kneel down and cry "in mighty prayer and supplication" for his soul until the Lord responded by manifesting Himself to Him (Enos 1:4–5).

26 "Because of thy faith in Christ."

27 Such faith seems to have been generated and nurtured through his reading and pondering of the words of his father, Jacob.

28 His faith did not arise from either hearing or seeing Christ, or from any other kind of manifestation of the Savior "in the flesh" (Enos 1:8).

29 His father's words.

30 Enos's faith and actions were also catalyzed and empowered by his pondering of the words of his father.

31 We may access those very same words right now—within the Book of Jacob and the Book of Alma.

32 No reason to suppose that the words of Jacob and Alma the Elder could not generate the same faith and actions within us. Positively put: we may have just a powerful manifestation of the Lord as Enos and Alma the Younger had—by exercising the same kind of faith in the words of Jacob and Alma the Elder, which we have available right now.

33 Alma charges his son Helaman to keep the plates sacred—just as he has.

34 Both Alma and Enos are aware that the words upon the plates they are preserving will have the same power to act upon future readers of this record as they did upon them. They know—from their own experiences—that the words of Jacob and Alma the Elder (as well as other prophets) can enable future readers to receive a full manifestation of the Savior so they can be

completely cleansed in His atoning blood. Therefore, both Enos and Alma the Younger pleaded with the Lord to preserve these plates and make them available for future readers.

35 "To a place that was called Mormon."

36 It was a place of pure water and a thick grove of trees—where they could feel safe and secure.

37 The same things taught in a temple: The plan of "Repentance, and redemption, and faith on the Lord" and an invitation to accept covenants—such as baptism, obedience (18:10, 19–20), sacrifice (18:9, 21–23), consecration (18:9, 13, 24–29)—"that [they] may be redeemed of God" and "that he may pour out his Spirit more abundantly upon [them]."

38 The same blessings as in the temple: The grace and Spirit of God, the hope of eternal life, and being sealed as children of God (18:13, 16, 22).

39 The waters of Mormon.

40 Complete transformation and rebirth—as they responded with great faith to the words of King Benjamin about Jesus Christ and His atoning mission.

41 He arranged to have his words transcribed so that those outside hearing range could read his words.

42 We have every reason to believe that those who read his words had an identical experience to those who heard his words.

43 We today are in the very same situation as those who could not hear but simply read King Benjamin's words. And we therefore have the opportunity to respond in the very same way.

44 We too may commit and consecrate ourselves completely to the will of the Lord, and we too may become "the children of Christ" as He spiritually begets us.

45 Just by reading from this record—including these words of King Benjamin—we can receive a full manifestation that Jesus is the Christ, and we can also know and receive the covenants of the Lord, which empowers us to walk His paths.

46 Mahonri actually saw and conversed with the premortal Christ—as one man to another. And Christ said that "never has man believed in me as thou hast."

47 The Lord personally promises that those who exercise faith in him—as they read of this account within the Book of Mormon—may have the very same manifestation of the Savior that Mahonri had (see Ether 4:7–8, 11–16).

48 "The very things which the brother of Jared saw."

49 "Then will I manifest unto them the things which the brother of Jared saw."

50 A full and complete visit and manifestation of the Savior and His atoning love.

51 When we accept and exercise faith in the record which the Lord will make available in the latter days; i.e., when we receive and exercise faith in the Book of Ether and the Book of Mormon (see all of the footnotes to this verse for further guidance).

52 The Lord uses very strong language to warn those against rejecting these words within the Book of Mormon: "and he that shall deny these things, let him be accursed, for unto them will I show no greater things." For similar warnings from the Lord about rejecting these words, see Doctrine & Covenants 20:14–15; 84:54–57; Alma 12:10–11; 3 Nephi 26:9–10.

53 We accept, value, exercise faith in, and apply to our lives the words we are now reading.

54 It can be said that we see the very "finger of the Lord" when we recognize His words in what we are reading; see Ether 4:12.

55 See Ether 2:12, where we learn that Jesus Christ "hath been manifested by the things which we have written."

56 In the same way Mahonri was brought back into His presence: "Because thou knowest these things ye are redeemed from the fall; therefore ye are brought back into my presence; therefore I show myself [i.e., manifest myself] unto you."

57 For both these scenarios: individuals are searching for a manifestation as powerful as that received by Enos and Alma the Younger. Yet, both Enos and Alma the Younger received their manifestations based on what they read in "the Book of Mormon"—specifically those words of Jacob and Alma the Elder which were what gave their sons the faith they needed. We have those same words with us today—within the Book of Mormon—which means we have the same key to unlock the same doors as Enos and Alma had. The second scenario is ironic since Jeff is ready to head to the woods in order to have the same experience Enos had, but the last thing he does is put his Book of Mormon on the shelf instead of in his backpack. It was from pondering the words of his father, Jacob (which we now have within our copies of the Book of Mormon) that enabled Enos to have his manifestation of the Lord—not just starving himself and kneeling for a full day. So, if we would desire to have the same experience as Enos, we should start not by going on a hike in the woods, but by going "for a hike in the Book of Mormon"—perhaps starting with Jacob's words in 2 Nephi 6–11.

The Very Things

We marvel that Mahonri pierced the veil
Conversing with the Savior face to face,
As one man to another, with no place
For doubt or darkness on that mountain trail.

Such rendezvous we may re-engage—
As we likewise ascend the same great height,
Uncover buried treasure, then invite:
"Reach down and touch these words upon a page":

I am he who was prepared; my grace
Now showers down upon you in a light
As full as any splashed on Shelem's mount
Or shone through palms nearby a Shomron fount.
No oak leaves in a battled grove more bright
As your reading and my visit interlace.

The Sacrament

As the congregation lament their sins,
Priests unravel the linen, rip and tear
Apart the bread of life, we watch him bear
Once more the soldier's' hammer as it pins

Hands and wrists to wood, the blood begins
Its path into this chapel, his nightmare
Recalled by us, newly made aware
Of the olive grindstone as it spins

And presses once more upon this altar
In its crooked motions, that now reclaimed
We declare enmity for what we were,
Our selves obliterated in his grace
Arising from bowed heads, new-named,
Love begetting love, as kin re-embrace.

Part II

Entering the Holy of Holies in the Temple of Mormon

Haven't we all at some time placed ourselves in nineteenth century Palmyra, pictured ourselves attending those various twilight camp meetings, felt ourselves being prompted to turn to the Lord for guidance, awakening one bright April morning to walk those same steps over a small creek bed and into the privacy of a newly budding grove of trees? Is it possible that the Lord has reserved the very same experience for each of us—and is just waiting for us inside such a grove?

INTRODUCTION

What Will Happen in This Part?

You'll open to some of the greatest manifestations of the Savior and His atoning mission ever recorded and have a chance to actually participate in them as you respond to some very personal and transforming questions about what you learn and experience during each of these manifestations.

You'll also consider the context of each of these manifestations: What events preceded and contributed to these great prophetic revelations of the Savior's redemptive sacrifice? In what way did the Book of Mormon prophets use other "scriptural temples" (e.g., the Brass Plates) as provocations, preludes, and catalysts to their own manifestations—which they then shared with us? What does this tell us about the role of the scriptures (including the Nephites' Brass Plates or our Old and New Testaments) in general and the Book of Mormon in particular?

What elements and events always accompany these manifestations of the Savior and His atoning sacrifice for us? Why are these elements and events essential parts of such manifestations? What particularly important activity or consequence always follows these great manifestations? What does this activity have to do with one of the central roles of the Book of Mormon (as stated on the title page)—"that they may know the covenants of the Lord"? In what way does the temple of Mormon fulfill the most sacred promises of the Abrahamic covenant?

Finally, we'll consider how the Lord telegraphs the grand and sacred purpose of all these things by arranging for each of them to occur at very deliberate physical locations within the temple of Mormon. Where did these great manifestations of the Savior and His atoning sacrifice take place? Why is that significant? What point is the Lord making by choosing such locations for such wonderful events?

What Do I Hope You Will Get out of This Part? How Do I Hope It Will Bring You Closer to the Savior and Help You to More Closely Follow Him?

My hope is that as you search the scriptures in response to the various questions in this part, you will actively participate in the greatest spiritual adventure of eternity, and that you will partake of the fruit of the tree of life that is being offered you through each one of these messianic manifestations—as you literally enter the most sacred precincts of the temple of Mormon. I hope this experience will help you better appreciate the great role of the Book of Mormon as the Manifestation of the Messiah—as well as understand how the Lord uses the scriptures as a powerful means of helping us know the Savior and of inviting us to come unto Him to be saved.

I also hope that you will simply appreciate the sublimity of the Book of Mormon (as described in the introduction) as you watch yourself enter the sacred various "towers, courtyards, and wings" that Elder Maxwell taught us "await [our] inspection" ("The Book of Mormon: A Great Answer to 'The Great Question,'" p. 13).

SOME OPENING QUESTIONS AS YOU BEGIN THIS PART:

- In this part, we are going to have you read some of the most sacred manifestations of the Savior ever written. Before you begin this journey into the sacred hallways of the temple of Mormon, it would help to pause first and invite the Lord's spirit to attend and guide you.

- What would you include on your list of the greatest manifestations of the Savior in the Book of Mormon?

- As you consider the context of these manifestations, what scriptures were these Book of Mormon prophets studying or teaching to others just before they shared their own witnesses or manifestations of the Savior?

- In what locale do we find these Book of Mormon prophets as they share these sacred witnesses of the Savior and His atoning sacrifice?

- What does this location tell us about the role of the Book of Mormon as the manifestation of the Messiah (see Doctrine & Covenants 109:5; 97:15–16)?

- What would you do or how would your life change if you were to walk out into a sacred grove this very day—just as the prophet Joseph did—and have the Savior personally descend from heaven and appear to you in a cloud of light and then converse with you as He did with Joseph? Why?

- You are about to enter the "temples" of Nephi, Jacob, Abinadi, Alma, Amulek, and Lehi. What might be some of your fondest hopes and anticipations as you embark on such a journey?

- What are some of the things you can do to help fulfill such anticipations?

OPENING SCENARIOS FOR PART 2

How would you respond to each of these right now? We'll have you return to these and respond again after you complete part 2.

Scenario #1

"They say the Lord is an impartial God—that He loves each of His children and would not give bread to one and a stone to another," Jeffrey said to himself for the umpteenth time, as he sat down to read the next chapter from the Book of Mormon. "Yet, how come Moses gets to see a burning bush and talk to God face to face? How come Peter, James, and John got to stand on the Mount of Transfiguration while past prophets and even Heavenly Father Himself conversed with them? And how come Joseph Smith gets to go into a grove of trees and have a pillar of light descend upon him as both the Father and the Son appear to him? And all we get today is a secondhand account? That sounds kind of partial to me."

Scenario #2

"How could those people in Jesus's day have been so blind?" Mary said to herself. "If I had lived then, I would easily have recognized the Savior. What a great time that would have been to be alive! I can hardly wait until the Millennium when I can have the same kind of closeness to the Savior as when He actually walked upon the earth."

ENTERING THE TEMPLE OF MORMON

Let's now give you a chance to discover just how powerfully and literally the Book of Mormon fulfills the great temple goal of making the Messiah manifest. Throughout this book so far, your personal participation has been crucial. Such participation is even more critical now. The more you take time to personally and prayerfully respond to the questions in this section, the more you'll actually enter the doors of the temple of Mormon, walk through various sacred wings and hallways—even within what might be considered the very Holy of Holies within this temple. As we all know, temple worship is not a "spectator sport" or passive activity. One moment you'll find yourself walking beside such Old Testament prophets as Moses, Abraham, Isaiah, Zenos, and Zenock; the next moment you may join the Nephite audience as Nephi, Jacob, Benjamin, Abinadi, or Alma reveal eternal and saving truths. You will walk through temple doors into the forests of Mormon and of Enos, upon the towers of Samuel and Nephi, the high mountain retreats of the Jaredites and Nephi, and the Zoramite hill of Onidah, into the very palaces and homes of kings and prophets, as well as those holy sanctuaries built in the lands of Nephi, Zarahemla, and Bountiful.[1]

We talk today about such things as having hypertextual experiences or of "entering the Ethernet." I think that the Lord was well ahead of modern Internet innovators in the many ways He invites us to spiritually become nested within increasing spiritual layers and dimensions of experience as we read the scriptures. I also think the Lord was well ahead of modern scientists who invite us to look at time and space in new and fuller ways. I think the kind of spiritual journey the Lord makes possible through the scriptures such as the Book of Mormon cuts across and transcends the usual boundaries and limits of space and time. The purpose of such journeys is not just entertainment, and not just added insight and experience; the purpose is to help us receive a powerful personal manifestation of the Savior, to accept His invitation to come unto him, to be reborn as we separate ourselves from the world, and to then make sacred covenants in response to such events. There is simply no greater adventure, no more heroic or significant quest, no more thunderous battle possible—than the one that takes place as you open the doors to the temple of Mormon.

All of this may sound a little strange, but I don't think it will seem as strange after you walk the following paths within the temple of Mormon—marvelous and wonderful, but no longer strange.

Notes

1 We often demonstrate how the prophecy in Ezekiel 37 (the sticks of Judah and Ephraim becoming "one" in our hands) by holding up the Bible and Book of Mormon together—or a "Quad" with these "sticks" literally sewn together. But as I invite you to see in this chapter, that great prophecy is marvelously fulfilled within the Book of Mormon by itself—where these two tribes' testimonies, witnesses, and manifestations of the Redeemer of Israel are already completely interwoven.

Our Own Sacred Grove

Like Joseph, we, too, would be saved but find
Ourselves and all the world cannot begin
To unravel the thorny knot of sin.
We hear the self-same testament remind

Us of a Savior who bids us leave behind
Anything profane and restore our kin-
Ship empyreal—through an expiation
Wrought in love, which alone can unbind

The cords of death. We then open the gate
To our own grove, mocked by pointing fingers
That jest and scorn, and unmitigated hate,
Which only prayer can dispel; we, too, see
A light flash through the leaves, which lingers
Upon us as we commune with divinity.

SECTION ONE

Exploring the Temples of Nephi, Jacob, Abinadi, Alma, Amulek, and Lehi

YOUR PARTICIPATION: QUESTIONS FROM CHART 1, COLUMN 1

In this part of the book, I'll present three different charts or lists of the greatest manifestations of the Savior and His atoning sacrifice by various prophets within the temple of Mormon and then invite you to prayerfully read these manifestations and respond to certain questions about them.

Remember, these are some of the most sacred moments in the entire Nephite record. So please feel no rush as you ponder these words. This is a great opportunity to allow the Holy Ghost once again to make the Messiah and His mission personally and powerfully manifest unto you—and for you to grow in that relationship with the Savior. Each one of the prophetic encounters from each of these rows is in itself a personal and direct encounter with the Savior.

This first chart will eventually contain four columns—each interrelated in very important ways. We'll start—in these next two sections—with two columns of these interrelationships. For the first column of this chart below, I'll list the chapters and verses where prophets such as Nephi (the first and second Nephi), Jacob, Abinadi, Alma, Amulek, and Lehi powerfully manifest the Messiah. For each manifestation I've listed, please prayerfully read the verses in the Book of Mormon, then answer the questions I've included below associated with that manifestation.

Your Responses to the Manifestations
Listed in Column 1 Below:

For each of these six manifestations of the Messiah . . .

How did Nephi (or Jacob, Abinadi, etc.) make the Messiah and His atoning mission powerfully manifest?

What do you learn about the atoning mission of the Savior from this manifestation?

How do you feel about the Savior after learning these things about him?

What do you plan to do with this knowledge and conviction that you have just gained in your mind and heart?

Note: I realize that to read and respond to each of the marvelous manifestations of the Messiah outlined in these three charts is a much more time-intensive task than can be accomplished by a typical book-reading experience. The most "sacred and sublime" experiences that await readers are in response to the four fundamental questions above for each of the eighteen manifestations in this section of the book. The great news is that you may proceed at your own leisure in enjoying and personally responding to these sublime manifestations of your Savior; and that you may respond quite differently to the same prophet's manifestation on different occasions—as moved by your own changing circumstances and the promptings of the Holy Ghost. There is no "expiration date" on such visitations with our Lord. The important point I would make through inviting you to respond to such questions is that we have the very same opportunity right now that these prophets had—to enter a current "scriptural temple" erected by the Lord for our own day and allow that spiritual foray to serve as a sacred catalyst for our personal manifestations of the Messiah, which we, then, likewise "pass on."

This prophet of the Lord from the Book of Mormon made the Messiah powerfully manifest in these verses, after having read or quoted . . .	. . . this prophet from a previous record or dispensation (and these specific chapters and verses from that previous prophet)
Nephi: 2 Nephi 25 (especially 2 Nephi 25:12–30)	What prophet did Nephi quote before giving us his manifestation (see 2 Nephi 12–24)? What does Nephi tell us was his reason for quoting from this prophet (see 2 Nephi 11:2, 4, 6–8)?
Jacob: 2 Nephi 9–10 (especially 2 Nephi 9 and 2 Nephi 10:3)	What prophet did Jacob quote before giving us this manifestation (see 2 Nephi 6:6–7, 16–18; 2 Nephi 7–8)? What does Jacob tell us was his reason for quoting from this prophet (see 2 Nephi 6: 4–5; 2 Nephi 9:1–4)?
Abinadi: Mosiah 15–16	What prophet did Abinadi quote before giving us this manifestation (see Mosiah 14)? What does Abinadi tell us was his reason for quoting from this prophet (see Mosiah 13:32–35)?
Alma and Amulek: Alma 33:12–23; 34:8–16, 30–37	What prophets did Alma and Amulek quote before giving us these manifestations (see Alma 33:3–14; 15–17; 18–21)? What reason do Alma and Amulek give for quoting from these prophets (see Alma 33:2–3, 12–15, 17–23; 34:1, 5–7)?
Nephi, son of Helaman: Helaman 8:13–24	What prophets did Nephi, the son of Helaman, quote before giving us these manifestations (see Helaman 8:13–20)? What reason does Nephi give for quoting from these prophets (Helaman 8:13–16, 18–20, 24–25)?
Lehi: 2 Nephi 2	Before giving us his manifestation, Lehi had listened to his son, Nephi, quote from what prophet (1 Nephi 20–21; 2 Nephi 1:1)? What reason did Nephi give for quoting from this prophet (1 Nephi 19:21–24; 22:10–12, 28–31; 2 Nephi 1:1)?

I'll provide below my own response to these four questions for Nephi's manifestation in 2 Nephi 25. But in the interest of space, I won't include in this book my own response to each of the manifestations. These responses—especially to the last two questions—are by their nature personal and varied. And even your own responses will change with each subsequent visit to the chambers of this temple. I think it would be nice for each reader to share her or his responses to these questions on the book's website.

A Personal Response to Nephi's Manifestation of the Messiah in 2 Nephi 25

How did Nephi make the Messiah and His atoning mission powerfully manifest?

It is amazing how much sacred clarity and plain knowledge we gain of the Savior in this one chapter. We not only confirm here His very name in full, "Jesus Christ," but all hesitations and ambiguities that the world today might try to foist upon us about the great, eternal, and divinely appointed roles He bore as the Messiah instantly dissolve as Nephi unimpeachably testifies that this same Jesus Christ is: 1) the "Son of God"; 2) the "Only Begotten of the Father"; 3) the very creator or the "Father of heaven and of earth"; 4) the One—and only One—who can "save," "atone," give "life," and "reconcile to God" all mankind; 5) Jehovah Himself, the "Holy One of Israel"; 6) the one and only prophesied "Messiah" as celebrated by all the prophets; 7) the great "end" or fulfillment of the law of Moses; and 8) the "source" to which all men "may look for a remission of their sins."

And Nephi further certifies some of the most sacred and concrete details of that Atonement: how Jesus Christ fulfilled His assigned messianic role through His rejection by men, sufferings on the cross, His actual death and placement in a tomb for three days, and then His sublime victory over death as Nephi sees in vision that He "shall rise from the dead, with healing in his wings."

Nephi also makes crystal clear the critical fuel of faith in the dynamics of redemption: Even though all shall rise from the dead because of Christ's victory over the grave, only "those who believe on His name" so that they may partake of His "grace," and thereby become "alive in Christ," and "worship the Father in His name, with pure hearts and clean hands," shall "be saved in the kingdom of God."

And furthermore, Nephi teaches me that the way I am to demonstrate such faith in Jesus Christ is by accepting this great testimony I am now reading—and thereby receive the same benefit that the children of Israel received as they faithfully "cast their eyes upon the serpent which [Moses] did raise up before them."

In fact, Nephi teaches me that I may be healed and redeemed right now by exercising the same kind of faith in these words that are even now being "raised up before [me]" by Nephi, an analogy he himself explicitly draws in the very same verse: "Behold, I say unto you [who are now reading these words], that as these things are true, and as the Lord God liveth, just as the Lord required Israel in Moses's day to "cast their eyes upon the serpent which he did raise up before them," even so Redemption today follows from receiving and believing the testimony I am now bearing of "this Jesus Christ." So sure and plain is this witness I am now receiving from Nephi that I will be justly judged by how well I receive and apply it in my life.

What do you learn about the atoning mission of the Savior from this manifestation?

I learn that there can be no salvation, no atonement, no forgiveness of sins, no transcendence of our fallen natures or of the demands of justice, no reconcilement with the Father, no resurrection, and no hope for eternal life in the kingdom of God, except through Jesus Christ.

And that because of His willingness to submit to the will of the Father and offer Himself as a sacrifice upon the cross, Jesus Christ alone emerged victorious over all things in eternity that could present an obstacle to my reconcilement with the Father or with my ability to follow my Savior, to have His very Spirit with me, and to take upon myself His name, words, thoughts, deeds, light, and life.

How do you feel about the Savior after learning these things about him?

I feel above all grateful. But also amazed at such willingness of our very God, Creator, and one perfect man to submit to such degradation, humiliation, sufferings, and sacrifices to reconcile my bad choices and make me whole again. I want to express that gratitude by doing what I think He wants most—to dedicate my life to be worthy of His presence and Spirit so that I may help others feel such love and receive these gifts from their Savior also.

Praise to the Lamb, slain from the foundation of the world to give me hope as I feel and act upon such love. Thank you, Lord, and thank you, Father, for sending us a Messiah.

What do you plan to do with this knowledge and conviction that you have just gained in your mind and heart?

I plan to do what I am confident He wants me to do: keep my covenants so that I can continue to know and feel what I do now, receive and always be guided by His Spirit, and dedicate my life to bearing witness of my Savior so that others too may come unto Him and be saved. I now turn my life over to You and seek your will and your glory and to bring others to enjoy the same relationship with their Savior and their Father.

QUESTIONS TO CONTEMPLATE

- Did you feel that you actually entered a sacred space as you explored these temple precincts? How? Why?
- Are you looking forward to returning to such places?
- Did you notice something very significant that preceded each of these great manifestations of the Savior in these temple precincts? What was it?
- Why do you think these things preceded these manifestations?

SECTION TWO

Exploring the Temples of Isaiah, Zenos, Zenock, Moses, and Abraham

YOUR PARTICIPATION: CHART 1, COLUMN 2

Now for the second column of this first chart. Something very interesting—that teaches us about the sacred role of the Book of Mormon for us today—preceded each one of those marvelous manifestations you read and responded to in column 1. To discover what that is, proceed to the questions in the right-hand side of the first chart from the last section—and respond to each question in that second column. As you do so, you will discover some surprising interconnections between those powerful messianic manifestations from the Book of Mormon prophets and other (previous) books of scripture.

After completing the questions in the second column, I invite you to consider the following three questions about the scriptures you just read in column 2 of this our first chart.

Your Turn: Chart 1, Column 2 Again

Where did Nephi (1) (or Jacob, Abinadi, Alma and Amulek, Nephi(2), or Nephi (1) again) likely gain access to these words of these other prophets?

What does this tell us about an important role the Brass Plates served for the people who lived during the Book of Mormon times?

What does this tell us about an important role the Book of Mormon serves for us today?

Some Possible Responses to the Questions from Chart 1, Column 2:

- What prophet did each Book of Mormon prophet quote before giving us his manifestation?

- What reasons did this Book of Mormon prophet give for quoting from this other prophet?

This prophet from the Book of Mormon made the Messiah powerfully manifest in these verses after having read or quoted from . . .	The following manifestations of earlier prophets (recorded on the Brass Plates) for the following reasons:
Nephi: 2 Nephi 25	The prophet Nephi quoted Isaiah (see 2 Nephi 12–24). His reason for quoting from this prophet (see 2 Nephi 11:2, 4, 6–8): "Behold, my soul delighteth in proving unto my people the truth of the coming of Christ" (11:4).
Jacob: 2 Nephi 9–10	The prophet Jacob quoted Isaiah (see 2 Nephi 6:6–7, 16–18; 7–8). His reason for quoting from this prophet (see 2 Nephi 6:5; 9:4): "that ye may learn and glorify the name of your God"; "that ye might know concerning the covenants of the Lord."
Abinadi: Mosiah 15–16	The prophet Abinadi quoted Isaiah (see Mosiah 14). His reason for quoting from this prophet (see Mosiah 13:32–35): to show "there could not any man be saved except it were through the redemption of God."
Alma and Amulek: Alma 33:12–23; 34:8–16, 30–37	The prophets Alma and Amulek quoted these prophets: Zenos, Zenock, Moses (see Alma 33:3–14, 15–17, 18–21). Their reasons for quoting from these prophets (see Alma 34:7): to show "that redemption cometh through the Son of God."

Nephi, son of Helaman: Helaman 8:13–24	Nephi, the son of Helaman, quoted these prophets: Moses, Abraham, etc. (see Helaman 8:13–20). His reason for quoting from these prophets (Helaman 8:15): to show that "as many as should look upon the Son of God with faith . . . might live."
Lehi: 2 Nephi 2	The prophet Lehi had just listened to his son, Nephi, quote from Isaiah (1 Nephi 20–21; 2 Nephi 1:1). The reason Nephi gives for quoting from this prophet (1 Nephi 22:12): that "they shall know that the Lord is their Savior and Redeemer."

Now, let's consider your responses those secondary questions (above) for Column 2:

We have seen how the Book of Mormon prophets turned to *previous sacred manifestations of the Messiah* from the Brass Plates as preludes in order to provoke and nurture *their* manifestations of the Messiah. In each case, these Book of Mormon prophets introduced these Brass Plate prophets as those ordained by the Lord to make the Messiah and His atoning mission and covenants manifest (that "they shall know the Lord is their Savior and Redeemer" as Lehi puts it).

Though these Book of Mormon prophets most often seem to turn to Isaiah as a springboard for their own powerful prophetic manifestations of the Savior and His atoning mission, they also turn to other Brass Plate prophets, such as Moses, Abraham, Zenos, and Zenock. Through this process, we learn how the Lord uses previous books of sacred scripture as the catalyst (or springboard, seedbed, tuning fork) for current manifestations.

This process teaches us much about the sacred role the Book of Mormon fills for *us today*: we turn today to the Book of Mormon prophets (which serve the same role for us as the Brass Plates served for the Nephites) as catalysts for our own most powerful manifestations of the Messiah. "The Bible is the Testament of the Old World; the Book of Mormon is the Testament of the New," taught President Gordon B. Hinckley. "One is the record of Judah; the other is the record of Joseph, and they have come together in the hand of the Lord in fulfillment of the prophecy of Ezekiel. (See Ezekiel 37:19.)

Together they declare the Kingship of the Redeemer of the world and the reality of His kingdom."[1]

Elsewhere, President Hinckley teaches about our reverence for the testimonies of both the Bible and the Book of Mormon: "We are sometimes told that we are not a biblical church. We are a biblical church. This wonderful testament of the Old World, this great and good Holy Bible is one of our standard works. We teach from it. We bear testimony of it. We read from it. It strengthens our testimony. And we add to that this great second witness, the Book of Mormon, the testament of the New World, for as the Bible says, 'In the mouth of two or three witnesses shall [all things] be established (2 Corinthians 13:1)."[2]

This parallel—and complementary—role of each record is suggested in other ways. For example, just as Nephi repeatedly refers to the plates that later become the Book of Mormon as "sacred," the guardians of the Brass Plates refer to them as "sacred" and "holy" (see Alma 37:2–3, 5). And the stated purposes of these respective sets of plates are identical (see Alma 37:8–10).

	Defining Quality of the Plates	Defining Purpose of the Plates
Brass Plates	Sacred or Holy: Alma 37:2–3, 14, 16	Make the Messiah manifest ("brought them to the knowledge of the Lord their God, and to rejoice in Jesus Christ their Redeemer") (Alma 37:8–10.) Make covenants available ("show[ed] forth his power" and "fulfilled his promises") Alma 37:14, 17–19
Plates of Nephi (Book of Mormon)	Sacred: 1 Nephi 19:5–6; Jacob 1:4, etc.	Ether 2:12, Title Page, etc. Make the Messiah manifest ("That they may know the covenants of the Lord")

Perhaps the following analogy can help clarify these interrelationships.

The Book of Isaiah : The Nephites

::

The Book of Mormon : Us Today

Or, in a more general sense:

The Brass Plates : The Nephites

::

The Book of Mormon : Us Today

Of course, we continue to benefit from studying the sacred words of the prophets of the Brass Plates, such as Isaiah (after all, the Lord commands all to search the words of Isaiah—because of their greatness and application to our own day). The Old Testament, New Testament, and the Book of Mormon unite as one to fulfill the Lord's words that in the mouth of three witnesses shall the truth be established (for good measure we also have the Doctrine & Covenants, Pearl of Great Price, and the records of all the conference addresses of the prophets and apostles of our dispensation). But this analogy may simply help explain why the Book of Mormon seems so much more accessible and clear to us today than does a prophet such as Isaiah. As Nephi himself taught us: "And I know that the Jews do understand the things of the [Brass Plate] prophets [such as Isaiah], and there is none other people that understand the things which were spoken unto the Jews like unto them, save it be that they are taught after the manner of the things of the Jews" (2 Nephi 25:5). Nephi then distinguishes the words of the Jews from his own prophecies: "But behold, I proceed with mine own prophecy, according to my plainness; in the which I know that no man can err. . . . For I know that they shall be of great worth unto them in the last days; for in that day shall they understand them; wherefore, for their good have I written them" (2 Nephi 25:7–8).

Isaiah and all of the prophets of the Brass Plates gave powerful manifestations of the Savior that we rejoice to search and receive—as I hope to show in your next chance for participation below, where we focus on the manifestations from these Brass Plate prophets. Certainly Isaiah 53 stands as one of the most powerful, intimate, and moving portraits of our Savior's love and condescension available anywhere. (In fact, I think each of our four standard works offers within them as a cornerstone a supreme testament of the atoning mission of the Savior. What would you list as that supreme testament of the Savior's loving sacrifice in each of these testaments: The Old Testament, New Testament, Book of Mormon, Doctrine & Covenants? Go to the endnote for one possible response.)[3]

But as the Lord has emphasized through both ancient and modern prophets, the Book of Mormon has a special purpose for our day in certifying and magnifying those earlier testaments: "For inasmuch as the knowledge of a Savior has come unto the world, through the testimony of the Jews, even so shall the knowledge of a Savior come unto my people . . . through the testimony of [the Nephite record]. . . . And for this very purpose are these plates preserved" (Doctrine & Covenants 3:16–17, 19; see also 1 Nephi 13:40; Ezekiel 37:17).[4]

Let's now take time to consider the great power of those earlier manifestations of the Messiah—from the Brass Plates, which contained much of what was later gathered in our Old Testament of the Bible.

Your Participation: Chart 1, Column 3

We'll now add a third column to our chart. For this third column, read the words of the prophet from the Brass Plates (in column 1 below) that were quoted by a Book of Mormon prophet. Since the purpose of quoting from that earlier prophet was to show how he made the Messiah and His atoning mission manifest (and the covenants available)—as a prelude or catalyst for the upcoming manifestation by the later prophet—write down how those words from the prophet of the Brass Plates helped make the Messiah manifest to all of the following: 1) the Book of Mormon prophet who quoted or read these words; 2) the people He was addressing; 3) you.

In this way, you have a chance to put yourself in the place of both the Book of Mormon prophet and his audience—as you see how these words (from the Brass Plate prophets, in column 1 below) make the Messiah manifest to you, and what difference such a manifestation will make in your life right now. So you'll be answering the questions in the right-hand column of the following table:

For each of these Brass Plate prophets below:	Answer the following questions[5]:
The prophet Nephi quoted: Isaiah (See 2 Nephi 12–24) The prophet Jacob quoted: Isaiah: (see 2 Nephi 6:6–7, 16–18; 7–8) The prophet Abinadi quoted: Isaiah (see Mosiah 14) The prophets Alma and Amulek quoted these prophets: Zenos, Zenock, Moses (see Alma 33:3–14; 15–17; 18–21) The prophets Nephi, the son of Helaman, quoted these prophets: Moses, Abraham, etc. (see Helaman 8:13–20) The prophet Lehi had just listened to his son, Nephi, quote from: Isaiah (1 Nephi 20–21; 2 Nephi 1:1)	How did this Brass Plate prophet make the Messiah powerfully manifest (to the Book of Mormon prophet, to his audience, and to you)? What do you learn about the atoning mission of the Savior from this manifestation? How do you feel about the Savior after learning these things about Him? What do you plan to do with this knowledge and conviction you have just gained in your mind and heart?

Some Verses to Consider in Response to the Questions from Chart 1, Column 3:

This prophet from the Book of Mormon made the Messiah powerfully manifest in these verses . . .	after having read or quoted this prophet from a previous record or dispensation (and these specific chapters and verses from that previous prophet) . . .	. . . which made the Messiah powerfully manifest in these ways:
I. Nephi: 2 Nephi 25		

How did Isaiah make the Messiah and His mission powerfully manifest (to the Book of Mormon prophet, to his audience, and to you) in these chapters (especially 2 Nephi 16)? See especially:

2 Nephi 16; Isaiah 6: Isaiah sees the Lord, receives a mission to bear witness and invite to come to Lord

2 Nephi 18; Isaiah 8: Turn to the Lord and His word and law for salvation—not to man or the world

2 Nephi 19; Isaiah 9: Messiah to be born to bring light and salvation to a wicked and fallen world

2 Nephi 29; Isaiah 10: Contrasting destiny of the wicked; remnant to be preserved and return

2 Nephi 21; Isaiah 11: To fulfill His covenants, the Lord will raise up a Savior and then an ensign in latter days

2 Nephi 22; Isaiah 12: The joy of redemption

2 Nephi 23–24; Isaiah 13–14: Contrasting state of the wicked and ultimate defeat of unrighteousness

| **II. Jacob: 2 Nephi 9–10**[6] | | |

How did Isaiah make the Messiah powerfully manifest in these chapters and verses?

"Thou shalt know that I am the Lord" (Isaiah 49:23; 2 Nephi 6:7)

"Isaiah speaks messianically" (chapter heading for Isaiah 50)

| **III. Abinadi: Mosiah 15–16** | | |

How did Isaiah make the Messiah powerfully manifest in this chapter? Perhaps the greatest messianic manifestation of the Old Testament: Isaiah 53 (see also Isaiah 54–57, 61–62)

IV. Alma and Amulek: Alma 33: 12–23; 34:8–16, 30–37
How did these prophets make the Messiah powerfully manifest in these verses?
The words of Zenos, Zenock, and Moses (see Alma 33:12–14; 34:6–7) quoted by Alma bore powerful manifestation and witness of the Savior and His Atonement
V. Nephi, son of Helaman: Helaman 8:13–24
How did these prophets make the Messiah powerfully manifest in these verses?
See especially Helaman 8:14–15
VI. Lehi: 2 Nephi 2
How did Isaiah make the Messiah powerfully manifest in these chapters and verses?
"I am he; I am the first, and I am also the last. Mine hand hath also laid the foundation of the earth. . . . Come ye near unto me" (1 Nephi 20:12–13, 16; 21:7–16)

QUESTIONS TO CONTEMPLATE

- Can you see how each of these Book of Mormon prophets turned to a different "scriptural temple" before receiving and then recording their manifestations of the Messiah?

- What might this all teach you about your own process of receiving your personal manifestations of the Messiah?[7] Did you notice something about the *physical* locations where these great manifestations of the Messiah occurred? What did you notice?

- What point do you think the Lord might be making by having these manifestation of the Messiah occur at these physical locations within the Book of Mormon?

NOTES

1 "The Power of the Book of Mormon," *Ensign*, June 1988, p. 6.

2 "Selections from Addresses of President Gordon B. Hinckley," *Ensign*, Mar. 2001, p. 64.

3 Perhaps these: Old Testament: Isaiah 53; New Testament: Luke 22; Book of Mormon: Mosiah 3; Doctrine & Covenants: Section 19.

4 On the particular power of the Book of Mormon to us today, President Ezra Taft Benson teaches "it was written for our day" and explains why "we must make the Book of Mormon a center focus of study": "The Book of Mormon is the keystone in our witness of Jesus Christ, who is Himself the cornerstone of everything we do. It bears witness of His reality with power and clarity. Unlike the Bible, which passed through generations of copyists, translators, and corrupt religionists who tampered with the text, the Book of Mormon came from writer to reader in just one inspired step of translation. Therefore, its testimony of the Master is clear, undiluted, and full of power. But it does even more. Much of the Christian world today rejects the divinity of the Savior. They question His miraculous birth, His perfect life, and the reality of His glorious resurrection. The Book of Mormon teaches in plain and unmistakable terms about the truth of all of those. It also provides the most complete explanation of the doctrine of the Atonement. . . . The Book of Mormon offers so much that broadens our understandings of the doctrines of salvation. Without it, much of what is taught in other scriptures would not be nearly so plain and precious" ("The Book of Mormon—Keystone of Our Religion," *Ensign*, Nov. 1986).

5 Below is my own response to the four questions on page 133 for 2 Nephi 12–24 (Isaiah 2–14):

How did this Brass Plate Prophet make the Messiah powerfully manifest (to the Book of Mormon prophet, to his audience, and to you?

Isaiah makes the Lord manifest as the promised Messiah, Born of a Virgin, the prophesied Stem of Jesse, "The Mighty God, the Everlasting Father, the Prince of Peace," upon whom "the spirit of wisdom, and understanding … of counsel and might … of knowledge" shall rest.

These chapters also make the Messiah manifest by presenting a wonderfully stark contrast between the ways of the Lord and the ways of the world, between the sacred and the profane, between that which brings us more in the presence of the Lord and those things that take us out of His presence.

Isaiah makes clear of what sins we must repent—in order to know and follow the Messiah:

Especially Isaiah makes clear the sin of pride and how so many other sins follow from pride (do all sins ultimately start and proceed from pride?)— including self-worship, ingratitude, neglect of the poor and the needy, immorality, materialism, lust, drunkenness, idolatry, and the seeking of the honors of men.

• "The daughters of Zion are haughty and walk with stretched-forth necks and wanton eyes"; and men are "wise in their own eyes" but "regard not the work of the Lord, neither consider the operation of his hands."

• "Wo unto the prudent in their own sight, who boweth not down … and humbleth not themselves… who walk with stretched-forth necks and wanton eyes."

• "They have cast away the law of the Lord … and have despised [his] word."

• "Wo unto them that turn away the needy.… to take away the right from the poor of my people, that widows may be their prey, and that they may rob the fatherless!"

What do you learn about the atoning mission of the Savior from this manifestation?

I learn the two most essential qualities of the atoning mission of the Messiah—His Justice and His Mercy.

1) What I learn about the Lord's Justice:

I learn that His Justice is above all else and that nothing can oppose or thwart His words and will. I learn that the Messiah is our creator as well as our great judge who sets the standards of punishments and rewards for our actions here and for eternity. I also learn that He cannot accept any degree of sin or unrighteousness. I learn that the consequences of sin and worldliness are harsh and terrible, but through His power and grace we may turn from them and walk instead in light and holiness.

• "The Lord of Hosts hath sworn, saying, surely as I have thought, so shall it come to pass; and as I have purposed, so shall it stand.… For the Lord of Hosts hath purposed, and who shall disannul? And his hand is stretched out, and who shall turn it back?"

• "The fear of the Lord shall come upon them and the majesty of his glory shall smite them," the "idols he shall utterly abolish," and "everyone who is lifted up … the proud and the lofty … the haughtiness of men … shall be brought low," and "the Lord alone shall be exalted in that day."

• "Say unto the righteous that it is well with them; for they shall eat the fruit of their doings. Wo unto the wicked, for they shall perish; for the reward of their hands shall be upon them!"

• "The Lord shall … wash away the filth of the daughters of Zion, and shall have purged the blood of Jerusalem from the midst thereof by the spirit of judgment and by the spirit of burning."

2) What I learn about the Lord's Mercy:

I learn that the Lord is ever anxious to redeem us from the world, to help us turn from idolatry and to escape the bonds of sin—and that through His grace we can be freed from such things. He wants us to see ourselves as His children, His people, with a divine origin and destiny—and to help us find true peace, true rest, and true happiness. His great charge to us all is to be holy, as He, our Lord, is holy.

• "In that day his burden shall be taken away from off thy shoulder, and his yoke from off thy neck, and the yoke shall be destroyed because of the anointing."

• "The people that walked in darkness have seen a great light; they that dwell in the lands of the shadow of death, upon them hath the light shined."

• "He will lift up an ensign to the nations … and will hiss unto them from the ends of the earth…. and shall assemble the outcasts of Israel, and gather together the dispersed of Judah."

• "The Lord will create upon every dwelling-place of mount Zion, and upon her assemblies, a cloud and smoke by day and the shining of a flaming fire by night…. and a tabernacle for a shadow in the daytime from the heat, and for a place of refuge, and a covert from the storm."

How do you feel about the Savior after learning these things about Him?

• I feel both gratitude—for His redeeming mission and mercy on my behalf; and fear of His steady hand of justice—with an awareness of the terrible consequences of sin and of how readily we fallen creatures fall into idolatry, pride, worldliness, and selfishness.

• I realize that I can always trust and rely upon the Savior—that my welfare and happiness here and hereafter are His constant concerns.

• And I realize that I am in the midst of a pervasive and ubiquitous battle in this life—between the forces of God and Satan, good and evil, light and darkness, righteousness and sin; and that I am always in danger and darkness whenever I am not clearly being led by His hand and have His Spirit with me.

What do you plan to do with this knowledge and conviction you have just gained in your mind and heart?

These chapters make me starkly aware of the battle that is raging—and I realize how much more committed I must be to following the Savior at all times and all places, to keeping my covenants that I may always remember Him, take upon myself His name, and have His Spirit and grace to guide me. I am more committed to being an instrument in His hand in helping others find and follow the Savior.

Isaiah also makes clear what our covenant relationship should be with the Messiah, what our duties and our worship should entail:

• We should be anxious to go up to His house so that He "will teach us His ways" and so that we "will walk His paths" and learn both the law and the word of the Lord.

• We should be aware that we have "all gone astray, everyone to his wicked ways" and therefore need the Lord's healing and Atonement.

• We should "walk in the light of the Lord" for in Him alone "I will trust, and not be afraid."

• We should hearken unto the prophets, so that we see with our eyes and hear with our ears, and understand with our hearts and thereby be converted and be healed.

• "O Lord, I will praise thee; though thou wast angry with me thine anger is turned away, and thou comfortedest me.... Praise the Lord, call upon his name; declare his doings among the people, make mention that his name is exalted."

6 My own response to the first 2 questions on page 134 for the Isaiah passages Jacob quoted (see 2 Nephi 6:6–7, 16–18; 7–8):

How did this Brass Plate prophet make the Messiah powerfully manifest (to the Book of Mormon prophet, to his audience, and to you)?

What do you learn about the atoning mission of the Savior from this manifestation?

In the first verses of Isaiah quoted by Jacob (2 Nephi 9:6:6–7, 18), the Brass Plate prophet promises that because of the "standard" (i.e., template, temple, ensign, covenant, Book of Mormon) set up by the Lord, the people of that day, "shalt know that I AM [i.e., shalt receive a full manifestation of Jehovah, the Messiah] and therefore "shall know that I the Lord am thy Savior and thy Redeemer, the Mighty One of Jacob."

And then, this great prophecy is directly fulfilled when Jacob includes two of the greatest messianic chapters of Isaiah (Isaiah 50–51), which makes him fully and sublimely manifest to us all—in the very first person words of the Messiah Himself!

In these chapters, we can hear the very personal, very immediate voice of the Lord as He pleads with us to simply accept him, to simply allow His atoning sacrifice to bless us, heal us, redeem us, to take from Him the gifts of love and salvation He is constantly extending to us, to recognize Him as our advocate, the source of our life, the author of the plan of salvation and eternal life; to awake from the slumber and chains this world and our complicity with it has placed around us; and to stop rejecting him—because of our shortsightedness, our preference for the things of this world, or because we either seek the honor of men or fear men:

• "Have I put thee away, or have I cast thee off forever? ... When I came ... when I called ... there was none to answer.... Is my hand shortened at all that it cannot redeem, or have I no power to deliver?"

• "Hearken unto me, ye that follow after righteousness. Look unto the rock from whence ye are hewn.... I am the Lord thy God ... the Lord of Hosts is my name.... [I] have covered thee in the shadow of mine hand, that I may plant the heavens and lay the foundations of the earth, and say unto Zion: Behold, thou art my people"

• "Awake, awake. Put on strength, O arm of the Lord…. Awake, awake, stand up, O Jerusalem…. Awake, awake, put on thy strength, O Zion; put on thy beautiful garments, O Jerusalem…. Shake thyself from the dust; arise, sit down, O Jerusalem; loose thyself from the bands of thy neck"

• "Fear not the reproach of men, neither be ye afraid of their revilings…. I am he; yea, I am he that comforteth you. Behold, Who art thou, that thou shouldst be afraid of man…. And forgettest the Lord thy maker, that hath stretched forth the heavens, and laid the foundations of the earth?"

We learn that His atoning love and mission is ongoing, never-ending, His hand never shortened, His pleadings never ceasing, His power always prevailing, and His sorrow at our rejection of His offerings always piercing.

We learn more of the condescension of God, of how far the Lord of Hosts would descend below all things in order to raise us above all things, and of the concrete and specific pains that would be part of His sacrifice:

• "I gave my back to the smiter, and my cheeks to them that plucked off the hair. I hid not my face from shame and spitting."

• "Behold, I have taken out of thine hand the cup of trembling, the dregs of the cup of my fury; thou shalt no more drink it again"

We are touched and moved as we learn how the Savior leaned upon His Father for strength during the atoning process (and how we can in the same way lean upon the Lord in our troubles):

• "For the Lord God will help me, therefore shall I not be confounded … and I know that I shall not be ashamed. And the Lord is near, and he justifieth me. Who will contend with me? Let us stand together. Who is mine adversary? … For the Lord God will help me. And all they who shall condemn me, behold. All they shall wax old as a garment, and the moth shall eat them up."

• "Who is among you that feareth the Lord, that obeyeth the voice of his servant, that walketh in darkness and hath no light?"

And we learn that the Atonement of the Savior will triumph:

• "The heavens shall vanish away like smoke, and the earth shall wax old like a garment….But my salvation shall be forever, and my righteousness shall not be abolished"

• "For the Lord shall comfort Zion, he will comfort all her waste places; and he will make her wilderness like Eden, and her desert like the garden of the Lord. Joy and gladness will be found therein, thanksgiving and the voice of melody"

• "Therefore, the redeemed of the Lord shall return, and come with singing unto Zion; and everlasting joy and holiness shall be upon their heads; and they shall obtain gladness and joy; sorrow and mourning shall flee away"

7 Even as we now read from the Book of Mormon, we participate in the very

same process as each of these Book of Mormon writers: as we encounter an inspired manifestation of the Messiah and His atoning mission, we have the chance to use that manifestation as the catalyst or springboard for receiving—and then sharing—our own manifestation. In this sense, each one of us finds ourselves somewhere upon one of the paths described by Lehi in his Vision of the tree of life: the Messiah has been made manifest unto us (by Lehi and other Book of Mormon Prophets) and we can use their witnesses as invitations to likewise taste of the fruit and likewise be filled with the Love of God. It should follow then that we would take Lehi's place and invite others to likewise partake.

The Stick of Ephraim

At last the day has dawned,
The angel's trumpet blew;
Ephraim rises from the dust
Introducing Christ anew.

The Lord brought forth a smith
To blazon coals in fire;
Buried words transformed into
Ephraim's temple spire.

Once dining in Emmaus
And standing by a tomb,
Today the Resurrected Christ
Appears in Ephraim's room.

Serpents raised to heal again,
Waters never letting,
Manna falling from the skies,
Caught in Ephraim's netting.

Let Judah celebrate
This long envisioned feat
Rolling forth with Ephraim's scroll,
These Witnesses now greet.

"My flesh is meat indeed—
Your hunger will assuage;
My blood is here for all to drink,
Who simply turn the page."

SECTION THREE

Temples within Temples within Temples

PHYSICAL LOCATIONS FOR THESE GREAT MANIFESTATIONS OF THE MESSIAH

In this book, we have been making the point that the Book of Mormon fulfills a temple role in that it serves as a sacred place where the Messiah may be made manifest—as we read about in Doctrine & Covenants 109:5; 97:15–16; 84:19. There is an interesting and powerful way that the Lord may help us to appreciate that great temple role of the Book of Mormon. What if the Lord conspicuously had each of these powerful manifestations from the Book of Mormon prophets we have been discussing so far (in the very first chart on page 123) occur in an actual physical temple (or else in a substitute temple, such as a sacred mount, hill, tower, or forest ["sacred grove"])?

Wouldn't the consistent designation—by the Lord—of such specific physical locations for each manifestation of the Savior's atoning mission help to overtly signify the role of the Book of Mormon as a great latter-day temple where the Messiah is made manifest—and the covenants made available?[1]

Can you think of any great manifestations of the Savior in the Book of Mormon that specifically took place at or near a temple?

What was the location for King Benjamin's witness? For Abinadi's? And where were the people gathered when the resurrected Savior appeared in glory to the Bountiful saints?

Can you think of any great manifestations of the Savior that specifically took place on a high mountain—when an actual temple wasn't available?

What was the location for Nephi's great manifestation? For the brother of Jared's? (See 1 Nephi 11:1: "an exceedingly high mountain"; Ether 3:1: a mountain of "exceeding height.")

Can you think of any great manifestations of the Savior in the Book of Mormon that took place at other locations where the "height" is conspicuously mentioned in the record?[2]

Can you think of any great manifestations of the Savior in the Book of Mormon that took place in a "sacred forest" (remembering that the greatest manifestation of the Savior in our dispensation took place in a "sacred grove")?[3]

In this next section, we'll consider the probable physical location for each of these wonderful prophetic manifestations we have studied so far (in the tables above) in the Book of Mormon.

Possible Responses to Chart 1, Column 4

The Physical Locations for These Great Manifestations

The Lord's prophet within this scriptural temple made the Messiah powerfully manifest, and the covenants available . . .	. . . while located within this actual temple (or substitute temple, such as a mountain, hill, or forest/grove), after having referenced or having quoted a manifestation of Messiah from . . .
2 Nephi 25–33: Nephi's wonderful manifestation of the Messiah, His Atonement, and His covenants	Temple built by Nephi (2 Nephi 5) (Occurred right after we read of this temple being built by Nephi, which seems a reasonable place for Nephi to 1) store and access the sacred brass plates; as well as his own sacred plates; and 2) receive important revelations)
2 Nephi 9–10: Jacob's great manifestation of the Messiah, His Atonement, and His covenants	Temple built by Nephi (Occurred right after we read of this temple being built by Nephi, which seems a reasonable place to suppose Jacob taught the "brethren," since he explicitly announces this location for his teaching of the "brethren" later [Jacob 2:2])

Mosiah 15–16: Abinadi's powerful manifestation of the Messiah, His Atonement, and His covenants	Temple built by Nephi (perhaps?), now occupied by Noah and his priests (Mosiah 11:10–11) as they question Abinadi
Alma 33: 12–23; 34:8–16; 30–37: Alma and Amulek testify to Zoramites of the Atonement	"Upon the hill Onidah": 32:4 (mounts or hills used as temples when other temples not available—as they were not to the poor Zoramites)
(Helaman 8:13–24): Nephi testifies to his people	"Nephi had bowed himself upon the tower which was in his garden": Helaman 7:10 (a substitute temple, perhaps as was the city wall upon which Samuel later manifested the Messiah)
2 Nephi 2: Lehi's climactic manifestation of the role of— and our need for—the Redeemer	Outside of the tent of Lehi (the tent serving as a type of tabernacle perhaps, where Lehi and his family earlier offered "sacrifices" and burnt offerings unto [the Lord]" (1 Nephi 7:22; 5:9)

SUMMARY FOR CHART 1, COLUMNS 1–4

To see a summary for chart 1, columns 1–4, putting all of these four columns we've made so far into a single chart, see page 306 in the appendix (chart 2.3.1).

Also see chart 2.3.2 in the appendix (page 310) to see how temples within temples serve as the foundation for the entire Book of Mormon.

NOTES

1 As interesting as the frequent correspondence between manifestations of the Savior and the physical locations of these manifestation at a temple is, I think it is much more valuable to consider the correspondence between these same manifestations of the Savior and the catalyst of previous scriptural temples (such as the quotations from the Brass Plates prophets) that always accompany and precede them. The presence of occasional physical temples is interesting and a lovely symbolic confirmation of the sacredness of both these manifestations and the role of the Book of Mormon itself as a

temple; however, the presence of these scriptural temples (such as Isaiah and other Brass Plates prophets) teaches us much more directly about the current role of the Book of Mormon as a scriptural temple (and therefore sacred catalyst) for our own manifestations of the Savior today. And I am aware that these physical temple locations are not always explicit—and sometimes rely upon probability and conjecture.

2 "The hill Onidah," a "tower," or "the walls of the city" in Alma 32:4; Helaman 7:10; 13:4.

3 See Enos 1:3 and Mosiah 18:30. For modern-day manifestations of the Savior received in temples and after reading from the New Testament, see Doctrine & Covenants 110; 137; 76:1, 23.

SECTION FOUR

Exploring the Temples of Enos, Alma (Elder and Younger), Ammon, and Helaman

LATER BOOK OF MORMON PROPHETS TURN TO EARLIER BOOK OF MORMON PROPHETS—AS CATALYSTS FOR MESSIANIC MANIFESTATIONS

As wonderful as that pattern demonstrates the idea that 1) the Book of Mormon is the Manifestation of the Messiah, and 2) the scriptures are the means the Lord uses in each dispensation to make the Messiah fully manifest, we have only begun to show how this pattern encompasses the various manifestations given in the Book of Mormon.

Because it turns out that the Book of Mormon prophets, as years and centuries passed, did not rely solely upon the Brass Plates as instruments for their own revelations and manifestations of the Messiah. Eventually, earlier manifestations of the Messiah from Book of Mormon prophets would serve as foundations, catalysts, or instruments for later manifestations of Book of Mormon prophets. In other words, earlier Book of Mormon prophets would serve the same function for later Book of Mormon prophets as the Brass Plates prophets once served for the earlier prophets.

Earlier Book of Mormon Prophets : Later Book of Mormon Prophets
::
The Brass Plates Prophets : Earlier Book of Mormon Prophets

Which brings us to another chart—and opportunity for your exploration of other celestial rooms within the temple of Mormon.

YOUR PARTICIPATION: CHART 2, COLUMNS 1 AND 2

In the first column, I'll list the chapters and verses where various Book of Mormon prophets such as Enos, Alma (the elder and younger), and Amulek gave us some of the greatest explanations and manifestations of the Messiah and His atoning mission. But now, in the second column, instead of the manifestations from the Brass Plates serving as instruments, foundations, or springboards, earlier manifestations from Book of Mormon prophets (such as Nephi, Lehi, Jacob, etc.) perform this role.

Once again, for each manifestation I've listed, 1) first answer the questions associated with that manifestation in column one, 2) then answer the questions associated with that manifestation in column two. (In column two, you may want to search for the relevant verses yourself before using the suggested verses provided after the questions—in parenthesis. As always, the more you search on your own, the more you will gain.)

Your turn to again prayerfully respond to questions about some marvelous and wonderful manifestations of the Savior:

How did Enos (or Alma, Ammon, Helaman, etc.) make the Messiah powerfully manifest in this part of the temple of Mormon?

What do you learn about the atoning mission of the Savior from this manifestation in this part of the temple of Mormon?

How do you feel about the Savior after learning these things about Him?

What do you plan to do with this knowledge and conviction that you have just gained in your mind and heart?

This prophet of the Lord from the Book of Mormon made the Messiah powerfully manifest in these verses, after having read or quoted . . .	. . . this earlier prophet from the Book of Mormon (and these specific chapters and verses from that previous prophet)
Enos: 1:4–8	
Alma the Elder: Mosiah 18:1–2, 7–22, 30	
Alma the Elder: Mosiah 26:14–33	
Alma the Younger: Mosiah 27:24–31; Alma 36:12–21	What prophet did Enos (or Alma 1 and 2, or Ammon or Helaman or Nephi and Lehi) reference before giving us his manifestation on the left?
Alma the Younger (see especially Alma 5:21, 27, 34, 38, 48–58) to the people of Zarahemla	
Alma the Younger (see especially Alma 7:7–27) to the people of the Church that were established in the land of Gideon	Where did this prophet likely gain access to these words of this prophet?
Alma the Younger and Amulek: Alma 9:26–28; 10:39–45; 12:22–35	What does this tell us about an important role the Book of Mormon serves for us today?
Ammon (Alma 18:36–41; 19:13, 29, 31) and the other sons of Mosiah (Alma 22:12–18)	
Helaman to his sons, Nephi and Lehi: Helaman 5:9–13	
Nephi and Lehi to the Lamanites while imprisoned: Helaman 5:40–48	

Possible Responses to Questions for Chart 2, Column 2

This prophet of the Lord from the Book of Mormon made the Messiah powerfully manifest in these verses, after having read or quoted . . .	. . . this earlier prophet from the Book of Mormon (and these specific chapters and verses from that previous prophet)
Enos: 1:4–8	What prophet did Enos reference before giving us his manifestation of Christ (see Enos 1:3)? The words of Jacob: "The words [of] my father [Jacob] sunk deep into my heart" (i.e., Enos received his manifestation of the Savior by exercising faith in the manifestations of the Savior he obtained from his father [which manifestations we know of as the Book of Jacob]).
Alma the Elder Mosiah 18:1–2, etc.	The words of Abinadi: "concerning . . . the redemption of the people . . . through the power, and sufferings, and death of Christ" (18:1–2)
Alma the Elder Mosiah 26:14–33	The words of Abinadi: "Thou art blessed because of thy exceeding faith in the words alone of my servant Abinadi" (Mosiah 26:15); "on what condition [is he] saved? . . . did not my father Alma believe in the words which were delivered by the mouth of Abinadi?" (Alma 5:10–11)
Alma the Younger: Mosiah 27:24–31; Alma 36:12–21	The words of Alma the Elder: "I remembered also to have heard my father prophecy [which prophecies we have recorded in the Book of Alma] unto the people concerning a Son of God, to atone for the sins of the world" (Alma 36:17). I.e., it was that which is contained in the Book of Mormon that manifested the Messiah so powerfully that Alma the Younger could then come unto Him and be saved.

Alma the Younger: Alma 5:21, 27, 34, 38, 48–58	Emphasizes the words of Abinadi and their power to manifest the power of the Savior and bring about "a mighty change" (5:7–13); and "the words of our fathers," the truth of which were "manifest[ed]" unto him (5:21, 44, 47) the words of Lehi about the tree of life (5:33–34, 62), Nephi (5:13, 21, 34, 37, 53, 62), Jacob (5:25–26, 33–39, 50–52, 55), and Benjamin (5:18, 26, 38)
Alma the Younger: Alma 7:7–27	See footnotes that show that Alma was quoting liberally from the Brass Plates—especially Isaiah and Psalms—as well as the words of Abinadi and Benjamin
Alma the Younger and Amulek: Alma 9:26–28; 10:39–45; 12:22–35	Words of Lehi and "the fathers" (see Alma 9:8–17)
Ammon, et al: Alma 18:36–41; 19:13, 29, 31	Both the Brass Plates and the record of Nephi (that portion of Book of Mormon available then) (see Alma 18:36–39)
Helaman to his sons	The words of King Benjamin and Amulek (Helaman 5:9–10)
Nephi and Lehi to the Lamanites	The words of Alma and Amulek (Helaman 5:41)

Now, just as with chart 1, let's consider the possible physical location for each of these great manifestations of the Savior and His atoning mission by Nephi (or Enos, Benjamin, Alma, Ammon, Helaman, etc.). Is there any indication that these great witnesses of the Lord were delivered in some kind of temple location? Turn to page 311 of the appendix to chart 2.4.1 to see a summary of (scriptural and physical) temples for chart 2 (now interlaced with the earlier manifestations from chart 1).

The Interrelationship among Testaments within the Book of Mormon

Just as the Book of Mormon prophets serve as instruments to

us in making the Messiah manifest, both earlier Book of Mormon prophets and the prophets from the Brass Plates served as instruments to the Book of Mormon prophets in making the Messiah manifest.

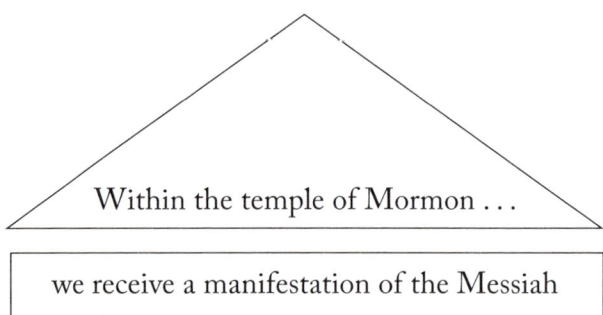

Within the temple of Mormon . . .

we receive a manifestation of the Messiah

through the instrumentality of the Book of Mormon prophets

who received a manifestation of the Messiah

through either

1) the instrumentality of the prophets of the Brass Plates (Isaiah, Zenos, Zenock, Joseph, Moses, etc.)

or

2) the instrumentality of earlier Book of Mormon prophets (Lehi, Nephi, Benjamin, Abinadi, etc.)

SECTION FIVE

Exploring the Temples of Nephi, Benjamin, Samuel, Bountiful, and Mahonri

S o far, we have shown how some of the great manifestations of the Messiah in the Book of Mormon were received by these prophets after they had read, studied, or quoted from earlier manifestations—revealed by prophets from either 1) the Brass Plates (chart 1) or 2) from earlier Book of Mormon prophets (chart 2). And we have seen how often these great manifestations just happen to occur within either actual temples or substitute temples (such as mountains, hills, towers, or forests).

Are there any other great manifestations of the Messiah in the Book of Mormon that you can think of—that we haven't yet considered? As we ponder the five following manifestations of the Messiah throughout the Book of Mormon (from Nephi, Benjamin, Samuel, the Brother of Jared, and from the Savior personally to those gathered in Bountiful), it seems that occasionally the Lord gives His prophets wonderful manifestations of His atoning mission directly through angelic ministers from the presence of God. As we consider these five manifestations, it is interesting that such direct manifestations are relatively rare in the grand order of things. And we also find that in the case of Nephi and Benjamin, their study and faithfulness of the words of previous prophets preceded their encounters with angelic messengers. We shall also find that though the Savior manifests Himself directly to the Nephites, at the same time He turns them to the Brass Plates prophets to certify His role as the Messiah.

Now turn to page 315 of the appendix to view chart 2.5.1, which is the possible responses to chart 3.

Let's now give you a chance to personally participate in these wonderful manifestations of the Savior and His atoning mission—be prayerfully responding to the following questions:

How did Nephi (or Benjamin, Samuel, Mohonri) make the Messiah powerfully manifest in these verses?

What do you learn about the atoning mission of the Savior from this manifestation?

How do you feel about the Savior after learning these things about him?

What do you plan to do with this knowledge and conviction that you have just gained in your mind and heart?

Final Chart: Summary of Charts 1–3

And now, turn to page 317 of the appendix (chart 2.5.2) to view the completed chart that combines all of our previous charts above—to show how consistently the Lord employs the pattern of making the Messiah manifest through 1) the words of previous prophets from previous scriptural records, and 2) within temples. Can you now see what I meant earlier by how the Lord is able to use the holy scriptures to take us upon spiritual adventures that transcend the world's boundaries of time and space? As we read and pondered the words of various Book of Mormon prophets, we literally found ourselves inside sacred temples that then brought us inside other sacred temples. And inside these temples, the most sacred of all temple purposes was fulfilled in our lives: the Messiah was made fully and plainly manifest unto us, and we had the opportunity to actually and literally receive Him and His great atoning gifts. Life just doesn't get any more "real"—or sacred—than that.

SECTION SIX

What Sacred Elements Accompany and Follow Such Manifestations of the Messiah?

W E HAVE just considered some of the greatest manifestations of the Savior and His atoning sacrifice in this sacred record, and, indeed, in all sacred writ. We have seen some marvelous congruencies that accompany each of these manifestations, which serve to point us to the sacred role of the Book of Mormon as an actual temple where the most sacred experience possible on earth occurs—the Savior, our Redeemer, the Messiah, Jehovah, is made fully manifest to us:

- Each Book of Mormon prophet's manifestation of the Atonement is preceded and guided by a manifestation from an earlier "scriptural temple" (either from the Brass Plates or earlier Book of Mormon prophets).

- Each manifestation takes place within either an actual temple or a "substitute" temple (some of the locations, of course, are surmised—based on previous patterns).

In this section we'll take a moment to consider several other sacred elements that consistently accompany each of these wonderful manifestations of the Savior in the Book of Mormon.

Since these manifestations of the Messiah are so sacred, we would expect that the Lord would make sure that certain certifications accompany each of them. Think of what you might expect from Latter-day Saint missionaries who canvass the world today to share their manifestations of the Messiah. *What might we expect from them—to accompany their testimonies of the Savior's atoning sacrifice?*

Wouldn't we expect these missionaries to include with their witnesses these other elements?

- A clear statement of their purpose in bringing you this witness—their "errand from the Lord"

- A clear statement of their authority to bear witness

- A statement of how they gained their personal knowledge of the truth of their message.

- A clear invitation to follow that person manifested as our eternal Savior and Redeemer

- A clear statement of the blessings (or consequences) that follow from accepting (or rejecting) this invitation

- An invitation to make covenants in order to be faithful to the truths they have heard and which they want to follow. (We'll focus more on this last specific element in part 3 of this book.)

Let's go back to each one of those powerful manifestations of the Messiah we have studied in this last section—and see if each of these elements accompanies each of these manifestations. There are a lot of manifestations in this chart. Just go ahead and choose several that you would like to consider and put the relevant scriptures in each square of chart 2.6.1 found on page 320 of the appendix. Then turn to chart 2.6.2 (page 324 to see some possible responses to those questions.[1]

Fruits of the Manifestations:
Obedience, Sacrifice, Consecration

Modern prophets and apostles have made clear that three of our primary temple covenants are obedience, sacrifice, and consecration.[2] Along with each of the great manifestations of the Messiah in the Book of Mormon, there seems to be a consistent pattern where the people addressed by the prophet are invited to demonstrate their willingness to obey, sacrifice, and consecrate their lives in response to the manifestations of the Messiah they receive. We can't be sure of the precise definitions of these three terms—and so my attempts below at describing each is tentative. Nevertheless, I think these Book of Mormon prophets do offer their listeners a chance to partake of each of the three covenants in one way or another. As far as interrelationships among these covenants, it appears that a willingness to obey precedes an ability to sacrifice; and that willingness to fully obey and sacrifice precedes an ability to fully consecrate our lives to the Lord.

In this section, I'll start by suggesting how prophets in some of the manifestations we have been enjoying also include invitations and exhortations to keep covenants of obedience, sacrifice, and consecration. I'll begin by giving a couple of examples from the words of these Book of Mormon prophets of what each of these covenants may include.[3]

Obedience

Especially obedience to the words of the prophets as they offer manifestations, testimonies, and invitations to come unto the Savior. The covenant of obedience—within the temple of Mormon—seems to consist of: 1) recognizing the prophets as designated oracles of the Father; 2) receiving their words as you would the words of the Lord; 3) having such faith in their testimonies and manifestations of the Savior that you submit to other ordinances (such as baptism) and covenants (such as sacrifice and consecration). The immediate reward of such obedience is the gift of the Holy Ghost and taking upon the name of Christ (though actually "waxing strong" in the Spirit of the Holy Ghost, instead of simply "receiving" it, seems to be part of those living the covenant of consecration; just as really acting in the name of Christ is distinguished from simply agreeing to "take upon the name of Christ"). All this is the "gate by which ye should enter" (2 Nephi 31:17–18).

> And now . . . hearken unto these words and believe in Christ . . . And if ye shall believe in Christ ye will believe in these words, for they are the words of Christ, and he hath given them unto me;
>
> And you that will not partake of the goodness of God, and respect . . . my words . . . I bid you and everlasting farewell. (2 Nephi 10, 14)

Blessed art thou, Alma, and blessed are they who were baptized in the waters of Mormon. Thou art blessed because of thy exceeding faith in the words alone of my servant Abinadi. And blessed are they because of their exceeding faith in the words alone which thou hast spoken unto them. (Mosiah 26:15–16)

Sacrifice

Allowing the Savior to "kill" the carnal, prideful, selfish man and being reborn as one concerned for the welfare of others, dedicated to lifting and blessing all, committed to fleeing Babylon. Sacrifice seems to focus upon three activities in particular: 1) leaving behind the "old man" with its carnal and vain desires as you take Christ's name upon you, and, therefore, learn to act more like Christ; 2) fleeing Babylon—or the world's values, enticements, and idols; getting rid of pride, selfishness, and love of vain things of world; and 3) taking upon you the burdens and seeking the welfare of others, particularly the poor and oppressed, seeking to bless others with the joy and abundance we have received through Christ.

> and consider themselves fools before God, and come down into the depths of humility. (2 Nephi 9:42)

> Wherefore . . . reconcile yourselves to the will of God and not to the will of the devil and the flesh. (2 Nephi 10:24)

> I trust that ye are not lifted up in the pride of your hearts; yea, I trust that ye have not set your hearts upon the riches and the vain things of the world; yea, I trust that you do not worship idols, but that ye do worship the true and living God, and ye look forward for the remission of your sins, with an everlasting faith, which is to come. (Alma 7:6)

Consecration

As we take upon ourselves His name and His Spirit, our will is "swallowed up in the will of the Father"; Consecration seems to be focused on three activities in particular: 1) relying completely upon the Savior, and therefore praying always and "feasting upon the word" in order to be always led by His Spirit; 2) living lives with constant thanksgiving and mindfulness of the blessings of the Lord; 3) bearing courageous witness of the Savior—at all times and in all places—even at the risk of being reviled and rejected.

> Ye must pray always and not faint . . . ye must not perform any thing unto the Lord save in the first place ye shall pray unto the Father in the name of Christ, that he will consecrate thy performance unto thee. (2 Nephi 32:9)

> . . . that ye may humble yourselves even to the dust, and worship God, in whatsoever place ye may be in, in spirit and truth; and live in thanksgiving daily, for the many mercies and blessings which he doth bestow upon you. Yea, and I also exhort you, my brethren, that ye be watchful unto prayer continually. (Alma 34:39)

> Ye must press forward with a steadfastness in Christ. . . . having a love of God and of all men . . . relying wholly upon the merits of him who is might to save. (2 Nephi 31:20, 19)

In some ways, these three covenants echo the progress of the Lord's beatitudes:

Obedience

"Blessed are they who shall believe in your words, and come down into the depths of humility and be baptized, for they shall be visited with fire and with the Holy Ghost, and shall receive a remission of their sins" (3 Nephi 12:2; this verse seems a good summation of the first four beatitudes [3 Nephi 12:3–6], which seem to echo the first four principles and ordinances of the gospel).

Sacrifice

"And blessed are the merciful, for they shall obtain mercy. And blessed are the pure in heart, for they shall see God" (3 Nephi 12:7–8).

Consecration

"And blessed are all the peacemakers [see Mosiah 15:14], for they shall be called the children of God. And blessed are all they who are persecuted [and reviled] for my name's sake, for theirs is the kingdom of heaven" (3 Nephi 12:9–12).

Turn to page 328 of the appendix for chart 2.6.3, which shows how each great manifestation of the Messiah we have studied so far also includes invitations and exhortations to keep covenants of obedience, sacrifice, and consecration.

With each manifestation of the Savior and His great atoning mission, we've invited you to consider what you learned, how you felt, and what you planned to do differently based on that sacred manifestation. Now that we've considered how the Book of Mormon prophets have focused upon the importance of three particular covenants—obedience, sacrifice, and consecration—perhaps you might like to consider your reactions to these manifestations in terms of these three covenants. Based on what these prophets have invited their audiences in the Book of Mormon to do, what might you include under each heading below?

How will I show greater obedience (as defined above) based on the manifestations of the Messiah I have received?

How will I show greater sacrifice (as defined above) based on the manifestations of the Messiah I have received?

How will I show greater consecration (as defined above) based on the manifestations of the Messiah I have received?

REVIEW QUESTIONS FOR THIS PART OF THIS BOOK:

- What pattern do we find precedes many of the great manifestations of the Messiah in the Book of Mormon?
- What are many of the Book of Mormon prophets reading or teaching before they bear their great witnesses or share their great manifestations of the Savior?

- Why is it appropriate that we should find this pattern in the Book of Mormon?

- In what physical location do we often find these Book of Mormon prophets when they share their manifestations of the Messiah?

- Why is it appropriate that we find them in these sacred locations?

- What does this say about the role of the Book of Mormon as the manifestation of the Messiah (see Doctrine & Covenants 109:5; 97:15–16)?

- If the Book of Mormon serves the role of a "scriptural temple" by making the Messiah fully manifest within its pages, would you expect earlier books of scripture (such as the New Testament) to serve similar roles?

- If you were to find the same pattern in the New Testament as you just discovered in the Book of Mormon, how might that pattern serve as a wonderful way that each of these testaments of the Savior supports the truth of each other—and become "one in our hands"?

- Can you quickly think of places in the New Testament in which the greatest manifestations of the Savior and His atoning mission occurred through the support of a previous "scriptural temple." The Old Testament? Where? How does this correspond to what we have just noticed about the Book of Mormon?

- Can you quickly think of places in the New Testament in which the actual physical location of a powerful manifestation of the Savior and His atoning mission was a temple? Where? How does this correspond to what we have just noticed about the Book of Mormon?

PERSONAL CHALLENGES FOR YOU

1. Write down some of the things you would do with your life, some of the commitments you would make in your life, some of the attitudes you would have in your life if you had walked into the Sacred Grove instead of the Prophet Joseph and received the same visitation (thought not the same calling) he received.

2. Now ask yourself this: Is reading these manifestations of the Savior in the Book of Mormon in any way less of a manifestation or visitation than you would have had in the Sacred Grove (see 3 Nephi 12:2)?

3. What opportunity and blessing do you have that goes beyond the opportunity and blessing you would have had in that grove?

4. Why should you celebrate and even prefer the opportunity you have now, through faith, to show that you recognize that the manifestation available in the Book of Mormon will affect your life and your commitment to the gospel—every bit as much as a personal, physical visitation would (see 3 Nephi 12:1–3, etc.)?

5. What are some of the ways that you can show this kind of faith?

Notes

1 I've only included here several examples with the wordings from the scriptural citations. For an expansion of this table—with wordings of all citations—see book's website.

2 See e.g., President James E. Faust, "Who Shall Ascend into the Hill of the Lord," *Ensign*, August 2001 and "To Reach Even Unto You," 1980, p. 82; Elder Bruce R. McConkie, "Obedience, Consecration, and Sacrifice," *Ensign*, April 1975; President Ezra T. Benson, *Teachings*, 1988, p. 121; President Gordon B. Hinckley, *Teachings*, 1997, p. 147; Elder D. Todd Christofferson, *Ensign*, October 2008.

3 Not only do we explicitly learn of these covenants through these admonishments of the prophets that accompany these manifestations of the Savior, we have also just spent time watching an entire family demonstrate (positively and negatively) how to actually embrace (Lehi, Sariah, Nephi, Sam, Zoram, some of the family of Ishmael) or reject (Laman, Lemuel, Laban, and some of the family of Ishmael) these covenants: obedience (Lehi [1 Nephi 1:4–5; 3:1–3, 20], Nephi [1 Nephi 2:16; 3:7]), sacrifice (Lehi [2 Nephi 2:2–4; 3:16]), consecration (Lehi [1 Nephi 1:18–20; 2 Nephi 2:1, 7], Nephi [1 Nephi 3:15], vs. Laman and Lemuel [1 Nephi 2:11–13; 3:5, 31]).

Words Matter

Covenants change when words change and the toll
Of an oath to God adjusts—the bounds
Of power bequeathed, as well as the grounds
For blessings and judgment. While on a stroll

In a dark Bavarian forest, drenched
In the Lord's very presence, I recall
Feeling guilty that such happiness should fall
Upon me. What right had I to be quenched

From all this world's woe? Then I felt unroll
Memory of the holy bread, that this joy
Is available to each who would employ
The very same words as I—every soul
Then nourished from the same buffet—
My strange guilt then finally swept away.

Reading from the Torah

"The Spirit of the Lord, is upon me," he read
As bleatings presage slit throats spewing fresh
Blood upon white linen vestments, burnt flesh
Chars on altars new-consumed; unleavened bread

Rains freely, while Sophars echo fierce songs
From across dead waters; and mothers wail
For toddlers tainted by a comet's trail
At birth; two more turtledove necks are wrung

And snapped; cold Horeb waters freely flow;
Lots are cast, Kapparah whispered in prayer;
Azazel chosen, anathema named,
Alone and exiled, all our sins in tow,
Herded to a high hill, caught in a snare,
Scourged and smitten, then spit upon, mocked, and maimed.

SECTION SEVEN

The Temples of Matthew, Mark, Luke, and John

Wouldn't it be interesting if the very same pattern of making the Messiah manifest we have just seen in the Book of Mormon was also followed in the Bible? In this section, you'll enter sacred precincts as you open to some of the greatest manifestations of the Savior and His atoning mission—as recorded in the New Testament. Just as was the case with the Book of Mormon, many of these New Testament manifestations—shared by the Savior Himself or by others through the Holy Ghost—will occur 1) through the instrumentality of another scriptural temple (the Old Testament); and 2) while located in an actual physical temple or in a "substitute temple," such as a mountain.

It is surprising to find that even while the Savior physically walked upon the earth, He often used the instrumentality of the Old Testament to manifest His role as the Messiah. It is also interesting to find how consistently the Lord places those who testify of His atoning mission in the New Testament record within temples.

All of this knowledge of how the New Testament served as a scriptural temple helps us better appreciate the current role of the Book of Mormon for us today as a great latter-day manifestation of the Messiah.

SOME OPENING QUESTIONS AS
YOU BEGIN THIS SECTION:

- In this part of the book, we are going to have you read some of the most sacred manifestations of the Savior ever written. Before you begin this journey into the sacred hallways of the temples of Matthew, Mark, Luke, and John, it would help to pause first and invite the Lord's spirit to attend and guide you.

- What would you include on your list of the greatest manifestations of the Savior and His atoning mission and sacrifice in the New Testament?

- When the Savior made His messianic mission clear, how did He sometimes use the Old Testament prophetic manifestations as instruments, springboards, or catalysts?

- In what sacred locations did many of the most sacred manifestations of the Savior and His mission occur in the New Testament? Examples?

- What does that tell us about the role of the New Testament as a scriptural temple in which the great temple role of making the Messiah fully manifest occurs (see Doctrine & Covenants 109:5; 97:15–16)?

- Why is it interesting that we find these same patterns in both the Book of Mormon and the New Testament?

- What does this tell us about the sacred role of the scriptures in general, as well as the Book of Mormon in particular, as the manifestation of the Messiah?

So far we've seen how the Book of Mormon serves as a great temple built for us in these latter days—as a place where the Messiah, Jesus Christ, can manifest Himself to us. Now that may seem a bit strange, that the Savior would choose this particular way of making Himself known to us—through a book. But we have seen how the greatest manifestations of the Messiah in the Book of Mormon (or the temple of Mormon) occurred in temples. And we have also seen how, while at those temple locations, the Book of Mormon often opened unto what we know of as the temple of the Old Testament (what the Book of Mormon writers considered the Brass Plates—which was their equivalent of our Book of Mormon—including the temples of Joseph, Zenos, Zenock, and Isaiah) as a means of making the Messiah manifest.

In each dispensation, the Lord provided a distinct scriptural temple that provided for the people of that dispensation the same blessings the Book of Mormon provides us: a manifestation of the atoning mission of the Savior—so that all may come unto Him, make covenants with Him, and thereby walk beside the Savior on the path to eternal life.

And we would expect to find in each of these scriptural temples the same pattern we found in the temple of Mormon:

- That the greatest manifestations of the atoning mission of the Savior will occur in actual temples or else in the Lord's preferred substitute temples of mountains.

- That within that scriptural temple, the prophets will use the scriptural temple of the previous dispensation as a primary means of accomplishing the two primary goals of a scriptural temple: making the Messiah manifest and making the covenants available. That is, even when the Savior physically walked the earth, He often chose to use the scriptures as the means of revealing Himself as the Messiah.

Let's take time now to search in the New Testament to see how this "scriptural temple" served as a sacred place of messianic manifestation to those who entered that sacred edifice and received its testimony during the centuries following its compilation (just as those who lived in New Testament times relied on the Old Testament as their "scriptural temple"). With that purpose in mind, I'd like to concentrate on just a couple of parts or "rooms" within the New Testament temple—the temples of Matthew, Mark, Luke, and John.

Our procedure will be the same as that we used with the Book of Mormon, though now from the point of view of those who relied upon a sacred witness other than the Book of Mormon.

USING THE OLD TESTAMENT AS A TEMPLE WITHIN THE NEW TESTAMENT

Strange as it may seem, we will now consider how, even when the Savior *physically* walked the earth, one of the most powerful ways He made Himself and His messianic mission manifest was *through the scriptures*. However, the scriptural temple to which He invited those of His day to enter, and in which He primarily chose to make Himself manifest back then was not the same as the one He uses most often today.

To which scriptural temple would you suppose the Savior pointed those of His day?

Before going further, take some time to think and search for places in the New Testament where the Savior used the Old Testament to make Himself and His mission as the Messiah powerfully and clearly manifest to those people of His day. *Then write them down and keep writing as ideas come to you as to how and why the Lord made Himself manifest in these ways.*

Did you check the topical guide? Which subheadings following "Jesus Christ" would be most helpful? Did you check these: "Mission of," "Prophecies about," or "Teaching Mode of"? Do any of these sections give places where Jesus used the Old Testament prophecies of the Messiah to make Himself manifest as the fulfillment of those prophecies? Where? How?

Not long after Christ's birth, certain people traveled from afar to find the child and worship Him as the promised Messiah. *How did they know He was the Messiah—before they even saw Him? What did they read that made the Messiah manifest to them (see Matthew. 2:1–6)?*

Manifesting Himself as the Messiah—in Nazareth: "This Day Is This Scripture Fulfilled in Your Ears"

When the Lord was first to make His mission as the Messiah fully manifest, how was it done? Perhaps one way to put it would be: how did the Lord let the scriptures fulfill their assigned task—to make the Messiah manifest?

We read that on one Sabbath day, "as his custom was, he went into the synagogue . . . and stood up for to read." And then, when the book of Isaiah was "delivered unto him," Jesus turned to a very significant passage: the passage of Isaiah that contained the very words the Messiah was to speak as He announced His mission of redemption to the world.

We can imagine the power of those words. For years, this audience had revered these words as some of the most sacred, hallowed verses of their entire canon of scripture—the very first-person announcement the Messiah was to utter. And now one of their neighbors, someone from Nazareth, was using them as if *he* were the "me" in these verses:

> The Spirit of the Lord is upon me, because he hath anointed me to preach the gospel to the poor; he hath sent me to heal the broken-hearted, to preach deliverance to the captives, and recovering of sight to the blind, to set at liberty them that are bruised. (Luke 4:16–19)

And so the scriptures fulfilled their task, and to all those gathered, they manifested clearly that the person now reading was the same as He of whom Isaiah prophesied would one day read these words.

As he closed the book, gave it to the minister, and sat down, we read that "the eyes of all them that were in the synagogue were fastened on him" (Luke 4:20)—as they realized that something truly earth-shattering had just occurred. We all can imagine the witness the Spirit must have born to those in that room as the Messiah Himself spoke these words. The scriptures themselves, explicitly revered so much by these people, and one of the most sacred passages from those scriptures were manifesting to these people clearly that the person they referred to as "Joseph's son" was the very Messiah.

But there was another personal witness immediately to follow. The Savior bore witness to those in the room that the words they had just heard read from the scriptures had just been fulfilled by the very person of whom those verses testified—the Messiah Himself: "This day," he said to them, "is this scripture fulfilled in your ears" (Luke 4:21).

So the Savior announced His messianic ministry and manifested Himself as the Messiah *by reading the scriptures and then pointing to them, saying: these words have just made the Messiah manifest.* And, as those scriptures make clear—I am he. As other Galileans, his audience already knew of that "fame of him" that sounded "through all the region round about," including stories of miraculous healings at Capernaum (Luke 4:14, 23). They knew of John's unwavering witness upon the river Jordan—as well, perhaps of a voice from heaven that announced Jesus as the anointed One, the very Son of God. But this "performance" in the sacred precincts of their own synagogue, desecrating the Torah itself (as they supposed), could not be countenanced: "And all they in the synagogue, when they heard these things, were filled with wrath, and rose up and thrust him out of the city, and led him unto the brow of the hill . . . that they might cast him down headlong" (Luke 4:28–29).

WALKING AND TALKING WITH THE RESURRECTED SAVIOR

"Did Not Our Hearts Burn within Us . . . While He Opened up the Scriptures?"

It is interesting how the scriptures were to make a more powerful impact in making the Messiah manifest than any other witness, even including the physical presence and physical activity of the Messiah. A wonderful example of this comes when the disciples, after the Savior's death, had given up hope of seeing Him again. It was all over; death had its victory. Even the assurances of the women, who saw the empty tomb and heard the angelic witness of the resurrection, could not revive their own faith:

> And they returned from the sepulcher, and told all these things unto the eleven, and to all the rest. . . . And their words seemed to them as idle tales, and they believed them not. (Luke 24:9, 11)

When "two of them" were later walking on the road to Emmaus, and "talk[ing] together of all these things which had happened," we learn that the resurrected Savior appeared to them physically: "Jesus himself drew near, and went with them" (Luke 24:15).

We read that "their eyes were holden that they should not know him" based on his physical appearance (Luke 24:16), perhaps requiring them to discern Him another way. *When did they finally receive a manifestation that it was the Messiah, their Savior and Redeemer, who walked and talked beside them?*

Let's let them tell us: "Did not our hearts burn within us, while he talked with us by the way, while *he opened to us the scriptures?*" (Luke 24:32; emphasis added). Yes, the Old Testament scriptures indeed should have made Him and His mission clearly manifest to them, as He had said to them during their walk together: "O fools, and slow of heart to believe all that the prophets have spoken" (Luke 24:25). So He let the scriptures again fulfill their assigned role: "And beginning at Moses and all the prophets, he expounded unto them in all the scriptures the things concerning himself" (Luke 24:27). As the Savior had enjoined them during His mortal ministry: "Search the scriptures, for in them ye think ye have eternal life; and they are they which testify of me" (John 5:39).

The Resurrected Lord Uses the Scriptures to Confirm His Role as the Messiah to the Gathered Apostles

Isn't it also interesting that when the resurrected Lord later physically appeared to the eleven apostles, even showing them "his hands and his feet," inviting them to "handle me and see" that "it is I myself," their faith still seemed unable to comprehend the fulness of the truth they were beholding: "And while they yet believed not for joy, and wondered" (Luke 24:36–41)? *How would the resurrected Messiah make Himself clearly manifest to these, His apostles?*

We watch the resurrected Lord open up the scriptures to them, showing how those words had testified of Him, and "that all things must be fulfilled, which were written in the law of Moses, and in the prophets, and in the psalms, concerning me" (Luke 24:44). Then He taught them how the scriptures had confirmed and made manifest His atoning mission, of which they had been witnesses:

Then opened He their understanding, *that they might understand the scriptures,*

> And said unto them it behooved Christ to suffer, and to rise from the dead the third day; And that repentance and remission of sins should be preached in his name among all nations, beginning at Jerusalem. (Luke 24:45–47)

The following chart shows examples of how the Lord, during His earthly ministry, often manifested Himself with the greatest power by quoting from the Old Testament (showing us how He let the scriptures fulfill their temple role of making the Messiah manifest—even when He was physically upon the earth!).

Summary Chart I

This great manifestation of the Messiah was made by the Savior as He physically walked upon the earth, as recorded in this scriptural temple . . .	. . . through the process or instrumentality of quoting from these Old Testament prophets . . .	with this result, or manifestation:
Luke 4:16–21 Jesus announces His mission as Messiah while in a synagogue in Nazareth	Isaiah 61:1–2: "The Spirit of the Lord is upon me, because he hath anointed me to preach . . . he hath sent me to heal the brokenhearted, to preach deliverance . . . to set at liberty"	"This day," he said to them, "is this scripture fulfilled in your ears" (Luke 4:21)
Luke 24:13–32 Jesus announces His mission as Messiah while on the road to Emmaus	"And beginning at Moses and all the prophets, he expounded unto them in all the scriptures the things concerning himself" (Luke 24:27).	"Did not our hearts burn within us, while he talked with us by the way, while he opened to us the scriptures?" (Luke 24:32)
Luke 24:36–41 Even the resurrected Christ, after speaking to them, and showing His hands and feet, used the scriptures to make Himself more powerfully manifest as the Messiah	"All things must be fulfilled, which were written in the law of Moses, and in the prophets, and in the psalms, concerning me" (Luke 24:44).	At first upon seeing Him physically: "And while they yet believed not for joy, and wondered" (Luke 24:41); Then, using the scriptures to manifest Himself: "Then opened he their understanding" (24:45)

TEMPLES WITHIN THE TEMPLE OF THE NEW TESTAMENT: A METONYMIC REMINDER OF ITS ROLE

To cue us to the New Testament role as a temple, wouldn't it be helpful if, like the Book of Mormon, some of the most powerful manifestations of the messianic mission of the Lord within that testament *occurred in a temple? As you consider the New Testament manifestations of the Savior's mission and Atonement, can you think of any that occurred in a temple?*

It turns out that just as the most powerful manifestations of the Messiah from the Book of Mormon occurred in a temple, some of the most direct and powerful manifestations of the Messiah within the New Testament also occur in a temple. *In the New Testament, what are the earliest temple activities and events recorded by the gospel writers? How did these temple events serve as moments when the future mission of the Messiah was made manifest?*

EARLY TEMPLE MANIFESTATIONS OF THE SAVIOR'S MISSION AS THE MESSIAH

John the Baptist's Role as an Elias (Harbinger of the Messiah) Announced in the Temple

For example, before he baptized Jesus in the Jordan River—in fact, before he was even born—the forerunner and harbinger of the Messiah began to fulfill His Elias role of making the Messiah manifest—*in the temple. How did he do this (see Luke 1)?*

While Zacharias "went into the temple" to perform his priestly duties, an "angel of the Lord" appeared and announced John's future birth and mission—to an astounded and then silenced father: "And many of the children of Israel shall he turn to the Lord their God" (Luke 1:8–9, 11, 16).

Later, when the priests "came to circumcise the child," John's role as Elias was again fulfilled when his father, recovering his voice, prophesied of the coming Messiah and of the glorious mission of his son in the fulfillment of the covenants:

Blessed be the Lord God of Israel; for he hath visited and redeemed his people. . . . As he spake by the mouth of all the holy prophets. . . . To perform the mercy promised to our fathers, *and to remember his holy covenant; the oath which he sware to our father Abraham.* . . . And thou, child, shalt be called the prophet of the Highest: for thou shalt go before the face of the Lord to prepare his ways. (Luke 1:68, 70, 72–73, 76; emphasis added)

While this last manifestation did not occur explicitly either in a temple or upon a mountain, the inspired writers did make note for us that the location of the home of John's parents was in "the *hill country*" in a city of Juda [or Judea] (Luke 1:39). The elevation becomes perhaps even more significant when we read that when Mary entered that same home, both she and her cousin, Elisabeth, along with the Holy Ghost, bore powerful witnesses of the messianic child she was carrying (Luke 1:39–55).

"Mine Eyes Have Seen Thy Salvation"

Heavenly Father arranged that the arrival of the Savior would take place, not in the Galilean town of Nazareth, but rather in a town much nearer Jerusalem and therefore much nearer to the temple—in the Davidic town of Bethlehem. Interestingly, Bethlehem is situated on a high prominent ridge (an elevation of over 2,500 feet), in the hills just south of Jerusalem. Though close to Herod's temple, the place of the promised Messiah's first mortal manifestation was a stable in the heights overlooking the temple in Jerusalem. The Lord also chose quite a different audience than the high priests and elders of the Jews: at His birth, angels heralded His coming by appearing to the humble shepherds, inviting them to come and behold their Savior, lying in a manger (Luke 2:4, 6–18).

Then, soon after Jesus's birth, how would the temple serve as the place for two other direct and powerful manifestations of the Messiah (see Luke 2)?

Both direct manifestations of Jesus's mission as the Messiah occurred at the time when Mary and Joseph came to "present" their first born child "to the Lord" (Luke 2:22). These manifestations would occur this time through two humble, elderly servants of the Lord. And the Lord seems to have Luke conspicuously highlight the sacred site of these great manifestations.

Simeon, to whom a view of the Savior had been promised before his death, "came by the Spirit *unto the temple*," and, upon seeing the child Jesus brought in by Mary and Joseph, "took the child up in his arms, and blessed God," and proclaimed

> Lord, now lettest thou thy servant depart in peace, according to thy word:
>
> > For mine eyes have seen thy salvation,
> >
> > Which thou hast prepared before the face of all people;
> >
> > A light to lighten the Gentiles and the glory of thy people Israel.
>
> (Luke 2:27–32)

Then the faithful centogenerian Anna, who for decades had "*departed not from the temple*, but served God with fastings and prayers night and day," likewise was ordained to bear witness at this time and place that Mary's new child was the promised Messiah, and "[speak] of him to all them that looked for redemption in Jerusalem" (Luke 2:37–38).

Finally, Luke returns us once more to the temple for the only other account we have of the pre-adult Savior—where the twelve-year-old shares with His parents His personal knowledge of His divine Sonship and great earthly mission: "Wist ye not that I must be about my Father's business?" (Luke 2:49).

LATER TEMPLE MANIFESTATIONS OF THE SAVIOR'S MISSION AS THE MESSIAH: THE FEASTS OF THE TABERNACLES, THE DEDICATION, AND THE PASSOVER

"Before Abraham Was, I Am"

Interestingly, whenever the Lord goes to Jerusalem for one of the three major festivals of Judaism (the feasts of the tabernacles, of the dedication, and the Passover), the Gospel writers make a point that He goes "up" to these, most obviously because of the geographical height of the city.

As the feast of the tabernacles approached, some of His apparently not-yet-convinced "brethren" prodded Jesus to follow their timetables and to get moving: "depart hence, and go into Judea."

Their encouragement, sadly, seemed tinged with a bit of skepticism and shorn of the reverence for the Messiah who happens also to have been their mortal brother—"If thou do these things, shew thyself to the world" (John 7:3–5).

Arriving in Jerusalem for the feast of the tabernacles (or the feast of booths or sukkot), Jesus first appears somehow "as it were in secret" and in the "midst of the feast . . . went up into the temple" (John 7:10, 14), where He makes crystal clear His messianic mission from the Father: "Then cried Jesus in the temple as he taught," testifying that "I am from him, and he hath sent me." Such plain declarations moved the Pharisees and chief priest to "sen[d] orders to take him" (John 7:28–29, 32).

Later, on the last "great day of the feast," likely during the customary "Water Drawing Festival," Jesus once again declares directly His divine mission and mandate, alluding to the miraculous gift of water flowing from rocks in the wilderness: "Jesus stood, and cried, saying, If any man thirst, let him come unto me, and drink. He that believeth on me, as the scripture hath said, out of his belly shall flow rivers of living water" (John 7:37–38).

The next day, after first going "unto the mount of Olives," Jesus "came again *unto the temple*" to teach and testify of His messianic mission. "I am the light of the world," He proclaimed, and "the Father that sent me beareth witness of me" (John 8:1–2, 12, 18; emphasis added). John then reemphasizes for us that "these words spake Jesus in the treasury, as he taught in the temple" (John 8:20).

Invoking the sacred name of Jehovah as His own, Jesus told those gathered there that He was indeed the anointed one of the Father: "If ye believe *not that I am he*, ye shall die in your sins. . . . When ye have lifted up the Son of Man, *then shall ye know that I am he*. . . . And that he that sent me is with me . . . for I do always those things that please him" (John 8:24, 28–29).

He then further testified to them that "If God were your Father, ye would love me: for I proceeded forth and came from God; neither came I of myself, but he that sent me," but their actions and hatred showed that "ye are of your father the devil" (John 8:42, 44). Finally, He announced His messianic role using words so sacred and explicit that His auditors reacted by taking up stones to cast at him: "Verily,

verily, I say unto you, Before Abraham was, *I am*" (John 8:58–59). At that point, John tells us, almost as if to conspicuously frame the location of such a sacred event: "Jesus hid himself, and went out of the temple" (John 8:59).

"I and My Father Are One"

During another important feast, "of the dedication" (what we today more familiarly call Hanukkah), the Savior again testified plainly of His redemptive role, while He "walked *in the temple* in Solomon's porch" (John 10:22–23; emphasis added). The Jews gathered there, those who had already dismissed His earlier clear revelations of His messianic mission, again taunted him, probably looking for words to condemn Him rather than for a witness of the truth: "How long dost thou make us to doubt? If thou be the Christ, tell us plainly" (John 10:24). "I told you, and ye believed not," the Lord responded. "I give unto [my sheep that hear my voice and follow me] eternal life. . . . My Father, which gave them me, is greater than all. . . . I and my Father are one" (John 10:25, 27–30).

Thinking that they successfully trapped Him into uttering blasphemy, a capital offense, they "took up stones again to stone him" (John 10:31, 33). Even still, the Savior attempts to lovingly reason with them, and help them get beyond their blind hatred in order to receive the gift the Father sent Him to bestow: "If I do not the works of my Father, believe me not. But if I do, though ye believe not me, believe the works: that ye may know, and believe, that the Father is in me, and I in him" (John 10:37–38).

Having received the plain witness they requested that He indeed is the Christ, they opted to dismiss such plainness, preferring instead to once more vent their hatred and "sought again to take him" (John 10:38).

"If Ye Believe Not His Writings, How Shall Ye Believe My Words"

Finally, during the approach of the most important feast of all, the Passover, the Lord again "went up to Jerusalem" (John 5:1) in order to manifest Himself in sublime light and truth. And on the holiest day of the week, during the holiest celebration of all Israel, the Lord enters the holiest place of all—the temple (John 5:14). And there, instead of accepting and worshipping the true Lamb slain from the foundation of the world, instead of allowing His blood to heal them that the destroying angel may "pass over" their houses and they may be redeemed from the captivity of sin, "the Jews did persecute Jesus, and sought to slay him," using as their latest pretext the arrogance (as they so defined it) displayed by Jesus when He profaned the Sabbath by healing a man who had suffered from an infirmity thirty five years (John 5:15–16). And then for thirty verses, the Lord leaves His audience no room for doubt that He is the very Son of God—and that all who now hear His words must bear the weight of eternal judgment, so absolute and clear and unimpeachable is the witness they now hear:

> Verily, verily, I say unto you, He that heareth my word, and believeth on him that sent me, hath everlasting life. . . . for the works which the Father hath given me to finish, the same works that I do, bear witness of me, that the Father hath sent me. And the Father himself, which hath sent me, hath borne witness of me. . . . I am come in my Father's name. . . . For had ye believed Moses, ye would have believed me: for he wrote of me. (John 5:24, 36, 43, 46)

"Who Eateth My Flesh, and Drinketh My Blood, Hath Eternal Life"

Though not of the same sacred heights as a temple, a synagogue is nevertheless a consecrated place (remember Luke 4; now see John 6:59). Perhaps the most sacred part of a synagogue is called the sanctuary, and the most sacred part of the sanctuary is the Ark or *Aron Kodesh* (meaning "holy cabinet"), which is simply a recession in the wall, containing the Torah scrolls. Further echoing its sacred relation to a temple, behind the doors of the Ark, we find an inner curtain called a parokhet, which was used in the Biblical temple to separate the Holy of Holies (*Kodesh Hakodashim*) from the main hall of the temple. Very fitting that behind such a veil, the Holy of Holies contains the scriptures—which, as we have seen—make the Messiah fully manifest. We have already seen the Savior use a synagogue at Nazareth to powerfully and incontrovertibly manifest Himself. Now we'll watch Him use a synagogue in Capernaum for the same purpose.

With all that in mind, we turn to one of the most powerful manifestations the Savior has given of Himself and His atoning mission, a manifestation that was so explicit and direct—and shocking to some—that it caused many of those who had been His "disciples" up to this point to turn back and "walk no more with him." We learn that this manifestation was given by the Savior "in the synagogue, as he taught in Capernaum" (John 6:60, 66, 59). These most sacred teachings in Capernaum occurred, interestingly, a day after two separate "mountain" visits the Savior made: 1) after He had miraculously fed a great multitude who had followed Him "up into a mountain," where He "sat with His disciples;" and then 2) when, after that miracle, knowing that those who had witnessed such a miracle would "come and take him by force, to make him a king," the Savior "departed again into a mountain himself alone" (John 6:3, 14–15). Interestingly also, the Lord will allow the scriptural types of Him provided hundreds of years earlier by the Old Testament prophets to bear witness of His divinity.

When the people are surprised to finally find Jesus again "on the other side of the sea," apparently at the Capernaum synagogue, the Lord will take the opportunity to let them know just exactly what role He, their Messiah, has come to fulfill and what true discipleship entails and the kind of faith it will demand from them. "Verily, verily, I say unto you, Ye seek me, not because ye desire to keep my sayings . . . but because ye did eat of the loaves, and were filled." He will now separate those who would follow Him as the source of their next easy meal: "Labour not for the meat which perisheth, but for that meat which endureth unto everlasting life, which the Son of man shall give unto you" (John 6:26–27). Showing their hearts and minds are as bound to this world as was Nicodemus's (see John 3:4–8), they respond to the Savior's invitation to partake of that true "bread of God," which "cometh down from heaven, and giveth life unto the world" by begging for manna as did the children of Israel in the wilderness: "Lord, evermore give us this bread" (John 6:32–34).

I imagine the Savior pausing after the first two sacred words of His reply, letting them settle upon—and whirl through—the ears, minds, and hearts of the scribes and Pharisees, as He virtually announces Himself as the Old Testament Jehovah and now their long-awaited Messiah: "*I am*," He tells them, "the bread of life; he that cometh to me shall never hunger; and he that believeth in me shall never thirst. . . . For I came down from heaven, not to do mine own will, but the will of him that sent me" (6:35).

The Jews then—almost on cue—"murmured at him," as if trying to outdo their ancestors in the wilderness for hard-heartedness: "Is not this Jesus, the son of Joseph, whose father and mother we know? How is it then that he saith, I came down from heaven?" (John 6:41–42). (I like Matthew's [13: 54–56] more detailed version of Jesus's local synagogue's reaction to His visit: "And when he was come into his own country, he taught them in their synagogue, insomuch that they were astonished, and said, Whence hath this man this wisdom, and these mighty works? Is not this the carpenter's son? is not his mother called Mary? and his brethren, James, and Joses, and Simon, and Judas? And his sisters, are they not all with us? Whence then hath this man all these things?") And the Lord seems to remind them of their faithless pedigrees when He responds by further emphasizing His role as the very Christ: "Your fathers did eat manna in the wilderness, and are dead. . . . I am the living bread which came down from heaven: If any man eat of this bread, he shall live for ever: and the bread that I will give is my flesh, which I will give for the life of the world" (John 6:49, 51).

"How can a man be born again when he is old? Can he enter a second time unto his mother's womb," was Nicodemus's version of these Jews' current spiritually tone-deaf response to their incarnate Lord: "How can this man give us his flesh to eat?" The mortal Messiah then gives perhaps his greatest and most plain and direct statement of his great atoning mission:

> Verily, verily, I say unto you, Except ye eat the flesh of the Son of man, and drink his blood, ye have no life in you. Whoso eateth my flesh, and drinketh my blood, hath eternal life; and I will raise him up at the last day. For my flesh is meat indeed, and my blood is drink indeed. He that eateth my flesh, and drinketh my blood, dwelleth in me, and I in him. As the living Father hath sent me, and I live by the Father: so he

that eateth me, even he shall live by me. This is that bread which came down from heaven: not as your fathers did eat manna, and are dead: he that eateth of this bread shall live for ever.

TEMPLE MOUNTS IN THE NEW TESTAMENT

Two of the Greatest Manifestations of the Messiah

We have seen in the Book of Mormon and also in the Old Testament that in lieu of a temple the Lord uses mountains as a natural substitute for those sacred buildings. Therefore, in keeping with this pattern, the Lord uses mountain settings in the New Testament for two of the greatest manifestations of the Messiah and His atoning mission.

Two manifestations stand out in their power and sacredness: the Transfiguration of the Lord when the Father Himself announced the divine mission of His Son, and the very act of Atonement—in Gethsemane.

And what did these places have in common—besides the power of their manifestations of Christ?

Each of these supernal manifestations of the Savior's atoning mission explicitly occurred in places designated as "mounts" or "mountains": the Mount of Transfiguration and the Mount of Olives or Olivet (see Matthew 17:1–5; Luke 22:39–44).

> And after six days Jesus taketh Peter, James, and John his brother and bringeth them up into an high mountain apart,
>
> And was transfigured before them: and his face did shine as the sun, and his raiment was white as the light. . . . [And] behold, a bright cloud overshadowed them; and behold a voice out of the cloud, which said, This is my beloved Son, in whom I am well pleased; hear ye him. (Matthew 17:1–2, 5)

> And he came out, and went, as he was wont, to the mount of Olives; and his disciples also followed him. . . .
>
> And he was withdrawn from them about a stone's cast, and kneeled down, and prayed, saying, Father, if thou be willing, remove this cup from me; nevertheless not my will, but thine be done. . . .
>
> And being in agony, he prayed more earnestly: and his sweat was

as it were great drops of blood falling down to the ground. (Luke 22:39, 41–42, 44)

Other Mountain Manifestations of the Messiah

Can you think of any other especially explicit moments in the New Testament when the Savior directly manifested Himself as the chosen Messiah or Christ? *Where did they occur?*

While traveling through Samaria, the Lord told a woman who gave Him water to drink that if she knew who it was who had requested the drink, "thou wouldst have asked of him, and he would have given thee living water" (John 4:10). This water, the Lord explained, shall be "a well of water springing up unto everlasting life" (John 4:14).

During their further conversation, a question arose as to the proper way to worship the Father, with the woman obviously feeling scorned by those who insisted that only in "Jerusalem is the place where men ought to worship" (John 4:20). The Lord's teachings to her seem similar to the words Alma and Amulek spoke to another despised group, the poorer Zoramites: that their worship need not be confined to a certain time or place (Alma 32:10–11; 33:2, 21–22). As the Lord said to the Samaritan woman: "the hour cometh, and now is, when the true worshippers shall worship the Father in spirit and truth; for the Father seeketh such to worship him."

The Samaritan woman then said that she was awaiting the time when "the Messias cometh, which is called Christ." She anticipated His coming, she said, because "when he is come, he will tell us all things." Then John records the Lord's glorious revelation of Himself as that promised Messiah: "I that speak unto thee am he" (John 4:25–26). A wonderful and direct revelation of His divine role. And according to John, where did this wonderful and direct manifestation of the Savior and His mission occur (see John 4:20–21)? Both the Samaritan woman and Jesus Himself describe the location as "in this mountain." How wonderful that the Samaritans, shunned by the Jews, barred from the temple of Herod, still awaiting the promises of redemption, would finally be granted their own manifestation of the Messiah in their own Samarian "temple."

OTHER TYPES OF TEMPLES IN
THE NEW TESTAMENT

Sometimes the substitute temple where the Lord makes His role as the Messiah manifest or fulfills that role may not be as clear-cut as a dedicated edifice or a "mount." But it is interesting how the Lord has His inspired record keepers add details that invite us to infer such sacred symbolism.

Feast of the Passover

For example, during what we know of as Christ's "last supper," He uttered some of the most sacred and somber words in all of scriptures about His role as our Redeemer. *In what ways did He powerfully manifest Himself as the true and literal Passover sacrifice that leads to redemption (see Luke 22:19–20; Mark 14:22–25; see also John 6:53–58)?*[1]

With such a powerful testimony of the imminent fulfillment of Israel's salvation through the sacrifice of His own body and blood—which, He had taught earlier, all men must "eat" and "drink" to receive eternal life—would we not expect, based on the patterns we have so far traced, for such a manifestation to occur in a temple or a temple substitute? Though neither in a temple building nor upon a mount, where do the Gospel writers explicitly note that this final Passover took place (see Luke 22:12; Mark 14:15)?[2]

The Scapegoat

Besides the slaying of the Passover Lamb, another powerful type or shadow of the future redemptive mission of the Messiah anticipated by Israel took place during the Day of Atonement. At this time, the "scapegoat" was chosen, upon whose head the sins of the people were vicariously laid.

From our perspective, when the Lord stands before Pilate and the Jewish leaders and people, displayed like the sacrificial lamb in so many past temple gatherings, and then taking upon Himself the sins of us all, the literal fulfillment of this sacred rite in Christ's condemnation is clear. With such clear temple echoes resounding, wouldn't we now expect such a messianic manifestation to occur in a substitute temple? Although the Gospel writers don't explicitly state so, it would make sense that Pilate would offer the crowds their choice of whom to release from prison at some height above such a mob.

Turn to page 341 of the appendix to see chart 2.7.1—examples of how some of the greatest New Testament manifestations of the Messiah and His atoning mission occurred in temple locations (a metonymic reminder from the Lord that the New Testament fulfills the most sacred roles of a temple), just as was the case with the Book of Mormon.

Satan's Attempted Perversion of These Patterns

It is interesting to note in the accounts of the temptations of the Savior in the wilderness: 1) Satan's efforts to pervert this pattern of the Messiah manifesting Himself most powerfully through "scriptural temples" rather than through more dramatic, "carnal" methods; and 2) how these attempts of Satan to pervert the true purpose of a temple occur at temple locations.

What are the three physical locations for these satanic temptations mentioned in Matthew's account (see Matthew 4:1, 5, 8; note the important JST of verses 5 and 8)?[23]

In these temptations in the wilderness, in what ways do you think Satan might be attempting to pervert the manner that Heavenly Father has ordained for His Son to manifest Himself?

Satan wants the Savior to demonstrate His divine Sonship through flashy, carnal maneuvers rather than through the divinely ordained means and processes (i.e., the scriptures, as the still, small voice of the Spirit bears witness). Like too many in our day, Satan wants the Savior to perform a "magic show act" to get people's attention and bedazzle their physical senses. "If thou be the Son of God, command that these stones be made bread," he entices the Creator of the universe, as if the Savior should act as a puppet on Satan's stage. In response, the Lord immediately emphasizes the role of the scriptures as the true source of life: "Man shall not live by bread alone, but by every word that proceedeth out of the mouth of God" (Matthew 4:4).

Inviting Him next to "Cast thyself down" from the temple pinnacle, Satan would have Him who binds souls unto eternal life within these sacred edifices perform a grandiose and dramatic demonstration of His divine Sonship. The Savior responds with words that apply to all carnal sign-seekers: "Thou shalt not tempt the Lord thy God" (Matthew 4:7).

Satan then takes out all stops, hoping that the sort of thing that impresses someone like him most—the glory, honor, flash, and dazzle of the world—might cause the Savior to lose focus on His mission: to do the will of His Father, who sent Him, and to glorify Him through obedience, consecration, service and sacrifice. "Get thee hence, Satan," the Savior answers—again pointing to the scriptures as the standard of both truth and action, "Thou shalt worship the Lord thy God, and him only shalt thou serve" (Matthew 4:10).[4]

A Scriptural Temple for Our Dispensation

Before leaving our discussion of the New Testament as a great "scriptural temple," we should note how the New Testament served as a prompt for those in our day to receive powerful manifestations of the Messiah, such as on the following occasions:

> Never did any passage of scripture [referring to James 1:5] come with more power to the heart of man than this did at this time to mine. It seemed to enter with great force into every feeling of my heart. I reflected on it again and again. (JS—H 1:12)

> By the power of the Spirit our eyes were opened and our understandings were enlightened, so as to see and understand the things of God. (Doctrine & Covenants 76:12; received after pondering John 5:29)

> And while we meditated upon these things [John 5:29], the Lord touched the eyes of our understandings and they were opened. (Doctrine & Covenants 76:19)

> As I pondered over these things that are written [in the New Testament, especially the Epistle of Peter], the eyes of my understanding were opened, and the Spirit of the Lord rested upon me. (Doctrine & Covenants 138:11)

REVIEW QUESTIONS FOR THIS PART OF THE BOOK:

- What pattern do we find precedes many of the great manifestations of the Messiah in the New Testament?

- How is this pattern similar to the pattern we find in the Book of Mormon?

- In what way does the Lord turn to the Old Testament prophecies of His atoning mission as a means of making His mission manifest?

- Why is it significant that, even while the Savior physically walked upon the earth, He often used the scriptures as a powerful means of making Himself manifest as the Messiah?

- What sacred locations often serve as the place for some of the great manifestations of the Messiah in the New Testament?

- Why is it appropriate that we find them in these sacred locations?

- What does this say about the role of the New Testament as the manifestation of the Messiah (see Doctrine & Covenants 109:5; 97:15–16)?

- How will you be sure that you "recognize" the Savior as He walks with you on your own roads to Emmaus each day?

- Imagine that you lived during the Meridian of Time—when the Savior physically walked the earth. According to what you've studied in this section and in the New Testament passages we've highlighted, what could you have done to make it more likely that you would have recognized and received the Savior as your Redeemer?

- In what way are we facing the exact same challenge today—and in what way is our solution the same as it would have been if we lived in the Meridian of Time? What is that solution?

RETURN TO SCENARIOS FROM THE INTRODUCTION TO PART II

Scenario #1

"They say the Lord is an impartial God—that he loves each of his children and would not give bread to one and a stone to another," Jeffrey said to himself for the umpteenth time, as he sat down to read the next chapter from the Book of Mormon. "Yet, how come Moses gets to see a burning bush and talk to God face to face? How come Peter, James, and John got to stand on the Mount of Transfiguration while past prophets and even Heavenly Father Himself conversed with them? And how come Joseph Smith gets to go into a grove of trees and have a pillar of light descend upon him as both the Father and the Son appear to him? And all we get today is a secondhand account? That sounds kind of partial to me."

Scenario #2

"How could those people in Jesus's day have been so blind," Mary said to herself. "If I had lived then, I would easily have recognized the Savior. What a great time that would have been to be alive! I can hardly wait until the Millennium when I can have the same kind of closeness to the Savior as when He actually walked upon the earth."[5]

NOTES

1 As He institutes the sacrament, He announces to His disciples that "This is my body which is given for you" and "This cup is the new testament in my blood, which is shed for you."

2 The Gospel writer describes the setting for this sacred occasion as "a large upper room."

3 "Then was Jesus led *up* of the Spirit into the wilderness"; "Then Jesus was taken up into the holy city, and the Spirit setteth him on the *pinnacle of the temple*"; "And again, Jesus was taken in the Spirit, and it taketh him up into an *exceeding high mountain*" (emphasis added).

4 Interestingly, each of these three temptations, taking place in "temple locales," might be seen as a perversion of three of the primary covenants we make in temples (obedience, sacrifice, and consecration—as listed by President James E. Faust in his general conference address). In the first temptation,

Satan would have the Savior obey him rather than the Father. In the second, Satan would have the Savior, who had come into the world as a sacrificial lamb—symbolically slain upon the altars of that very temple—counterfeit such a sacrifice, and then invite angels to prevent any discomfort or pain. Perhaps this was Satan's way of prepping for the Savior's later trip to Gethsemane and upon the Cross, hoping the Savior might recall such options while in much greater distress. Third, Satan seems clearly anxious to have the Savior betray his complete consecration to the worship, service, and glory of the Father, transferring such allegiance to the worship, service, and glory of him who envied glory so much that he rebelled rather than serve or worship anyone but himself.

5 For first scenario: In each of these instances (Moses, the Apostles, Joseph Smith) the Lord powerfully manifests Himself to His servants in what may be called a temple setting—which is designated as the place where the "Son of God may manifest himself" (see Doctrine & Covenants 109:5). Each of us today has the very same chance and invitation from the Lord to receive as powerful a manifestation of the Savior's atoning love and sacrifice on our behalf—every time we open the gates to the temple of Mormon.

For second scenario: The Savior is making Himself just as powerfully manifest—within the pages of the Book of Mormon—to each of us today as He did to those who walked and talked with Him in the Meridian of Time, during His earthly ministry. We have the same challenge today of exercising faith and thereby "seeing Him," receiving Him as our Savior, and following Him as anyone has ever had.

Gethsemane

Remove, Abba, this bitter cup I pray;
Though all things are possible to thee,
Let my will be swallowed in thine this day;

I am that Lamb, whom from birth thou must slay
And for this cause planted Gethsemane;
Remove, Abba, this bitter cup I pray;

Sins barking and gnashing at their captive prey,
Unleashed by Elohim's divine decree;
Let my will be swallowed in thine this day;

My soul sorely pressed that mercy repay
Each drop of justice demanded of thee;
Remove, Abba, this bitter cup I pray;

How raw must these sufferings be to convey
All defaults stand redeemed by agony?
Let my will be swallowed in thine this day;

Thou, too, must bear each lash sent my way--
Thine hands and thine feet soon nailed to a tree;
Remove, Abba, this bitter cup I pray;
Let my will be swallowed in thine this day.

Ten Ways of Looking 1 Nephi 1:11

"And the first came and stood before [me] and gave [me] a book, and bade [me] that [I] should read"

Among all the visits of God to earth,
One recurs each time
I turn a page.

Why visit Peter, Joseph, and
Alma but not me, I complained;
Then I turned a page.

I felt the leaves rustle,
Saw the sun break through
The page.

First a meadow of new wheat,
Then a trickling stream,
Across the page.

Jerome, Wycliffe, and Tyndale
Have waited centuries for me
To turn this page.

I smell the morning mists,
Hear suspicious feet,
As I turn the page.

Men choose self over soul,
Trade now for forever,
Page after page.

I squint in the April light
As leaves float on cold streams
Against the page.

I hear echoes from eons before
Race toward eons ahead
Upon the page.

I wonder what brought me here
Before this strange foreboding gate,
Knowing he is waiting for me
To turn the page.

Part III

"That the Promises Might Be Fulfilled": The Book of Mormon and the Abrahamic Covenant

"For the Lord God will fulfill his covenants which he has made unto his children; and for this cause the prophet has written these things. . . . Wherefore, [the Messiah] shall manifest himself unto them in power and great glory. . . ." —2 Nephi 6:13, 14–15

"And for this very purpose are these plates preserved, which contain these records—that the promises of the Lord might be fulfilled, which he made to his people." —Doctrine & Covenants 3:19

"When you read the Book of Mormon, concentrate on the principal figure in the book—from its first chapter to the last—the Lord Jesus Christ, Son of the Living God. And look for a second under girding theme: God will keep His covenants with the remnants of the house of Israel. The Book of Mormon is a crucial component of that covenant."[1] —Russell M. Nelson

"This messenger [Moroni] proclaimed himself to be an angel of God, sent to bring the joyful tidings that the covenant which God made with ancient Israel was at hand to be fulfilled, that the preparatory work for the second coming of the Messiah was speedily to commence; that the time was at hand for the gospel in all its fulness to be preached in power, unto all nations that a people might be prepared for the Millennial reign." —History of the Church, 4:536–37.

WHAT WILL HAPPEN IN THIS PART?

Although we turn to the temple for various temporal and eternal goals, in this book we have been focusing on just two temple goals which the Book of Mormon helps fulfill—and which the Book of Mormon writers themselves have emphasized—starting with the title page:

1) A place where the "Son of Man may manifest Himself" (Doctrine & Covenants 109:5; see also Doctrine & Covenants 110:7); and

2) A place where covenants—especially the Abrahamic covenant—are offered and accepted (Doctrine & Covenants 109:67).

I would like to show how these two temple roles may be interrelated—how one of the roles is fulfilled through the other. But to get there, we need to first talk a bit about covenants.

With that purpose in mind, please consider the following questions:

- What are some of the most important roles of a temple?[2]
- What is a covenant?
- How is a covenant related to these two words: temple and template?
- What always accompanies those who make covenants? Why?
- In what way does the Book of Mormon serve as a sacred template?
- How is the Abrahamic covenant fulfilled?
- How is the fulfillment of this covenant related to the priesthood?
- How does a manifestation of the Messiah help fulfill the Abrahamic covenant?
- What role do the scriptures play in the fulfillment of the Abrahamic covenant?
- What role does the Book of Mormon play in the fulfillment of the Abrahamic covenant?
- In what way does the Abrahamic covenant grant power to those who receive it through receiving the Book of Mormon?

WHAT I HOPE YOU WILL GET OUT OF THIS PART

I hope you'll have a better understanding of the nature of sacred covenants in general, and of the "new covenant" of the Book of Mormon in particular. Through this understanding, I hope you'll be better able to come unto the Savior and look to Him for both our standard of our actions and our power to meet these standards.

Scenario # 1

I have a relative who has spoken with the missionaries often, and recognizes the unusual spirit that accompanies members of the Church.

"Terry, one day I will read the Book of Mormon and when I do I will know it is true," he said. "And I will then know for sure that the church you belong to really is true also."

"Well, _____, what is stopping you? Go ahead and read it."

"I can't right now."

"Why not?"

"Because I just don't think I am capable of living the kind of life that I would need to if I joined this church."

How might you respond to this person?

How might your response involve the idea of covenants in particular, and the Abrahamic covenant in general? (We'll get back to your responses to Marty at the end of this section.)

Scenario # 2

The missionaries asked a couple of us recent converts to join with them as they taught an investigator. They had just taught the principle of the Word of Wisdom. Since tobacco and alcohol were so cheap overseas, many GIs had become addicted to these things.

The other convert with us that day was a big, burly Army cook. He told how he had been smoking several packs of cigarettes and drank a bottle of whiskey each day for years. Like so many others, he had often tried to quit his smoking but always returned to the habit. But now that he was starting to gain a testimony of the truth of the restored gospel; he knew he had to make some changes.

One day, he said, he brought a bag full of his "booze and butts" to the missionaries and said: "If this gospel is true, I should be able to give you this bag of stuff and never have a desire to use these things again."

What do you think happened? Why?

NOTES

1 Elder Russell M. Nelson, "A Testimony of the Book of Mormon," *Ensign*, Nov. 1999, emphasis added.

2 Some possible roles of a temple you may have listed below. Note that the last 5 roles of a temple may only be fulfilled within consecrated and dedicated physical temple edifices. (Two particularly excellent and readily available sources of information about the roles of temples published by the Church are the March 1993 issue of *Ensign* magazine, and *Temples of the Church of Jesus Christ of Latter-day Saints* by Gordon B. Hinckley (Salt Lake City, Ensign Press, 1988).

A temple, among other things, is a place where you may:
• powerfully feel the Spirit and presence of the Lord and be invited to follow Him
  • gain perspective on the true purpose of life
  • gain an understanding about the creation of the earth and its purpose
  • gain an understanding of the plan of salvation and happiness that Heavenly Father has prepared for His children
  • learn of the standards that will be used to judge our faith and actions in this life
  • gain an understanding about the origin and tactics of the adversary
  • gain an understanding about the great choices we make in life between God and the adversary, truth and error, right and wrong, and how we can make the right choice among these alternatives
  • learn how you can separate yourself from the world
  • learn how you can cleanse yourself from the world
  • gain power to follow the Lord and keep His commandments
  • gain power to represent the Lord in serving others
  • gain an understanding about the nature of the Priesthood, its authority from the Lord, and its power to overcome Satan and lead us to the Savior
  • participate in the great gathering and uniting of the Lord's people
  • have your heart turned to the fathers (or parents), and have the hearts of the fathers (or parents) turn to the children
  • Be sealed as a family through the proper authority

• Receive essential temple ordinances through proper authority
• Make essential covenants through proper authority
• Serve as vicarious substitutes so that those on the other side of the veil may receive necessary ordinances
• Gather, serve, and unite with other saints in our Heavenly Father's House

Which of those temple blessings you listed above also come from your study of the Book of Mormon? In this book, I have been focusing on just two very significant temple roles that the Book of Mormon powerfully fulfills for us. Through the fulfillment of these two goals, many other of the blessings you listed will also become available. However, there will always be certain blessings and ordinances that can only be fulfilled inside a physical temple.

Professor Moroni on a Panel

You say we are mere creatures of the earth
Byproducts of cold centuries of change,
Bent only on survival, moved by strange
Delusions that we lived before our birth.

Then how meaningless all talk of worth,
Of goodness, hope, or love—beyond the range
Of chemistry; and how easy to exchange
Such tales for truth and confirm their dearth:

Just read these words and put them to this test:
Do they invite you: walk with holy might?
Grant you power to sever the profane?
Let you taste the bread of life and light—
Because you've clearly entered his domain?
You're mind now set, your knees can do the rest.

SECTION ONE

What Is a Covenant?

I n our activity as members of Christ's Church, what are some "covenants" we have made or which we regularly make? Did you include such things as baptism, the sacrament, the priesthood, the Sabbath, and the many covenants we make in the temple, culminating in the wonderful blessings of celestial marriage?

As you consider each of the various covenants we take upon ourselves, what are some of the things that they all have in common?

For now, we'll consider two very important qualities shared by each covenant we make.

QUALITY NUMBER ONE OF COVENANTS

Let's just take the sacrament covenant for a moment as an example of other covenants.

In the sacrament covenant, we make certain _____ to _____, and the fulfillment of these leads to certain _____ from _____.[1]

Under what circumstance must the sacrament prayer be repeated?[2]

Why do you think it needs to be repeated under that circumstance?[3]

What does the fact that it is a covenant have to do with the need for each word to be exact?[4]

What would happen if some people made the sacrament covenant using different words than other people? Would that be fair? What principle would then be violated? Why? How?[5]

How does this same principle of consistency, exactness, and fairness hold for all other sacred covenants we make (such as baptism and temple covenants)?[6]

In what way does a covenant serve as a standard or basis upon which we each can base the rightness of our decisions in life?[7]

In what way does a covenant serve as a standard or basis upon which a fair and righteous judgment of our lives can be determined?[8]

Why must that standard of judgment be the same for each individual?[9]

Why is it appropriate that so many covenants take place in a temple? How does the origin of the word temple (see definitions below), and its relation to the word template ("temple" comes from the Latin templum, from which we also derive "template") further clarify why a temple is an appropriate location for making covenants?

Temple

From Latin *templum,* itself derived from the Indo-European root *tem-,* "to cut, divide." Latin *templum* probably referred originally to the fact that temples were on sacred ground that was "divided" or separated from ordinary ground.[10]

Tem·plate

"A pattern or gauge, such as a thin metal plate with a cut pattern, used as a guide in making something accurately, as in woodworking or the carving of architectural profiles."[11]

So our temples become standards, templates, or patterns for our actions—which draw us nearer to the sacred or to our divine potential and separate us from the profane, carnal, and worldly.

The Words *Standard* and *Ensign*

So, one important quality of a covenant is to serve as standard, or template upon which each person can measure his or her faithfulness. Such a standard, of course, must be the same for each person. Each word must be exact and precise because it wouldn't be fair to judge one person's faithfulness or to make one person's opportunity to receive blessings (in the case of the Sacrament Covenant the blessing is the gift of the Lord's spirit) based on a standard that varies in any way from another's. "Ordinances instituted in the heavens before the foundation of the world, in the priesthood, for the salvation of men, are not to be altered or changed," taught the prophet Joseph Smith. "All must be saved on the same principles."[12]

We learn that the Lord would raise a standard or ensign in the latter days—unto which all will gather to receive the word of the Lord as well as His covenants and manifestation (2 Nephi 15:26; 21:10; 29:2; Doctrine & Covenants 45:9). The Lord uses of both "standard" and "ensign" apply very well to two sacred edifices: physical temples and the Book of Mormon (and other scriptural temples). In Isaiah, the Lord exhorts all the inhabitants of the earth to "see" the ensign He lifts "on the mountains" and "hear" when He "bloweth a trumpet" to reveal His "dwelling place (Isaiah 18:3–4; see also 11:12). Instead of turning to false standards devised by men ("wizards that peep and that mutter"), the Lord tirelessly invites His children to accept only one standard: "the Lord of hosts himself; and let him be your fear, and let him be your dread [and your only] sanctuary" (Isaiah 8:19, 13–14). And then the Lord immediately reveals where we can access this standard (i.e., the Lord Himself): "Should not a people seek unto their God? . . . to the law and to the testimony [of the prophets]" (Isaiah 8:19–20).

The Lord echoes both these frustrations and solutions in modern scriptures—the people will not seek Him for a standard and will not look for Him where He chooses to make Himself available (manifest): "I am Alpha and Omega . . . a light that shineth in darkness and the darkness comprehendeth it not. I came unto my own, and mine own received me not, but unto as many as received me gave I power . . . to obtain eternal life." How do we find and receive Him today? The same as always: "Even so I have *sent mine everlasting covenant unto the world*, to be a light to the world and *to be a standard for my people*, and for the Gentiles to seek to it, and to be a messenger before my face to prepare the way before me. Wherefore, *come ye unto it*, and with him that cometh I will reason as with men in days of old, and I will show unto you my strong reasoning" (Doctrine & Covenants 45:9–10; see also). Later the Lord tells some of His disciples that their minds had "been darkened" because they did not do two things, which He fully interlaces as being one and the same thing— 1) come unto Him and receive His voice; and 2) receive and apply as standards for their actions "the new covenant, even the Book of Mormon" (84:57, 51, 54, 60).

The two most common definitions of "standard" also conflate and join these two "edifices." First of all, a standard is an acknowledged measure of comparison for establishing value, or a recognized model of excellence.[13] A second meaning of standard comes from the Middle English word *estandard* (rallying place) and refers to a flag or banner or ensign of a nation, a chief of state, or an army. The Lord seems to be combining these definitions as He sets up both temples and the Book of Mormon as rallying banners or flags to which His people gather for strength, safety, testimony, and the very presence and counsel of their King and Savior; as well as a sure criterion to base the value and truth of their actions.

QUALITY NUMBER TWO OF COVENANTS

What covenants or promises do we make when we are baptized? (see Doctrine & Covenants 20:37; Mosiah 18:8–10)

What always follows the baptismal covenant (see the end of Mosiah 18:10; Doctrine & Covenants 84:64)? Why?

When we make certain promises in the Sacrament Covenant, what does the Lord grant us at the same time, in return? Why?

When the Lord gives us commandments or covenants, He also always gives us the _____ to keep those commandments or covenants (1 Nephi 3:7; 17:3; 1 Nephi 10:17; Doctrine & Covenants 93:20; Jacob 4:7).[14]

A great example of this process occurs to the people who gathered at the temple to hear King Benjamin's message. At the end of his discourse, they celebrated together the knowledge they had gained: "Yea, we believe all the words which thou hast spoken unto us; and also, we know of their surety and truth" (Mosiah 5:2). Because of this knowledge, they were willing to enter into a sacred covenant, the result of which was described by King Benjamin:

> And now, because of the covenant which ye have made ye shall be called the children of Christ, his sons, and his daughters; for behold, this day he hath spiritually begotten you; for ye say that your hearts are changed through faith on his name; therefore, ye are born of him and have become his sons and his daughters. (Mosiah 5:6–7)

We all have seen examples of the power of covenants to motivate people to rise "above themselves" or to exceed their expected, "natural" potential.

We saw this on September 11, when, while hundreds rushed to escape burning buildings, hundreds others rushed to enter them. These firefighters and police officers ignored their own safety and risked their lives—sometime with a very clear recognition that they would likely not leave the building again—because of promises they had made.

What is about making a solemn covenant that has the power to transform and empower people? I think Robert Bolt in his play *A Man for All Seasons* captures some sense of that solemnity and power. In many ways, the theme of the entire play centers upon people's attitudes toward covenants, both between men—and with God. While imprisoned in The Tower for not signing an edict certifying the moral and legal reality of King Henry's latest marriage, Thomas More's family obtains permission to visit him—by promising to try to convince him to sign. In the play, the following dialogue takes place, in which More teaches his daughter, Meg—as well as us—the solemnity of covenants:

MORE: "You want me to swear to the Act of Succession?

MARGARET "God more regards the thoughts of the heart than the words of the mouth." Or so you've always told me.

MORE Yes.

MARGARET Then say the words of the oath and in your heart think otherwise.

MORE What is an oath then but words we say to God? When a man takes an oath, Meg, he's holding his own self in his own hands. Like water. And if he opens his fingers then-he needn't hope to find himself again.

As the conversation continues, Thomas More teaches his daughter why all of her logic and argumentation would avail her nothing—because his motivation for being faithful to his conscience transcends such tools:

MARGARET: Haven't you done as much as God can reasonably want?

MORE: Well, Meg, ... finally... it isn't a matter of reason; finally it's a matter of love.

This ideas of "love" as the greatest motivation for keeping covenants reminds me of a discussion my companion and I had in Flanders. We were teaching a couple in Flanders about the Law of Tithing. "Each member of the Church gives 10 percent of his increase or income to the Lord as a tithe," we explained. The discussion led to the idea that in order to participate in the most sacred activities of the Church, such as temple worship, we have to be full tithe payers. "Do they have a copy of your financial records?" the woman asked. "No," we said, "it is all based on our word." "Then why not just pay only five percent?" she asked. "I mean, nobody is going to know, right?" Our answer didn't make a lot of sense to her at that time, but is the strongest possible enforcement of each and every covenant we make with the Lord. "We wouldn't feel right if we paid less than ten percent," we told her. It is our love for the Lord and our gratitude for His generosity that opens our wallets, not some ledger someone keeps.

Thomas More's attitude toward covenants is contrasted with others' in the play, such as the "seagoing principles" of his son-in-law, Will Roper, whose commitments seem rather malleable and subject to situations or arguments:

MORE: Will, I'd trust you with my life. But not your principles. You see, we speak of being anchored to our principles. But if the weather turns nasty you up with an anchor and let it down where there's less wind, and the fishing's better. And "Look," we say, "look, I'm anchored!" (Laughing, inviting ROPER to laugh with him) "To my principles!"

The strongest contrast, however, is between Thomas More and his former friend, Richard Rich, who when asked if he would compromise sacred trusts, answered: "It depends upon what I was offered."

So, two essential qualities of covenants are: 1) covenants serve as standards or templates—to judge the rightness of our decisions, as well as to serve as a just standard to judge our faithfulness; and 2) covenants are always accompanied by the power to keep those covenants. Now, with these two qualities of *covenant* in mind, let's turn to the Book of Mormon.

"THE NEW COVENANT"

How does the Lord sometimes refer to the Book of Mormon (see Doctrine & Covenants 84:57; 2 Nephi 29:2; 2 Nephi 2:6; 1 Nephi 21:22)? In what ways does the *first* quality of covenants discussed above (consistency, exactness, fairness, and standardization) hold for the Book of Mormon as a covenant? How is the Book of Mormon Covenant, in this respect, like the Sacrament Covenant? *Why is it important that each person receives the very same words as any other person when they receive the Book of Mormon as a covenant?*

ACCORDING TO MODERN PROPHETS: THE BOOK OF MORMON COVENANT

- President Ezra Taft Benson on why the Lord called the Book of Mormon the "new covenant" ("The Keystone of Our Religion," *Ensign,* Jan. 1992).

- President Benson on the Book of Mormon as a standard for Israel: ("The Book of Mormon Is the Word of God," *Ensign,* Jan. 1988, p. 4)

What is the ultimate standard (i.e., template) upon which the faithfulness of all of our actions and attitudes will be based, and upon which all of our blessings and judgments will be determined (see 2 Nephi 31:12; 3 Nephi 27:27; 12:48; Matt. 5:48; John 13:15; 14:6; Ether 5:4; 4:10–12, 18; Lev. 19:2; and quotes below)?[15] Why?[16]

In what way does the Lord fulfill both qualities of a covenant we have considered so far (see Doctrine & Covenants 20:12; 3:2; 35:1; 76:4; 1 Nephi 10:18; Mormon 9:9; Moroni 8:18; Alma 7:20; and then see John 15:5; Moroni 10:32; Ether 12:27)?[17]

ACCORDING TO MODERN PROPHETS:
CHRIST AS COVENANT

What do we learn from each of these modern prophets about "Christ as Covenant"?

- President Ezra Taft Benson on setting our sights always on the life of Christ as our exemplar and standard to judge all other choices in life: ("Life Is Eternal," *Ensign*, June 1971, p. 34 and *Ensign,* May 1986, p. 78).

- President Benson on how our emulation of the life of Christ is the only measure of true greatness: ("Listen to a Prophet's Voice," *Ensign,* January 1973, p. 57).

- President Joseph F. Smith on how the main purpose of our existence is to conform to Christ's example and standard: (*Teachings of the Presidents of the Church: Joseph F. Smith* [1998], 151).

Just as there is only one name by which we all can be saved (Mosiah 3), there is only one ultimate standard upon which each of must judge our actions and attitudes: the Savior, Jesus Christ. Any other standard falls short. With that in mind, let's turn again to the Book of Mormon.

Where do we learn that the Book of Mormon also serves as standard (template) upon which our actions and attitudes will be judged?[18]

What do these scriptures tell us about the role of the Book of Mormon?[19]

What do these scriptures tell us about the consequences of our attitudes toward the Book of Mormon?[20]

Why would the Book of Mormon be a suitable standard (template) for judgment (2 Nephi 33:10–15; 25:18, 26, 29; 31:17; 1 Nephi 14:1; 13:40–42; 15:14–15; Doctrine & Covenants 3:16–20; 20:9, 17–36; Mormon 7:8–10; Ether 2:12)?[21]

In what ways does the Book of Mormon achieve the second quality of covenants (above): blessing us with power?[22]

Since the word covenant is sometimes translated as "testament," in what ways are the New Testament and the Book of Mormon both covenants and testaments? In what ways does a testament of Christ become a covenant with Christ?[23]

How do all of these things fit with the words we read in the

Book of Ether: that Jesus Christ "hath been manifested by the things which we have written" (Ether 2:12)?

NOTES

1 promises . . . God . . . blessings . . . God.

2 Whenever it is misspoken (e.g., words added or omitted).

3 If the words changed, the Covenant would then change.

4 A covenant is a uniform standard God makes available for all His children—it is a standard both for our actions and for future judgment of those actions.

5 The principle of fairness or justice would be violated since the standard, template, or criterion would no longer be uniform for all.

6 The words for each covenant must be consistent for each person—and therefore each covenant is made by each person using the exact same words.

7 Each covenant becomes our standard to measure and evaluate our actions.

8 Since each covenant is used a template for our actions, each covenant will also serve as the basis for the Lord's judgments of these actions.

9 In order for justice to prevail.

10 www.thefreedictionary.com/temple.

11 *The American Heritage Dictionary of the English Language*, Fourth Edition, 2000 by Houghton Mifflin Company. Updated in 2003.

12 *History of The Church of Jesus Christ of Latter-day Saints*, ed. B. H. Roberts, 2nd ed., 5.

Though fairness and justice demands each and every person receive the exact same covenant or standard, it is also important to remember that the Lord sees and treats each of us as His individual son or daughter as we make these covenants with him. The Lord did not forget either the ninety nine or the one. A single woman in a jostling crowd tugging at His gown merits His whole attention. Zacchaeus, perched above the crowd atop a tree branch joins the Savior for dinner. A wayward woman at a desert well in Samaria receives the Savior's personal concern and divine witness. Each of over ten thousand gathered at Bountiful received the wonderful privilege of individually feeling their Redeemer's wounds and love.

13 See http://dictionary.reference.com/ search?q=standard.

14 Power.

15 The one true standard is the Lord Himself.

16 He is the light and life of the world, the only perfect man, the one anointed by the Father as our Savior and exemplar, and the one and only way and path to eternal life.

17 He provides us an unimpeachable and unchangeable standard we can always rely upon as well as providing us the power and grace to meet His standard.

18 See Doctrine & Covenants 20:13–15; 84:57; 2 Nephi 25:22; 29:11; Words of Mormon 1:11; Mosiah 3:23–24; Moroni 10:27; Ether 5:4, 6; 2:11)?

19 The Book of Mormon is the means we use to come unto the Lord, receive Him as our standard, and then through exercising faith in this manifestation of Christ, receive grace and power from Him to walk His paths and remain in His presence.

20 By accepting or rejecting the Book of Mormon, we accept or reject Christ— as well as His redeeming grace and power.

21 The Book of Mormon is the very manifestation of Christ, and is therefore a reliable, unchanging standard for our actions and judgment as well as access to the Lord's grace and power in order to accomplish those actions.

22 See e.g., John 15:5; Moroni 10:32; Ether 12:27 as well as those statements from modern prophets about the power available through the Book of Mormon—in section 7 of part 1 of this book.

23 A testimony or testament of the Savior by the prophets is the Lord's decreed means by which we 1) receive a manifestation of the Messiah and 2) then accept Him and His words and will as our standards. Our reward for such acceptance is the grace and power to live according to such standards as we continue to exercise faith in that testament, covenant, and manifestation.

SECTION TWO

The Abrahamic Covenant: Making the Messiah Manifest through the Priesthood and the Scriptures

"THROUGH THY MINISTRY MY NAME SHALL BE MADE KNOWN IN THE EARTH": THE MINISTRY OF ABRAHAM TO MANIFEST THE MESSIAH

With these ideas of covenants, testaments, and the Book of Mormon as the "new covenant," let's consider how all of these things relate to a very important covenant—the Abrahamic covenant.

We have all heard of the Abrahamic covenant. The scriptures—both ancient and modern have taught us the importance of this covenant, and that we should all do our best to understand and fulfill this covenant in our lives. There are many crucial aspects of the Abrahamic covenant, but right now I would like to consider only one aspect, one that relates to the main subject of this book, and one which the Book of Mormon prophets—and the Lord Himself during His visit to the Nephites—continually emphasize. I would like to consider *how a significant part of the Abrahamic covenant is fulfilled by having the Messiah made manifest through the scriptures.*

Where do we learn about the Abrahamic covenant? Where in the scriptures would you expect to go to learn most about that covenant?

Let's go right to the Book of Abraham to learn more about that covenant.

According to this record, what were the very first promises given to Abraham by the Lord?

Do you remember when Abraham recorded that the false priests of Elkenah "laid violence upon me that they might slay me" (Abraham 1:13)? When he called upon the Lord, the Lord sent an angel to loose his bands and deliver him. At that time, the Lord spoke to Abraham and made these two very important promises to him:

1) that the Lord would put upon Abraham His "name, even [His] priesthood," so that "[His] power shall be over [Abraham]"; and

2) that through Abraham and his "ministry" the Lord "shall be *made known in the earth forever*" (Abraham 1:18–19).

Can you think of any ways that these two promises may be interrelated, or how the fulfillment of one of these promises promotes or enables the fulfillment of the other?

In other words, wasn't Abraham promised that through him and his *ministry* the Lord would be *made manifest* to all others on the earth? How would you define "ministry"? Or in still other words, Abraham was promised that through the *priesthood* ("*ministry*") that would be given to him, the Messiah would be made manifest to all future generations. It would be worthwhile to see how the ministry of the priesthood makes all these things possible.

Nephi's Definition of "Ministry" and the Purpose of the Plates: *"Come unto [Christ] and Be Saved"*

With this idea of "ministry" in mind, look up what Nephi has to say about the purpose of the plates (see 1 Nephi 9:3; 19:3). Then look up how he defines what his "ministry" is (1 Nephi 6:4). *How do Nephi's statements coincide with the promises made to Abraham?*

How do Nephi and his priesthood ministry help fulfill the Abrahamic covenant?

(Note here that when Nephi takes time to describe the purpose of the record he is keeping, he is emphatic in noting that he has "received a commandment of the Lord" that the specific purpose of the plates is to preserve an account "of the *ministry* of my people" (1 Nephi 9:3; 19:3). He clearly describes for us what that "ministry" is when he emphasizes that "the fulness of mine intent is that I may persuade men to come unto the God of Abraham, the God of Isaac, and the God of Jacob, and be saved" (1 Nephi 6:4)).

"Even the Key of the Knowledge of God": How Does the Priesthood or Ministry Make the Messiah Manifest?

The Melchizedek Priesthood . . . is the channel through which all knowledge, doctrine, the plan of salvation, and every important matter is revealed from heaven. . . .

It is the channel through which the Almighty commenced revealing His glory at the beginning of the creation of this earth, and through which He has continued to reveal Himself to the children of men to the present time.[1]

Wonderful promises indeed. And these promises lead to another question: *how do you suppose the priesthood would help make the Messiah manifest?*

There are many answers to this question. I would like to consider just one very important way that the scriptures teach us how the priesthood of Abraham would make the Messiah manifest: through worthy priesthood holders of the seed of Abraham (the prophets, seers, and revelators such as Moses, Isaiah, Luke, John, Nephi, Alma, Mormon, and Joseph Smith and so many others like them) the revelations known as the scriptures were received, recorded, compiled, and made available to all people. And through these scriptures, the Messiah is then made manifest to all people. Then, through receiving a manifestation of the Messiah, all of the blessings of eternal life become available—thereby fulfilling the great promise of the Abrahamic covenant.

As we receive the manifestation of the Savior through the Book of Mormon (available to us through the ministry of the priesthood) and accept the covenants, we may receive the blessings promised to Abraham, and then we help further fulfill the Abrahamic covenant by bringing the Book of Mormon and its manifestation of the Savior and the covenants to others.

Figure 1 The Abrahamic Cycle of Blessings

The Abrahamic covenant, the priesthood, and the Book of Mormon

Through the ministry and priesthood of Abraham all the world will be blessed (Abraham 2:11).

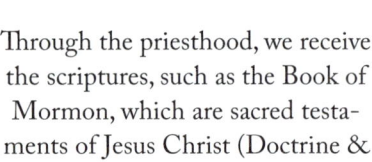

Through the manifestation of the Messiah via the Book of Mormon, we experience the Savior's atoning love and are moved to share these blessings by sharing the Book of Mormon, which makes the Savior manifest to others. Thereby, we personally become part of the fulfillment of the Abrahamic covenant (Moroni 8:25–26; Enos 1:6, 13).

Through the priesthood, we receive the scriptures, such as the Book of Mormon, which are sacred testaments of Jesus Christ (Doctrine & Covenants 84:36; John 5:39).

Through the scriptures, such as the Book of Mormon, the Messiah is made manifest, and an opportunity becomes available to receive the Savior and make covenants (Doctrine & Covenants 84:19–21), thereby receiving the promised blessings.

THE LORD'S VISIT TO ABRAHAM IN CANAAN: AN EMPHASIS UPON THE PRIESTHOOD

Let's consider how this connection between the priesthood passed through the seed of Abraham and the scriptures is further explained by the Lord as He again spoke to Abraham.

It turns out that after saving Abraham from the priests of Elkenah, and sending him to the land of Canaan, the Lord appeared unto Abraham. *In this next visit, how did the Lord emphasize the role of the priesthood in the fulfillment of the Abrahamic covenant (Abraham 2:11)?*

We see that in this visit to Abraham, the Lord reiterated the promises He had made earlier, this time emphasizing the role of the priesthood that would be transferred and continued through Abraham:

> [I]n thee (that is, in thy priesthood) and in thy seed (that is, thy priest-
> hood), for I give unto thee a promise that this right shall continue in
> thee, and in thy seed after thee . . . shall all the families of the earth be
> blessed, even with the blessings of the Gospel, which are the blessings
> of salvation, even of life eternal. (Abraham 2:11)

We learn here that *through the priesthood*, which continues through Abraham's Seed, the blessings of salvation and eternal life will become available to all the families of the earth.

How the Priesthood of Abraham Makes Salvation Available: Through the Priesthood "the Power of Godliness Is Manifest"

All of which leads naturally to this question: *how* will the priesthood of Abraham accomplish this task? Where would you turn if you wanted to learn more about the role of the priesthood (see e.g., Doctrine & Covenants 84:19–21; Alma 13:16)? *What do you learn about the role of the priesthood from the scriptures?* If we turn to the section in the Doctrine & Covenants that contains what is known as the "oath and covenant of the priesthood," we read that "this greater priesthood . . . holdeth the keys of the mysteries of the kingdom, even the *key of the knowledge of God*," such that through the ordinances and authority of the priesthood "*the power of godliness is manifest*" (Doctrine & Covenants 84:19–21). Along these lines, Alma says that "these ordinances were given . . . that thereby the people *might look forward on the Son of God*, it being a type of his order, or it being his order, and this that they might look forward to him for a remission of their sins, that they might enter into the rest of the Lord" (Alma 13:16).

Might one very important example of these ordinances and authorities of the priesthood be the recording and dissemination of the scriptural revelations? And thereby, *through the recording and dissemination of the scriptures*, the priesthood of Abraham *makes the Messiah manifest* to the world. And when the world thereby receives this manifestation of the Savior, the blessings of salvation and eternal life also become available—as well as the power to live them—thereby helping to fulfill the grand purpose of the Abrahamic covenant. "Search the scriptures," the Lord teaches us, "for in them ye think ye have eternal life: and they are they which testify of me" (John 5:39). "And this is life eternal," we learn from the Lord's intercessory prayer, "that they may know thee the only true God, and Jesus Christ, whom thou hast sent" (John 17:3). "And also all they who receive this priesthood, receive me, saith the Lord" (Doctrine & Covenants 84:35). The Lord has made it clear that when we receive His prophets and priesthood holders, we receive Him (see Matthew 10:40; Doctrine & Covenants 1:38; Doctrine & Covenants 68:8- 9; Doctrine & Covenants 84:36; Doctrine & Covenants 112:20). And certainly, one of the primary ways we receive His priesthood is to receive and embrace the scriptural testaments of the Savior.

This priesthood function—of bringing to pass the blessings of the Abrahamic covenant through receiving and disseminating the scriptures—is summarized well in these words of Moroni, as he describes the office of angelic ministers (which includes all of the Book of Mormon writers):

> And the office of their ministry is, to call men unto repentance, and to fulfill and to do the work of the covenants of the Father which he hath made unto the children of men, to prepare the way among the children of men, by declaring the word of Christ unto the chosen vessels of the Lord, that they may bear testimony of him;
> And by so doing, the Lord God prepareth the way that the residue

of men may have faith in Christ, that the Holy Ghost may have place in their hearts, according to the power thereof;

And after this manner bringeth to pass the Father the covenants which he hath made unto the children of men. (Moroni 7:31–32)

In the Book of Acts, we see how well the centurion Cornelius seemed to understand this priesthood function when, in response to his prayers, an angel bade him to send for Peter. After calling "together his relatives and close friends," he greeted Peter in his enthusiasm by falling down at his feet. Peter then corrected Cornelius and "took him up, saying, 'Stand up; I myself also am a man'" (Acts 10:24–26). Cornelius explained his actions by reciting the angelic visit and commands: "Immediately therefore I sent to thee, and thou hast done well that thou art come. Now therefore are we all here present before God, to hear all things that are commanded thee of God" (Acts 10:33).

Peter then confirms the sacred priesthood stewardship Cornelius understood so well by giving one of the great manifestations of the Messiah recorded in the New Testament, testifying:

How God anointed Jesus of Nazareth with the Holy Ghost and with power, who went about doing good, and healing all that were oppressed of the devil; for God was with him.

And we are witnesses of all things which he did both in the land of the Jews and in Jerusalem; whom they slew and hanged on a tree;

Him God raised up the third day, and shewed him openly;

Not to all the people, *but unto witnesses chosen before of God*, even to us, who did eat and drink with him after he rose from the dead;

And he commanded us *to preach unto the people*, and to *testify* that it is he which was ordained of God to be the judge of the quick and the dead.

To him give all the prophets witness, that through his name whosoever believeth in him shall receive remission of sins. (Acts 10:38–43)

Paul, too, taught this sacred function of the priesthood—to make the Messiah manifest in fulfillment of the Abrahamic covenant:

For whomsoever shall call upon the name of the Lord shall be saved.

How then shall they call on him in whom they have believed? and how shall they believe in him of whom they have not heard? and *how shall they hear without a preacher?*

And how shall they preach, except they be sent? As it is written, How beautiful are the feet of them that preach the gospel of peace, and bring glad tidings of good things! . . .

For then faith cometh by hearing, and hearing by the word of God.

But I say, Have they not heard? Yea, verily, their sound went into all the earth, and their words unto the ends of the world. . . .

But Esaias is very bold, and saith, I was found of them that sought me not; *I was manifest unto them* [in Isaiah (65:1) this reads: "I said, *Behold me, behold me*"] that asked not after me. (Romans 10:13–15, 17–18, 20)

And in the Book of Mormon, Abinadi's persecutors quote the very same passage of Isaiah that Paul quotes (see Romans 10:15 and Mosiah 12:21), and then Abinadi responds by showing how that passage refers to the priesthood office of making the Messiah and His Atonement manifest.

Interestingly, the passage from Isaiah (52:7) quoted by both Paul and Abinadi to teach the priesthood function of making the Messiah and His atoning sacrifice ("the power of godliness") manifest, is preceded by a very significant verse that further emphasizes this priesthood role: "Therefore *my people shall know my name*; therefore *they shall know* in that day *that I am* he that doth speak: *behold it is I*" (Isaiah 52:6). And as we saw

How beautiful upon the mountains are the feet of him that bringeth good tidings, that publisheth peace; that bringeth good tidings of good, that publisheth salvation; that saith unto Zion, Thy God reigneth!

Figure 2. The Relationship among the Abrahamic Covenant, the Ministry of the Priesthood and the Book of Mormon.

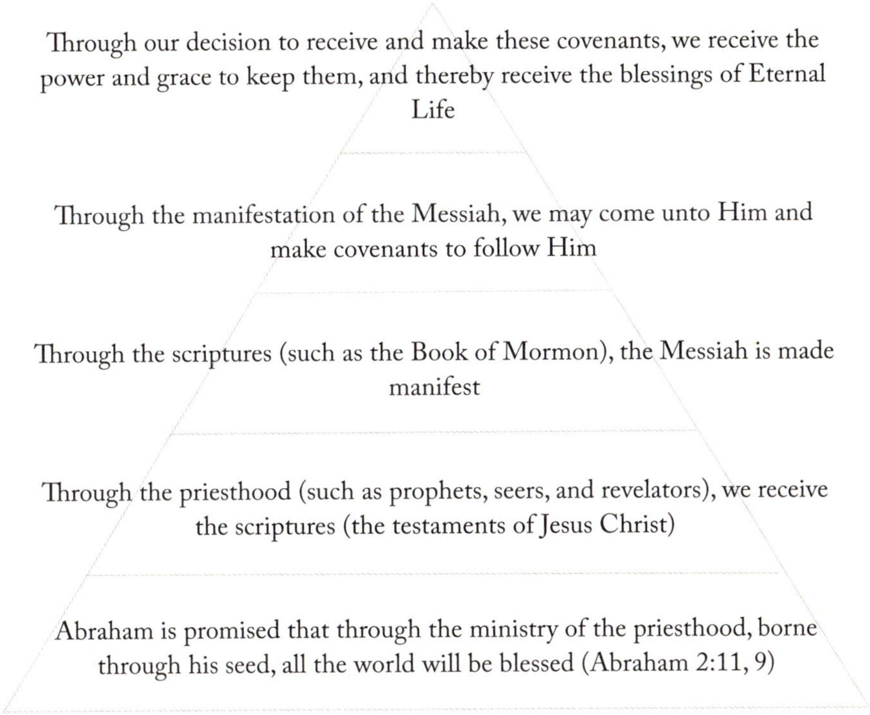

Through our decision to receive and make these covenants, we receive the power and grace to keep them, and thereby receive the blessings of Eternal Life

Through the manifestation of the Messiah, we may come unto Him and make covenants to follow Him

Through the scriptures (such as the Book of Mormon), the Messiah is made manifest

Through the priesthood (such as prophets, seers, and revelators), we receive the scriptures (the testaments of Jesus Christ)

Abraham is promised that through the ministry of the priesthood, borne through his seed, all the world will be blessed (Abraham 2:11, 9)

Note how through the priesthood (passed down through Abraham), which brings forth the scriptures (such as the Book of Mormon), the Messiah can be made manifest, and the blessings of the gospel and eternal life thereby made available

Notes

1 Joseph Smith (History of the Church, 4:207).

Translating the Book of Mormon Today

Each of us imagines we could assume
The role of Oliver, should we translate
Nephite etchings, avoiding the same fate
Of expecting words instantly to bloom.

We know much better lately than presume
Reformed Egyptian on an ancient plate
Could be alchemized to a purer state
Through wish alone. And yet, how oft' in a tomb

Has that book remained interred, each writer
From the dust with dust encumbered still,
Waiting for extraction through modern seers'
Faith, those words of life unquickened in biers
Ourselves create, its sacred sheen no brighter,
As another day's assignment we fulfill.

SECTION THREE

How the Book of Mormon Helps
Fulfill the Abrahamic Covenant—By
Making the Messiah Manifest

C an you think of anywhere else in our scriptures that further
emphasizes this role of the scriptures in making the Messiah manifest, and thereby making available and fulfilling
the Abrahamic covenant? *Specifically, can you think of anywhere in
the scriptures where the role of the Book of Mormon in fulfilling these
Abrahamic promises is made clear? Where and how is this connection
made between 1) fulfilling the Abrahamic covenant and 2) making the
Messiah manifest through the Book of Mormon? You may want to notice
also how consistently the prophets associate the blessing of power with the
fulfillment of the Abrahamic covenant through the Book of Mormon.*

ACCORDING TO NEPHI

*"In that day he shall manifest himself to them in word, and also in power,
in very deed" as part of "the covenant which should be fulfilled in the
latter days."*

Nephi often emphasizes the interrelationship between the future
arrival of the Book of Mormon and the fulfillment of the blessings of
the Abrahamic covenant. Speaking to his brethren about the vision
of the tree of life, he taught that in the latter days "shall the fulness
of the gospel of the Messiah [remembering that the Lord emphasizes to us that the Book of Mormon contains the "fulness of the
gospel of Jesus Christ" (Doctrine & Covenants 20:9; 14:10; JS-H
1:34)] come unto the Gentiles," so that thereby the remnant of his

seed may "*come to a knowledge of their Redeemer*" that "they may know how to come unto him and be saved" (1 Nephi 15:14). Nephi then emphasizes that these blessings obtained through the coming forth of the Book of Mormon are part of "the covenant which should be fulfilled in the latter days; which covenant the Lord made to our father Abraham, saying: In thy seed shall all the kindreds of the earth be blessed" (1 Nephi 15:18).

This great role of the Book of Mormon in blessing the nations by making the Messiah manifest is further taught by Nephi as he records the words an angel spoke to him about the role his record will play in making the Messiah manifest:

> These last records, which thou hast seen among the Gentiles, shall establish the truth of the first, which are of the twelve apostles of the Lamb, and shall make known the plain and precious things which have been taken away from them; and shall make known to all kindreds, tongues, and people, *that the Lamb of God is the Son of the Eternal Father, and the Savior of the world*; and that all men must come unto him, or they cannot be saved. . . .
>
> And the time cometh that *he shall manifest himself unto all nations*, both unto the Jews and also unto the Gentiles, and after he hath manifested himself unto the Jews and also unto the Gentiles, then he shall manifest himself unto the Gentiles and also unto the Jews, and the last shall be first, and the first shall be last.
>
> And it shall come to pass, that if the Gentiles shall hearken unto the Lamb of God in that day that *he shall manifest himself to them in word, and also in power, in very deed* . . . (1 Nephi 13:40–42; 14:1)

"Wherefore, the Lord God will proceed to make bare his arm in the eyes of all nations, in bringing about his covenants"

Later, Nephi reemphasizes this covenant-fulfilling role of the Book of Mormon and the restoration of the gospel when he teaches his brethren that this "marvelous work among the Gentiles" shall "be of great worth unto our seed," and also "of great worth unto the Gentiles" and unto "all the house of Israel" in "making known of the covenants of the Father of heaven unto Abraham, saying: In thy seed shall all the kindreds of the earth be blessed" (1 Nephi 22:8–9). Such blessings, Nephi stresses, become available only when the Book of Mormon fills its ordained role: i.e., *when the Lord is made manifest*:

And I would, my brethren, that ye should know that all the kindreds of the earth cannot be blessed unless he shall *make bare his arm* in the eyes of the nations.

Wherefore, the Lord God will proceed to make bare his arm in the eyes of all nations, in bringing about his covenants and his gospel unto those who are of the house of Israel.

Wherefore, he will bring them again out of captivity . . . and they shall be brought out of obscurity and out of darkness; and they shall *know that the Lord is their Savior and their Redeemer, the Mighty One of Israel.* (1 Nephi 22:10–12)

"The day will come that it must needs be expedient that they should believe these things" and *"look not forward any more for another Messiah."*

Speaking of the Jews, Nephi anticipates the day that they will again be blessed through the restoration of the covenants, and makes clear how the fulfillment of those covenants will occur through the knowledge of the Messiah made available by the coming forth of the Book of Mormon:

Wherefore, the Jews shall be scattered by other nations.

And after they have been scattered, and the Lord God hath scourged them by other nations for the space of many generations, yea, even down from generation to generation until they shall be persuaded to believe in Christ, the Son of God, and the atonement, which is infinite for all mankind—and when that day shall come that they shall believe in Christ, and worship the Father in his name, with pure hearts and clean hands, and look not forward any more for another Messiah, *then, at that time, the day will come that it must needs be expedient that they should believe these things* [i.e., the Book of Mormon]. (2 Nephi 25:15–16)

Nephi makes clear that such covenantal blessings in the latter days will be available to both Jew and Gentile. "For, behold, I say unto you that as many of the Gentiles as will repent are the covenant people of the Lord; and as many of the Jews as will not repent shall be cast off." What finally defines "the covenant people of the Lord"? Those who rely upon the Lord's mercies: "for the Lord covenanteth with none save it be with them that repent and believe in his Son, who is the Holy One of Israel" (2 Nephi 30:2). These latter day blessings of the covenant are only contingent upon belief in the

Savior—as He will be made manifest in the Book of Mormon:

> For after the book of which I have spoken shall come forth, and be written unto the Gentiles, and sealed up again unto the Lord, there shall be many which shall believe the words which are written; and they shall carry them forth unto the remnant of our seed. . . .
>
> Wherefore, they shall be restored unto the knowledge of their fathers, and also to the knowledge of Jesus Christ, which was had among their fathers. (2 Nephi 30:3, 5).

According to Jacob

"The Messiah . . . will manifest Himself unto them in power and great glory" to *"fulfill his covenants which he has made unto his children"* when they *"come to that which will give them the true knowledge of their Redeemer"*

In his panoramic testimony of the latter-day blessings awaiting the House of Israel, Jacob clearly teaches us how the Abrahamic covenant becomes fulfilled when the Messiah is made manifest through the Book of Mormon. "Our children shall be restored," writes Jacob, "that they may come to that which will give them the true knowledge of their Redeemer" (2 Nephi 10:2).

Jacob's testimony starts with the words of Isaiah, as the great Old Testament prophet foresees the day when a latter-day "standard" will be set up among the Gentiles, through which, the Lord says, the people "shalt know that I am the Lord" (2 Nephi 6:6–7).

Jacob then teaches about two different occasions—and two different means—when Israel would receive direct and powerful manifestations of the Savior, or "know that I AM" (2 Nephi 6:7 added caps). The first manifestation, a physical manifestation, occurs during the Lord's mortal ministry. The Lord, Jacob says, "has shown me that the Lord God, the Holy One of Israel, should manifest himself *in the flesh*; and after he should manifest himself they should scourge and crucify him" (2 Nephi 6:9; see also Jacob 4:11;).

Then, after being scattered, a time well after the Lord's physical presence upon the earth, we learn that the Lord will reach out again in order to "fulfill his covenants which he has made unto his children" (2 Nephi 6:11–12). On this second occasion, something other than a manifestation "in the flesh" will occur, though with no less power or presence: the Messiah "will *manifest himself unto them in power and great glory*," that they thereby "shall know that the Lord is God, the Holy One of Israel" and "shall come to a knowledge of their Redeemer" (2 Nephi 6:14–15, 11).

The Lord's prophets regularly make this distinction between the Lord's physical manifestations ("in the flesh"; see also e.g., 1 Nephi 15:30, 2 Nephi 25:12; 32:6; Enos 1:8; 1 Timothy 3:16, etc.) and other manifestations. See e.g., in 1 Nephi 14:2, where Nephi prophecies that in the latter-day restoration of the Church through "the Gentiles," the Lord "shall manifest himself unto them in word, and also in power, in very deed"; 1 Nephi 10:11: "and after he had been slain he should rise from the dead, and should make himself manifest, by the Holy Ghost, unto the Gentiles," as well as those scriptures included in the introduction to this book. As described by the Book of Mormon prophets, manifestations "in the flesh" invariably refer to the Lord's mortal ministry in the Meridian of Time. In this book, I am suggesting that those other manifestations available to us—through our explorations with the temple of Mormon—are no less, and indeed may be more, immediate, vivid, and powerful.

Jacob then fulfills his own prophecies when he makes the Messiah and his mission fully manifest "in power and great glory" (2 Nephi 9, 10). Throughout his testimony, Jacob stresses that his words now make the Messiah fully manifest unto us, and invites us to come unto him:

"O, my beloved brethren, give ear to my words. Remember the greatness of the Holy One of Israel" (2 Nephi 9:40).

"O, then, my beloved brethren, come unto the Lord, the Holy One" (2 Nephi 9:41).

"Come unto that God who is the rock of your salvation" (2 Nephi 9:45).

"Hearken diligently unto me, and remember the words which I have spoken; and come unto the Holy One of Israel" (2 Nephi 9:51).

"It must needs be that Christ—for in the last night the angel spake unto me that this should be his name—should come . . ." (2 Nephi 10:3).

According to Lehi—and Joseph of Egypt

"The covenants of the Lord" will be "remembered" when "the Messiah should be made manifest . . . in the latter days, in the spirit of power" through" the thing, which the Lord shall bring forth by the [choice seer's] hand."

Father Lehi received great knowledge and visions of the Lord's latter-day work of restoration, particularly about how the covenants of the Lord would be fulfilled through the manifestation of the Lord made available by means of the Book of Mormon. Part of Lehi's knowledge came through the Brass Plates, which included the prophecies of Joseph of Egypt. From these prophecies, Lehi learned the Lord would raise up a "righteous branch unto the house of Israel" and also "a choice seer" (2 Nephi 3:5, 7). Through this branch and seer, "the covenants of the Lord" would be "remembered" when *"the Messiah should be made manifest . . . in the latter days, in the spirit of power"* (2 Nephi 3: 5–6). Through this manifestation, the blessings of the Abrahamic covenant (Abraham 2:11) become available: "For the thing, which the Lord shall bring forth by the [choice seer's] hand, by the power of the Lord," wrote Joseph, "shall bring my people unto salvation" (2 Nephi 3:15).

According to the Savior

"then will I fulfill the covenant which the Father hath made", when "these sayings . . . shall be manifested unto the Gentiles" that they "may be brought to a knowledge of me, their Redeemer."

This sacred role of the Book of Mormon in the fulfillment of the Abrahamic covenant *through making the Messiah manifest* was also strongly and clearly emphasized by the Lord when He visited the Nephites in Bountiful. The Lord promised that the "fulness of these things," or the record of the Nephites, shall come unto the Gentiles in the latter days. The Gentiles thereby would base their belief in the Savior, not on the physical sight and sound of the Lord, as had the Jews and Nephites, but instead upon the truth of the record of the

Nephites—as the Holy Ghost bore witness (3 Nephi 16:7, 6). By rejecting this record, the Lord taught, the Gentiles would "reject the fulness of my gospel" (3 Nephi 16:10):

> And I command you that ye shall write these sayings after I am gone . . . *that these sayings which ye shall write shall be kept and shall be manifested unto the Gentiles*, that through the fulness of the Gentiles, the remnant of [the seed of the Jews], who shall be scattered forth upon the face of the earth because of their unbelief, may be brought in, or may be brought to a knowledge of me, their Redeemer.
>
> And then will I gather them in from the four quarters of the earth; and *then will I fulfill the covenant* which the Father hath made unto all the people of the house of Israel. (3 Nephi 16:4–5)

"Therefore, when these works . . . shall come forth from the Gentiles" He will *"show forth his power"* unto *"the fulfilling of the covenant which he hath made unto the people who are of the house of Israel"* and they shall *"be brought to the knowledge of the Lord their God."*

In the days when the Book of Mormon comes forth, the scattered people of the Lord will be gathered to the full knowledge of the Messiah: Through the "fulfilling of the covenant which the Father hath made unto this people," the Savior taught, "shall the remnants which shall be scattered upon the face of the earth be gathered . . . and they shall *be brought to the knowledge of the Lord their God*, who hath redeemed them" (3 Nephi 20:12–13). Further, the Lord taught that "when the fulness of my gospel shall be preached," then shall the words of Isaiah be fulfilled that "the Father hath *made bare his holy arm* in the eyes of all the nations; and all the ends of the earth shall see the salvation of the Father," and "they shall believe in me, that I am Jesus Christ, the Son of God, and shall pray unto the Father in my name" (3 Nephi 20:11, 30–31, 35).

In fact, the Lord emphasizes that America was set up as free land for the express purpose that the Book of Mormon might be made available as a means of finding and coming to the Lord—in fulfillment of the Abrahamic covenant: "that these things which I declare unto you" might "come forth . . . that the covenant of the Father may be fulfilled" (3 Nephi 21:2, 4).

Therefore, when *these works* and the works which shall be wrought among you hereafter shall come forth from the Gentiles. . . . that *he may show forth his power* unto the Gentiles, for this cause that the Gentiles, if they will not harden their hearts, *that they may repent and come unto me.* . . .

And when these things come to pass that thy seed shall begin to know these things—it shall be a sign unto them, that they may know that the work of the Father hath already commenced *unto the fulfilling of the covenant* which he hath made unto the people who are of the house of Israel. . . .

For in that day, for my sake shall the Father work a work, which shall be a great and marvelous work among them; and there shall be among them those who will not believe it, although a man shall declare it unto them. . . .

Therefore it shall come to pass that whosoever will not believe in my words, who am Jesus Christ, which the Father shall cause him to bring forth unto the Gentiles, and shall give him power that the shall bring them forth unto the Gentiles . . . they shall be cut off from among my people who are of the covenant. (3 Nephi 21:5–7, 9, 11)

"At that day . . . my words shall hiss forth unto the ends of the earth, for a standard unto my people, which are of the house of Israel" and to show *"that I am God and that I covenanted with Abraham."*

Of course, these were the same blessings—and the same standard of judgment (i.e., the Book of Mormon) for those who are accounted as accepting the covenant—that the Lord had promised to Nephi and Lehi almost 600 years earlier:

At that day when I shall proceed to do a marvelous work and a wonder among them, that I may *remember my covenants* which I have made unto the children of men. . . . And also, that I may remember the promises that I have made unto thee, Nephi, and also unto they father, that I would remember your seed; and that the words of your seed should proceed forth out of my mouth unto your seed; and my words shall hiss forth unto the ends of the earth, *for a standard unto my people*, which are of the house of Israel. . . .

For I command all men . . . that they shall write the words which I speak unto them; for out of the books which shall be written I will judge the world. . . .

And I will show unto them that that fight against my word and against my people, who are of the house of Israel, that I am God and that I covenanted with Abraham that I would remember his seed forever. . . .

Wo unto them that turn aside the just for a thing of no worth and revile against that which is good, and say that it is of no worth! . . .

Yea, wo be unto him that saith: We have received, and we need no more! (2 Nephi 29:1–2, 11, 14; 2 Nephi 28:16, 27)

Through Nephi, the Lord also makes clear that the Book of Mormon's testimony and witness (or manifestation) of the Savior will be so explicit that our acceptance or rejection of that book will be the same as the acceptance or rejection of the Savior, and our decision will be judged as such: "And the words which I have spoken shall stand as a testimony against you; for they are sufficient to teach any man the right way; for the right way is to believe in Christ and deny him not; for by denying him ye also deny the prophets and the law" (2 Nephi 25:28). And conversely, "by denying the prophets [in the Book of Mormon], ye also deny Christ."

According to Mormon

"And for this intent shall they go—that they may be persuaded that Jesus is the Christ . . . unto the fulfilling of his covenant."

The great prophet and abridger of the Nephite records, Mormon, paused in his lamentations for the wickedness and destruction of his people to look forward to our day when his record "shall come forth according to the commandment of the Lord." Just as Nephi and the Savior before him, Mormon clearly taught that the glorious purpose of this future record would be to fulfill the Abrahamic covenant through making the Messiah manifest "unto the remnant of the house of Jacob" (Mormon 5:13, 12):

> And for this intent shall they go—that *they may be persuaded that Jesus is the Christ*, the Son of the living God; that the Father may bring about, through his most Beloved, his great and eternal purpose . . . *unto the fulfilling of his covenant*;
>
> And also that the seed of this people may more fully believe his gospel, which shall go forth unto them from the Gentiles. (Mormon 5:14–15)

"Then," Mormon writes, "will the Lord remember the covenant which he made unto Abraham and unto all the house of Israel" (Mormon 5:20).

"that they may bear testimony of him . . . to fulfill and do the work of the covenants of the Father."

In a letter to his son, Mormon writes about the ministry of angels (which, it turns out, includes all of the Book of Mormon writers), which ministry includes helping to fulfill the "covenants of the Father" by bearing testimony of Christ:

> And the office of their ministry is, to call men unto repentance, and to fulfill and to do the work of the covenants of the Father which he hath made unto the children of men, to prepare the way among the children of men, by declaring the word of Christ unto the chosen vessels of the Lord, that they may bear testimony of him;
>
> And by so doing, the Lord God prepareth the way that the residue of men may have faith in Christ, that the Holy Ghost may have place in their hearts, *according to the power thereof;*
>
> And after this manner bringeth to pass the Father the covenants which he hath made unto the children of men. (Moroni 7:31–32)

"And as [the Lord] hath covenanted with all the house of Jacob . . . they shall know their Redeemer who is Jesus Christ, the Son of God"

It is appropriate that this great prophet and abridger of the Nephite records should make clear to us the explicit relationship between the fulfillment of the Lord's covenants and the manifestation of the Savior made available through the book that bears His name:

> And as [the Lord] hath covenanted with all the house of Jacob, even so shall the covenant wherewith he hath covenanted with the house of Jacob be fulfilled in his own due time, unto the restoring all the house of Jacob unto the knowledge of the covenant that he hath covenanted with them.
>
> And then shall they know their Redeemer who is Jesus Christ, the Son of God.
>
> Yea, and surely shall he again bring a remnant of the seed of Joseph to the knowledge of the Lord their God. (3 Nephi 5:25–26, 23)

According to Moroni

The final Nephite prophet and record keeper sealed his testimony with this invitation to us: that we partake of the blessings of the Abrahamic covenant by receiving the Savior as He has been made manifest in the book we have been reading:

And awake and arise from the dust, O Jerusalem . . . that thou mayest no more be confounded, *that the covenants of the Eternal Father which he hath made unto thee, O house of Israel, may be fulfilled.*

Yea, come unto Christ, and be perfected in him, and deny your-selves of all ungodliness; and if ye shall deny yourselves of all ungodli-ness, and love God with all your might, mind and strength, then is his grace sufficient for you, that by his grace ye may be perfect in Christ; and if by the grace of God ye are perfect in Christ, ye *can in nowise deny the power of God*" (Moroni 10:31–32).

According to Modern Revelation

In the Doctrine & Covenants the Lord also makes clear how the Book of Mormon helps fulfill the Abrahamic covenant through helping people come to "the knowledge of a Savior" (i.e., making the Messiah manifest), just as the Bible did before the Book of Mormon:

For inasmuch as the knowledge of a Savior has come unto the world, through the testimony of the Jews, even so shall the knowledge of a Savior come unto my people . . . through the testimony of [the Book of Mormon prophets] . . .

. . . And for this very purpose are these plates preserved, which con-tain these records—*that the promises of the Lord might be fulfilled*, which he made to his people."

And that the Lamanites [as well as the non-Lamanites, we can assume] might come to the knowledge of their fathers, and that they might know the promises of the Lord, and that the may believe the gospel and rely upon the merits of Jesus Christ, and be glorified through faith in his name, and that through their repentance they might be saved. (Doctrine & Covenants 3:16–17, 19–20)

In another section of the Doctrine & Covenants the Lord declares the blessings that become available through the words that He gave to the prophet Joseph Smith "by the Comforter" (including the Book of Mormon?). These words, we learn, help fulfill part of the Abrahamic promises in that they "manifest that Jesus was crucified by sinful men for the sins of the world, yea, for the remission of sins unto the contrite heart" (Doctrine & Covenants 21:9).

Summary Chart: How the Book of Mormon Helps Fulfill the Abrahamic Covenant—By Making the Messiah Manifest

According to this prophet,	Through this scriptural temple (the Book of Mormon) the Lord will . . .	. . . fulfill the Abrahamic covenant (with its gift of power) by . . .	. . . Making the Messiah Manifest (or "known") in this way:
Nephi in 1 Nephi 13–15	In the latter days "shall the fulness of the gospel [i.e., the Book of Mormon] of the Messiah come unto the Gentiles" . . .	. . . and thereby fulfill "the covenant which should be fulfilled in the latter days; which covenant the Lord made to our father Abraham, saying: In thy seed shall all the kindreds of the earth be blessed" (1 Nephi 15:18) . . . "in that day that he shall manifest himself to them in word, and also in power, in very deed" 14:1	in fulfillment of which, the remnant of his seed may "come to a knowledge of their Redeemer" 1 Nephi 15:14 "and shall make known to all kindreds, tongues, and people, that the Lamb of God is the Son of the Eternal Father, and the Savior of the world; and that all men must come unto him, or they cannot be saved. . . . 1 Nephi 13:40–42

Nephi in I Nephi 22	This "marvelous work among the Gentiles" shall "be of great worth unto our seed," and also "of great worth unto the Gentiles" and unto "all the house of Israel" (1 Nephi 22:8).	in "making known of the covenants of the Father of heaven unto Abraham, saying: In thy seed shall all the kindreds of the earth be blessed" (1 Nephi 22:9),	"And I would, my brethren, that ye should know that all the kindreds of the earth cannot be blessed unless he shall make bare his arm in the eyes of the nations," so that "they shall know that the Lord is their Savior and Redeemer" (1 Nephi 22:10–12)
Nephi in 2 Nephi 25, 30	The day will come that it must needs be expedient that they should believe these things [i.e., the Book of Mormon]. (2 Nephi 25:16; 26:14; 27:6, 13–14) so that	they may become "the covenant people of the Lord" and "be persuaded to believe in Christ, the Son of God, and the atonement, which is infinite for all mankind" (2 Nephi 30:2; 25:15) and thereby . . .	"be restored . . . unto the knowledge of Jesus Christ, which was had among their fathers" (2 Nephi 30:5)

Jacob in 2 Nephi 6, 10	The Lord will grant the Book of Mormon so that all may "come to that which will give them the true knowledge of their Redeemer" 2 Nephi 10:2	in order to "fulfill his covenants which he has made unto his children" (2 Nephi 6:12), in fulfillment of which . . .	"The Messiah . . . will manifest himself unto them in power and great glory" (2 Nephi 6:14) that they thereby "shall know that the Lord is God, the Holy One of Israel" and "shall come to a knowledge of their Redeemer"(2 Nephi 6:15,11)
Lehi (and Joseph of Egypt) in 2 Nephi 3	Through "the thing, which the Lord shall bring forth by the [choice seer's] hand" [i.e., The Book of Mormon] (2 Nephi 3:15) . . .	"The covenants of the Lord" will be "remembered," (2 Nephi 3:5) when . . .	"the Messiah should be made manifest . . . in the latter days, in the spirit of power" (2 Nephi 3:5)
The Savior in 3 Nephi 16	When "these sayings [i.e., The Book of Mormon] . . . shall be manifested unto the Gentiles" (3 Nephi 16:4)	"then will I fulfill the covenant which the Father hath made" (3 Nephi 16:5) . . .	that they "may be brought to a knowledge of me, their Redeemer" (3 Nephi 16:4)

The Savior in 3 Nephi 20–21	"Therefore, when these works . . . shall come forth from the Gentiles" (3 Nephi 21:5; see also 3 Nephi 21:2–4, 11) . . .	. . . he will "show forth his power" unto "the fulfilling of the covenant which he hath made unto the people who are of the house of Israel" (3 Nephi 20:12; see also 3 Nephi 20:22; 21:4, 7, 22, 25)	"and they shall be brought to the knowledge of the Lord their God, who hath redeemed them" (3 Nephi 20:13; see also 3 Nephi 20:30–31, 35; 21:11, 25, 27).
The Savior in 2 Nephi 29	"The words of your [i.e., Nephi's] seed should proceed forth out of my mouth unto your seed; and my words shall hiss forth unto the ends of the earth, for a standard unto my people, which are of the house of Israel" (2 Nephi 29:2)	"that I may remember my covenants which I have made unto the children of men" (2 Nephi 29:1) . . .	. . . to show "that I am God and that I covenanted with Abraham" (2 Nephi 29:14)
Mormon in Mormon 5	"And for this intent shall [The Book of Mormon] go" (Mormon 5:14)	"unto the fulfilling of his covenant" ("that the Father may bring about, through his most Beloved, his great and eternal purpose") (Mormon 5:14; see also 5:20)	"that they may be persuaded that Jesus is the Christ, the Son of the living God" (Mormon 5:14)

Mormon in 3 Nephi 5	While speaking of the purposes of the plates (3 Nephi 5:9–19), Mormon promises that	"as [the Lord] hath covenanted with all the house of Jacob, even so shall the covenant where-with he hath covenanted with the house of Jacob be fulfilled in his own due time" (3 Nephi 5:25)	"And then shall they know their Redeemer who is Jesus Christ, the Son of God . . . . Yea, and surely shall he again bring a remnant of the seed of Joseph to the knowledge of the Lord their God" (3 Nephi 5:26, 23)
The Savior in Doctrine & Covenants 3	"And for this very purpose are these plates preserved, which contain these records—" (Doctrine & Covenants 3:19)	"that the promises of the Lord might be fulfilled, which he made to his people" (Doc-trine & Cov-enants 3:19)	"And that the Lamanites [as well as the non-Lamanites, we can assume] . . . may believe the gospel and rely upon the merits of Jesus Christ . . . that through their repentance they might be saved" (Doctrine & Cov-enants 3:20)

It is astounding how consistently—and intimately—the Lord associates these three events (as we see in the chart below): 1) the coming forth of the Book of Mormon; 2) the fulfillment of the Abrahamic covenant; and 3) the Manifestation of the Messiah. The Lord leaves no room for doubt that these last two sacred events take place as each of us "enters" the scriptural temple of Mormon.

THE NEW AND EVERLASTING COVENANT

In summary, let's just consider a couple of significant ways that the Book of Mormon is a covenant.

1) As all covenants, the Book of Mormon is a "template," a standard by which our expectations and faithfulness can justly be measured and judged—since this standard remains consistent for every single person, and since this standard is sufficient for us to fully know and follow the Lord.

When the Lord's servants speak or write under the influence of the Holy Ghost, their words become scripture (see Doctrine & Covenants 68:4). From the beginning, the Lord has commanded His prophets to keep a record of His revelations and His dealings with His children. He said:

> I command all men, both in the east and in the west, and in the north, and in the south, and in the islands of the sea, that they shall write the words which I speak unto them; for out of the books which shall be written I will judge the world, every man according to their works, according to that which is written. (2 Nephi 29:11).

Nephi tells us that its contents "shall go from generation to generation as long as the earth shall stand; . . . and the nations who shall possess them [the teachings of the Book of Mormon] shall be judged of them according to the words which are written" (2 Nephi 25:22).

2) It is a covenant since it helps fulfill the Abrahamic covenant by making the Messiah fully manifest, so that we can thereby come unto Him and be saved.

Shared Qualities and Blessings among Various Sacred Covenants:

Let's now give you a chance to summarize what we have discussed in this section about the covenants of the Lord and the qualities that each of these covenants share. Using the headings provided in chart 3.3.1 on page 344 of the appendix, fill in each square in the chart by finding scriptures that describe that particular quality of that particular covenant. After you have completed this chart, I have provided a version with some suggested scriptures in chart 3.3.2

(again, it would be most effective for you if you *prayerfully fill in the chart first with your own ideas*, and then afterwards consult the completed chart for comparison).

REVIEW QUESTIONS FOR THIS SECTION:

- What were the first promises made to Abraham (see Abraham 1:13, 18–19)?

- How might these two promises be interrelated?

- How did Nephi define the purpose of the plates that became the Book of Mormon? How does Nephi define "ministry" (see 1 Nephi 9:3; 19:3, 6:4)?

- How do Nephi and his "ministry" help fulfill part of the Abrahamic covenant?

- What did we learn about the role of the priesthood from the Lord's second visit to Abraham (see Abraham 2:11)?

- What do we learn about the role of the priesthood from other books of scriptures (see Doctrine & Covenants 84:19–21; Alma 13:16)?

- What does the Lord teach us about the role of the scriptures (see John 5:39; Alma 33:14; 2 Nephi 25:26, etc.)?

- How do these descriptions of the role of the priesthood and the role of the scriptures interrelate and converge or coincide (dovetail)?

- How does the Book of Mormon use the priesthood to help fulfill the Abrahamic covenant?

- How does the Book of Mormon make it possible for us to receive the blessings of the Abrahamic covenant?

- What is the greatest blessing that results from accepting and keeping the Abrahamic covenant? Would that be worth it to you?

- According to the scriptures, what role does the priesthood or ministry of Abraham and his descendants play in the fulfillment of the Abrahamic covenant?

- According to the Book of Mormon prophets, what roles does

the Book of Mormon play in the fulfillment of the blessings of
the Abrahamic covenant?

- Based on these scriptures, what very important decision are you
  making as you read and study the Book of Mormon? What
  opportunity awaits you? What important consequences can
  you expect?

- Why is the Book of Mormon referred to as "the new and
  everlasting covenant"? How is the Book of Mormon similar
  to other covenants, such as the Sacrament Covenant and the
  Temple Covenants?

- Why is the Book of Mormon, like other covenants, a perfectly
  "fair" means of judgment? In what ways is the Book of Mormon
  a "standard"?

- Considering the purpose of the Book of Mormon in the fulfillment of the Abrahamic covenant, why would you say that the
  Book of Mormon contains "the fulness of the gospel"?

- What kind of total commitments to the Lord would you be
  willing to make right now?

- Can you think of anything that might cause you to hesitate or
  be half-hearted in those commitments? What? Why?

- Do you believe that the Lord really can reach out to you directly
  from the pages of the Book of Mormon? Do you believe He
  really is doing that right now?

RETURN TO THE OPENING SCENARIOS

Scenario # 1

I told my relative: "When the Lord lets you know these things
are true, He will also give you the power to do those things He told
you are true. You can count on that."

Scenario # 2

The cook testified that since then he has felt no desire to either
smoke or drink. (Though he continues to exercise faith and common

sense by staying away from all activities and locations that might again provoke such temptations.)

PERSONAL CHALLENGES FOR YOU

1. What will you do now that you have studied these things?

2. In what ways does it seem more urgent for you to study, receive, and follow the teachings in the Book of Mormon?

Discussion Threads from This Section You May Enter on the Companion Website

1. What are some of the ways that our acceptance or rejection of the Abrahamic covenant is determined by our attitude and embrace of the teachings in the Book of Mormon?

2. How does this relation between receiving the blessings of the Abrahamic covenant and the purpose of the Book of Mormon motivate you to share the Book of Mormon with others? What exciting role are you able to play when you share the Book of Mormon with others? What are some of the ways that you can share this testament of Christ with others?

3. What are some of the ways you have recognized through your own experiences that the Book of Mormon contains the "fulness of the gospel"? How has the Messiah been made fully manifest to you through the Book of Mormon?

4. In what ways have you felt infusion of power as you committed to keep some covenant with the Lord? What is some specific area in your life where you would like to receive greater power? What weakness would you like to strengthen? What habit would you like to kick? Based on what you've learned about covenants in this section, how can the blessings promised to Abraham and the blessings available in the Book of Mormon (the presence and power of the Savior and His Atonement) help you find the power and grace to make these changes?

SECTION FOUR

Nephi's First Panoramic Vision:
An Invitation to Us

YOUR PARTICIPATION: WHAT WILL YOU DO WITH THE COVENANTS AND MANIFESTATIONS NOW BEING OFFERED TO YOU?

What Will Happen in This Section?

In an earlier section, we introduced the concept of "Self-Referentiality," and showed how often the Book of Mormon talks about itself. In this section, such self-referentiality will become thunderous. And one more kind of self-referentiality will be introduced: the Book of Mormon will spend a lot of time talking about *you*. The Book of Mormon (i.e., the prophets within the Book of Mormon—inspired by your Heavenly Father) has seen you, cares about you, and wants to help you make the right decisions—as well as teach you how significant these decision are. In this section, Nephi (i.e., the Lord, through Nephi) will show you how people throughout time have treated the manifestations and covenants that are now being offered to you. He will clearly show some of the main weapons and tactics the world and the adversary will marshal in an effort to keep you from accepting these manifestations and covenants.

And then the decision will be entirely yours. Between you and the Lord. You will have the chance to treat such things differently—as Nephi "cries from the dust" unto you and offers these manifestations and covenants anew. Nephi has waited nearly 1,500 years to get your attention. As has the Messiah whom He is making plainly manifest. They both hope you are listening.

What Do I Hope You Will Get out of This Section? How Do I Hope This Section Will Bring You Closer to the Savior and Help You to More Closely Follow Him?

My hope is that as you enter these two visions of the prophet Nephi, you will actually see yourself involved in the most important struggle now and in eternity. I hope you'll decide to receive the great atoning love of the Savior available within these pages of the temple of Mormon and then also partake of the sacred covenants (with their gifts of grace, direction, and power) that follow from such manifestations—which are now being offered you.

After hearing his father share the vision of the tree of life, Nephi requests and receives from the Lord the opportunity to "behold the things which [his] father saw" (1 Nephi 11:3). Fortunately, Nephi recorded that vision in detail (in 1 Nephi 11–15) and then expanded on its teachings by reading and commenting to his brethren upon Isaiah (see 1 Nephi 19, 22)—so that *we, too, have a similar opportunity* today. With that opportunity comes an enormous responsibility: because Nephi's words are so plain and powerful, we will, as he did, receive a full and viable manifestation of the Messiah, as well as a fair and just invitation to receive the covenants that follow such a manifestation. And what is that invitation? That we will come unto the Savior, recognize and receive Him as our Redeemer and dedicate our lives to following Him and keeping His commandments. In a very real sense, the hinges of eternity will move as you open the door upon these chapters.

So I feel I should warn all those who decide to continue upon this path: prepare yourself spiritually for this journey. Please pause now and ask the Lord to guide you with His Spirit, to fortify you against any forces that would oppose such a journey and to grant you the faith and courage to hold tight to the iron rod of His words. Be assured that whatever decision you make as you read from these chapters will affect your spiritual destiny—in this life and beyond. Yes, it is that consequential.

I invite you, as usual, to read each chapter, asking the Lord to guide you as you read and then to guide your pen as your write responses to the questions I pose (below) for each chapter. Though I supply suggested scriptural references after each question, you will be better off if you first search the chapter yourself for answers—and then later use the references for additional guidance.

Nephi's first panoramic vision (1 Nephi 11–22) describes the reactions of various groups to whom the Messiah is made manifest and to whom the covenants are offered. Each person now reading is included in one of those groups. Particularly, Nephi is both warning and inviting us, as *we now read*, to avoid earlier reasons for rejecting these blessings, and to fully accept the clear manifestations that are now within the pages of this scriptural temple. Think of your entrance into the temple of Mormon and your actual participation as you walk these sacred halls and chambers—through your study of these chapters and your answers to these questions.

Before Beginning

Since you will essentially be receiving the same vision Nephi received, how can you be sure you are guided by the same power he was (see 1 Nephi 10:17)? *And how does Nephi emphasize that we, today, while reading this account of this vision, have the very same opportunity that he had?[1]*

Do you really believe Nephi? How will you show it?

How does Nephi let you know that eternal consequences hang upon your actions right now?[2]

Finally, what does Nephi do to certify the validity of the experience he is now sharing with you?[3]

Entering Nephi's Vision Today as You Read and Respond

I'll give you a chance further below to respond to each of the questions first from Column 1 and then from Column 2. As you respond, you will actually enter Nephi's vision—in which he has already included you. You will have a chance to then respond the same or differently than those Nephi has seen.

In this Chapter.	. . . The manifestation of the Messiah and the covenants are offered to some group of people	The manifestations and covenants are then either accepted or rejected by this group:
1 Nephi 11	Unto whom are these manifestations and covenants of the Messiah offered in this chapter (see 1 Nephi 11:24–31)? In what way are we now in the same situation as this group from a previous dispensation? What choice are you now making even as you read this chapter?	What does this group do with these manifestations and covenants that are presented to them? (See 11:32–36) Why did this group react the way they did to these offerings from the Lord (see 11:35–36)? How does this chapter serve as a warning and lesson for us today? How will you make sure that your choice is better than theirs?
1 Nephi 12	Unto whom are these manifestations and covenants of the Messiah offered in this chapter (see 1 Nephi 12:6–12)? In what way are we now in the same situation as this group from a previous dispensation? What choice are you now making even as you read this chapter?	What does this group do with these manifestations and covenants that are presented to them (12:4–5, 15–23)? Why did this group react the way they did to these offerings from the Lord (see 12:16–18)? How does this chapter serve as a warning and lesson for us today? How will you make sure that your choice is better than theirs?

1 Nephi 13 (and parts of 1 Nephi 14)	Unto whom are these manifestations and covenants of the Messiah now offered (see especially 1 Nephi 13:16–30)?	Since you are in this group, how are you now reacting to the manifestations and covenants currently being offered to you?
	Through what sacred record are these things first offered (13:20–25)? What are the limitations of this sacred record (see especially 13:26–29, 32)?	How are you making sure you overcome the obstacles that prevented the groups mentioned in the last two sections from receiving these things?
	Through what other sacred record does the Lord next make these things available to this group (see 13:32–42; 14:1–2, 5–8)?	
	In what way does this chapter teach you that the Book of Mormon is the Manifestation of the Messiah (see especially 1 Nephi 13:34–36, 40–41; 14:1)?	
	What choice are you now making even as you read this section?	

| 1 Nephi 14 | Unto whom are these manifestations and covenants still being offered in this section? What is your relation to this group?

So, according to this and the last section, in what way is the Lord offering His manifestation and covenant to you now?

What choice are you making right now (14:5–7, 10)?

According to these verses, what are the consequences of your choice (see 14:2)?

In what way does this section teach you that the Book of Mormon is the Manifestation of the Messiah (see especially 1 Nephi 14:1–2, 7, 17)? | What do you learn in this section about the opposition you can expect from the world and the adversary as you weigh your choices about accepting or rejecting these manifestations and covenants (see especially 1 Nephi 14:3–4, 10–13)?

Who does the Lord clearly teach you is the ultimate source of the opposition you must face as you consider your response to these manifestations and covenants? How does this knowledge help you? |

| 1 Nephi 15 | What is your relation to the group that is being offered the manifestations and covenants in this section?

According to this section, what responsibility do you (and other members of this group) have in these latter days (see especially 15:12–20; 13:42)?

How does this section serve as a mission call to you as you read?

What will do about the call that is being proffered to you right now (15:18)?

In what way does this section teach you that the Book of Mormon is the Manifestation of the Messiah (see 1 Nephi 15:13–14, 17–18)? | What do you learn in this section about how you can best exercise faith in what is now being made manifest to you ("the fulness of the gospel," see 15:13) and offered to you ("the covenants," so that you may know "how to come unto him and be saved" see 15:14–16, 18)? (See 15:21–25).

How is your faith in the power of the Book of Mormon related to your ability to know "how to come unto him and be saved" (15:13–14)?

What do you learn in this section about how "high the stakes are" as we make the choice about accepting or rejecting the manifestations and covenants being offered to us right now (see 15:26–36)? |

1 Nephi 19	In this section Nephi summarizes again the rejection of the Messiah by which groups (see 1 Nephi 19:8–14)? How will the Lord then "remember the covenants" and help the earth "see the salvation of the Lord" (see 19:15, 17–19)? In what way does this section teach you that the Book of Mormon is the Manifestation of the Messiah?	According to Nephi, why did these groups reject the Messiah and His covenants (see 19:7)? How can we avoid doing the same thing today (see especially Doctrine & Covenants 84:54–57)? In what ways might we be said to "take lightly" the Book of Mormon? Would we take it lightly if we think that the Manifestation of the Messiah offered through it is not sufficiently plain, full, or powerful (see 2 Nephi 33:11, 14, 4, 2–3; 32:6; Jacob 4:14; Doctrine & Covenants 3:12, 16–19; Enos 1:13, 18; Ether 4:4, 7–8, 10–12)?
1 Nephi 22	In this section Nephi summarizes the scattering of which groups of his covenant people (22:3–5, 7)? According to Nephi, why were they scattered (19:5)? Who will help gather these groups "in the days to come" (see 22:6, 8)?	What else will the Lord restore at this time (22:9)? What does the Lord tell us will be necessary in order for that restoration to occur (22:10, 12)? How might the Book of Mormon help the Lord accomplish both of those goals? In what way does this role of the Book of Mormon coincide with the idea that the Book of Mormon is the Manifestation of the Messiah?

HERE IS ONE EXAMPLE OF HOW THESE QUESTIONS FROM 1 NEPHI 11 COULD BE ANSWERED

Unto whom are these manifestations and covenants of the Messiah offered in this section (see 1 Nephi 11:24–31)?

In 1 Nephi 11, Nephi sees how the Messiah makes Himself manifest to the House of Israel during His earthly ministry, from His virgin birth, through His ministry and rejection, then judgment and crucifixion. His role as Messiah is attested through His miraculous birth in fulfillment of the prophecies; through the testimony of John the Baptist, accompanied by a divine confirmation when "the heavens open[ed], and the Holy Ghost [came] down out of heaven and [abode] upon him in the form of a dove"; by the "power and great glory" of His ministry and teachings, witnessed by "multitudes"; and by the "multitudes of people" who were miraculously healed "by the power of the Lamb of God."

What does this group do with these manifestations and covenants that are presented to them? (See 11:32–36.)

Despite such manifestations that Jesus is the Messiah, he is "cast out from among them" and then taken, judged, and crucified "for the sins of the world. The people then also fought against the Church leaders that Jesus had called to represent him, bear witness of him, and build His Church.

Why did this group react the way they did to these offerings from the Lord (see 11:35–36)?

These people who rejected the Savior were part of that same group of people in the "great and spacious building" Lehi saw in his vision of the tree of life—and therefore full of "the pride of the world" and "the wisdom thereof."

In what way are we now in the same situation as this group from a previous dispensation?

We just received from Nephi a testimony that the person we read about in the New Testament is indeed the Christ, the promised Messiah, the Lamb of God, slain from the foundation of the world, the very "Redeemer of the world." We also received testimony that those apostles who bore witness of Him throughout the New

Testament are indeed His authorized testators and servants and that we will be responsible for how we receive their words and witnesses.

What choice are we now making even as we read this section?

And now, two millennia later, we find ourselves in the same situation as those who lived during Christ's day: do we fully accept this person, Jesus Christ, whose words and works we read about in the New Testament—all of which is now confirmed by this additional witness from Nephi—as our Lord and Savior? Do we now take hold of this "rod of iron," follow its path to the "fountain of living waters" and to "the tree of life," and thereby taste "of the love of God," and then "fall down at his feet and worship him"? Or do we, as others in that day, "cast him out," and allow our worldly pride and wisdom, as well as the feelings of shame in our Savior provoked by the scoffings from those in the "great and spacious building" to persuade us to join them?

How does this section serve as a warning and lesson for us today? How will you make sure that your choice is better than theirs?

We are now given a double witness of the truth of Jesus Christ's role of the promised Messiah and Redeemer—from both the New Testament witnesses and Nephi—and we have a chance to treat this Messiah quite differently from those who rejected Him during His earthly ministry. Our attitude and reception of these words of Nephi become our attitudes and reception toward the Messiah Himself. We now have the chance to covenant and commit ourselves to obey, sacrifice, and consecrate our lives to following and serving the Messiah—all because of our exploration of this one sacred chamber within the temple of Mormon.

SUMMARY OF NEPHI'S FIRST PANORAMIC VISION OF THE VARIOUS GROUPS TO WHOM:

1) The Messiah is made manifest and
2) The covenants are offered (by means of the Book of Mormon) throughout Israel's history, and the glorious culmination of His efforts in the latter days.

Above all, note how Nephi emphasizes the instrumentality of the Book of Mormon in these sacred events—and our current receptions of these very blessings as we now read from this record.

Summary of Nephi's Panoramic Vision of the Various Groups to Whom the Messiah is Made Manifest and to Whom the Covenants are Offered	
1 Nephi 11 To the Jews	Nephi sees the Messiah's great Manifestation and Covenant to the Jews (see especially 11:24–31), and the rejection of these things (see 11:32–36) . . . . . . .even as they are now offered to us—through the Book of Mormon—as we now read
1 Nephi 12 To the Nephites	Nephi sees the Messiah's great Manifestation and Covenant to the Nephites (see 12:6–12), and their rejection of these things (12:4–5, 15–23). . . . . . . even as they are now offered to us—through the Book of Mormon—as we now read

| 1 Nephi 13 (and parts of 1 Nephi 14) To the Gentiles | Nephi sees the Messiah's Renewed Manifestation and Covenant in the latter days—this time to "the Gentiles" (i.e., Ephraim, meaning us). After the persecution of the early "saints" and long years of apostasy (1 Nephi 13:9), the Lord's spirit guides some Gentiles to America, empowers and preserves them (13:12–13, 16, 19, 30).
The covenants and manifestation were first offered via the Bible (see especially 13:16-30), even with its limitations—i.e., the taking away of many plain and precious parts (13:26-29), and later via the Book of Mormon (see 13:32-42; 14:1-2, 5-8), which "shall contain my gospel … and my rock and my salvation" and which "shall make known to all kindreds, tongues, and people, that the Lamb of God is the Son of the Eternal Father, and the Savior of the world; and that all men must come unto him, or they cannot be saved. And they must come according to the words which shall be established by the mouth of the Lamb" (1 Nephi 13:36, 40–41)
So the Lord makes very clear that his ordained way for us to find, know, and follow the Savior is through the scriptures, and especially in our day, through the Book of Mormon, which restores the plain and precious parts removed from the Bible, and which contains the fulness of the Gospel. And by accepting these manifestations of the Messiah, we enter into covenant with the Lord and thereby may "be numbered among the house of Israel" and be "a blessed people upon the promised land forever" (1 Nephi 14:2) |
| 1 Nephi 14 Opposition to the Restoration and to Book of Mormon | Nephi sees, during the days of the days of the Gentiles, the intense opposition arranged by "the devil" to these Renewed Manifestations and Covenants (see 14:3-4, 11–13), as well as the power of the Lord to accomplish these things (14:14–17) through, among other things, the instrumentality of the Book of Mormon (14:1–2), through which "the Lamb of God in that day… shall manifest himself unto them in word, and also in power, in very deed." |

1 Nephi 15 From the Gentiles to all of Israel via the Book of Mormon	Nephi describes how the Gentiles (i.e., Ephraim) will take this Renewed Manifestation and Covenant to Lehi's seed (15:12–17) and to the entire House of Israel (15:18–20), thus bringing the manifestation and covenants to a full circle (see also 1 Nephi 13:42) through, among other things, the instrumentality of the Book of Mormon (see 15:13–14): "they shall come to the knowledge of their Redeemer and the very points of his doctrine, that they may know how to come unto him and be saved"
1 Nephi 19 How the Book of Mormon will restore a manifestation of the Messiah	Nephi summarizes again the rejection of the Messiah by the Jews (19:8–14; see also 1 Nephi 11, 12) and their future restoration of the knowledge (manifestation) of their Redeemer by means of the Book of Mormon (19:15–19): "And I, Nephi, have written these things unto my people, that perhaps I might persuade them that they would remember the Lord their Redeemer. Wherefore, I speak to all the house of Israel, if it so be that they should obtain these things" Nephi also then explains why so many reject the Messiah— as he equates the undervaluation ("setting at naught"), rejection, and "trampl[ing] under [our] feet" of these words he is now writing with doing the same things to "the very God of Israel" when we "hearken not to the voice of his counsels" or the words of his servants—contained in the scriptures (see 1 Nephi 19:7). Nephi thereby makes clear that these words we are now reading contain the full manifestation of the Savior and his gospel and our acceptance or rejection of them becomes our acceptance or rejection of him.

1 Nephi 22 How the Book of Mormon will re- store and fulfill the covenants	Nephi summarizes the scattering of Israel (22:3–5) and their gathering by "the Gentiles" (22:6–8, 25), unto the fulfilling of the Abrahamic covenant (22:6, 9, 11) through the instrumentality of the Book of Mormon (22:10–12), which will "make bare his arm" (or make the Messiah manifest) so that "all nations" shall "know that the Lord is their Savior and their Redeemer" Nephi also details the two choices all must make when these things are set before them, and how they can depend upon Him for power over their enemies (22:13–19, 22–28)

NOTES

1 We, like Nephi, must be guided "by the power of the Holy Ghost, which is the gift of God unto *all* who diligently seek him. . . . For he is the same yesterday, to-day, and forever; and the way is prepared for all men from the foundation of the world. . . . For he that diligently seeketh shall find; and the mysteries of God shall be unfolded unto them, by the power of the Holy Ghost, as well as in these times as in times of old, and as well as in times of old as in times to come" (1 Nephi 10:17).

2 "Therefore remember, I man, for all thy doings thou shalt be brought into judgment" (1 Nephi 10:20).

3 He states his authority—given by divinity: "And the Holy Ghost giveth author- ity that I should speak these things, and deny them not" (1 Nephi 10:22).

SECTION FIVE

Nephi's Second Panoramic Vision and Invitation to Us

Through the instrumentality of the Book of Mormon, we can choose to accept or reject the covenants and manifestation of the Lord in Nephi's second panoramic vision (2 Nephi 25–33), which will be offered to Ephraim (the Gentiles, us) in the latter days. Once again, think of your entrance into the temple of Mormon and your participation as you walk these sacred halls and chambers—through your study of these sections and your answers to these questions.

In his earlier panoramic vision, Nephi has shown how throughout history, groups have rejected the Manifestations of the Messiah—and the covenants—that were offered to them. Now he shifts directly to our day—where we have a chance to learn from the mistakes of groups in his earlier vision.

So Nephi is both warning and inviting us, as *we now read*, to avoid earlier reasons for rejecting these blessings, and to accept the clear manifestations that are now within the pages of this scriptural temple.

I'll give you a chance further below to respond to each of the questions first from column 1 and then from column 2. As you respond, you will actually enter Nephi's vision—in which he has already included you (chart 3.5.1 on page 348). You will have a chance to then respond the same or differently than those Nephi has seen. But neutrality will not be an option. This chart (3.5.2) is found on page 351 of the appendix.

Chiastic Summary of 2 Nephi 25–33: How the Book of Mormon Fulfills the Abrahamic Covenant by Making the Messiah Manifest

Chiasmus of 2 Nephi 25–33: Central message of these chapters: The Book of Mormon makes Christ manifest and brings us to Him			
25	I am making Christ plainly manifest to you in the last days; therefore, by accepting these words (i.e., the Book of Mormon), you accept Christ (25:16-26)	33	The Spirit is plainly making manifest to you that these words you are reading (the Book of Mormon) are the words of Christ: therefore, the Messiah has been made clearly manifest to you, and you will be accountable for that witness
26	You now must choose between two clear alternatives: either follow Christ as manifested by the Book of Mormon and the Holy Ghost (26:8, 13-16) or follow the adversary (26:10, 22)	32	You must daily choose among two alternatives: follow Christ by feasting upon his words (i.e., the Book of Mormon) and receiving the Holy Ghost through prayer (32:3-4, 9) or follow the adversary (32:8), who teaches you to deny the truth as clearly manifested
27	The Book of Mormon saves people from Apostasy (27:25, 35)—and brings them to Christ through faith in its words (27: 6—14; 23-29)	31	Follow Christ (and be baptized) by exercising faith in my words(i.e., the Book of Mormon)—for I am manifesting Christ just as John the Baptist did (31:11,17)
28	Why people won't repent and believe the Book of Mormon (28:4, 16, 26-32), and what happens (28:19-24, 28-32)	30	What happens when people do repent and believe the Book of Mormon (30:2, 5-6)
Central chapter of these chapters: 29: The Book of Mormon fulfills the Abrahamic covenant by making the Messiah manifest and bringing us to Him			

It is astounding how consistently—and intimately—the Lord associates these three events (as we see in the chart below): 1) the coming forth of the Book of Mormon; 2) the fulfillment of the Abrahamic covenant; and 3) the Manifestation of the Messiah. The Lord leaves no room for doubt that these last two sacred events take place as each of us "enters" the scriptural temple of Mormon.

AFTERWORD

My Waters of Mormon

"Perhaps the perfect pattern . . . is to teach what is found in the scriptures and then to put a seal of living reality upon it by telling a similar thing that has happened in our dispensation and to our own people, and —most ideally, to us as individuals." —Bruce R. McConkie

WHAT WILL HAPPEN IN THIS SECTION?

The goal for this book has been to show how and why the Book of Mormon serves as a great latter day temple in order to accomplish two purposes announced on its title page: to make the Savior manifest and thereby to help fulfill the Abrahamic covenant. It seems appropriate—especially in light of President Benson's challenge found in the Preface of this book—to share my first entrance into the sacred hallways of the temple of Mormon.

Each conversion to the Savior is an extremely sacred experience, and of necessity words have their limitations. Some things are so sacred that they cannot adequately be put into words; other things we all must choose to keep private. Within those limitations, I hope that these experiences simply will show how sacred that book is and how important and exciting it is to put that book in the hands of our brothers and sisters everywhere who only "are kept from the truth because they don't know where to find it" (D & C 123:12).

Preliminary Questions for This Section

- How does the Lord prepare investigators to be receptive to the gospel?

- What are those searching for the gospel often looking for?

- What must each convert acknowledge—about himself and his situation—in order to be receptive to the gospel?

- In what ways does each convert follow a similar path that Joseph Smith followed?

- What is a testimony?

- How do we gain a testimony?

- What do investigators need to understand about a testimony?

- What does the Lord expect of us as we are seeking a testimony from Him?

- Why is the Book of Mormon so important to those investigating the truth of the restored gospel?

- After baptism, what are some things we can do to help a new convert?

I Walked Down the Long Hallway

I passed the barracks for Delta, Charlie, Bravo, and Alpha companies before reaching my own building and walking up the stairs to Headquarters Company, First Battalion, Fifty-Fourth Infantry, Third Brigade, of the First Armor Division—"Old Ironsides," according to the triangular patch of a tank on my olive drab fatigues. All the combat support platoons—medics, mechanics, clerks, cooks, and engineers—were assigned to HQ.

I walked down the long hallway, duffle bag on my shoulder, escorted by another medic, Kurt Haefen, a skinny little guy from Queens, who always carried nunchaka sticks and a mini-machete tucked away somewhere. Kurt relayed the most popular topic of conversation—what a hole I had walked into. The concrete-floored barracks were leftovers from the Third Reich's Panzer divisions, and you could understand how a tanker might feel comfortable here. By the standard American unit of measurement, each building was about two football fields long and two first downs wide.

Near the end of the hall, at an open door, Kennebrew, another medic in an OD green t-shirt and patched blue jeans sat on his cot, bouncing to something in his headphones. A mirror on his lap, a switch blade in his hand, he was separating a big pile of white powder into smaller piles and then scraping these piles into baggies, tapping the cigarette in his mouth to the beat of the music. My escort shouted to get past the music: "Brew, got a new doc here." Brew still didn't look up, just finished twist-tying a half-filled bag of white powder, removed his headphones, then turned and smiled and tossed the baggie my way. "Freebie for the Newbie." I caught the gift and held it for a moment. This had not happened to me before.

I can still see that cellophane bag full of white powder in the air headed toward me. The barracks abounded in speed, heroin, and an East European version of today's meth. The medics were big dope users. For one, they had the needles and syringes. For another, about every other medic seemed to have gone straight from Woodstock to the U. S. Army Recruiting Center. I wasn't really religious. Or at least I wasn't a practitioner. I stopped going to Our Lady of Lourdes Church midway through high school. But something told me this didn't make a lot of sense. "No thanks," I said, and tossed the baggie back. Brew laughed and got back to his music and pharmacology.

A few weeks later, I may have met someone who didn't toss the baggie back. While I was on duty at the base dispensary, we were called to bring an ambulance over to an Artillery company barracks. Another medic, another skinny kid, this one from California, just seventeen years old, parted his dirty-blonde hair down the middle and walked around with glassy, bloodshot eyes most of the time, had not been out of his room all weekend. They knocked on the door and got no reply, were ready to break in, and wanted a medic present when they did. Maybe to take away the body. At about two in the morning, the CQ (Command of Quarters) assigned for that night called us.

The MPs brought in a huge battering ram—two cops grabbing the handles on either side—and woke up a lot of people. The medic was kneeling up against the end of his bed, his back to us, a needle and syringe sticking out of his left arm. He'd probably been there for a while. When we leaned him back, his bent legs and arms stuck up in the air. We unwrapped the OD green body bag, broke his arms and legs, zipped it up, and drove him off to the base coroner. Very sad.

We left Brew and moved to the last room, where my new roomie was focused on the latest *Playboy* foldout. A few other medics came in to see the new Band-Aid. "We're headed off base tonight," a taller one, holding a water pipe, said. "Prostitution is essentially legal here," he assured me. "Just need about forty bucks. Comin'?" I declined, and knew I had failed another test of friendship.

"Not Very Comfortable Right Now"

In my room, alone, I took out a pen and opened up a spiral notebook. It was the first time I had written a letter to myself. "Aren't we supposed to be comfortable in the world we are living in?" I scribbled, "because right now I am not very comfortable." I really didn't know where I was headed, but I knew I had to keep writing. "Society dictates much of your life's activity, but it is imperative not to let it dictate your feelings, your attitudes. Society tends to become more selfish, more immoral, and more violent every day, and so if I want to be comfortable in society, I must become more selfish, more immoral, and more violent." I never really talked much about God, but he came up in the next sentence. "God does not want us to become comfortable in the world at that price. We have the God-given responsibility to resist the material goals of society. Since He has given us the responsibility, He will also give us the power. He will give us the power to be comfortable without becoming a part of the world."

I decided to hang on to these words. The only thing that was more important to me now was what I needed to know next—*how* I would get this power from God. Because I knew I didn't have that power, and I knew I needed it.

It was kind of strange that the barracks would have this kind of atmosphere, because surrounding the barracks was one of the most astoundingly beautiful cities on the planet—Bamberg, Germany. Cobblestone streets crossed various little bridges over two rivers that intersected the ancient Cathedral town. One of the world's great symphony orchestras regularly performed here. A long line of colorful old houses hugged both shores of the Regnitz river downtown, forming what they called "Kleine Wien," or "Little Venice." One of my favorite walks meandered up the hills past an old castle, including a mote and drawbridge, St. Mikkelsberg Church with its big square and gardens, and then followed a small branch of the river to the quiet outskirts where a flock of long-necked swans always greeted me.

On the weekends in the summer, you could always find a "volksmarch" in the surrounding countryside, where you'd join lederhosened families, groups of youth, elderly couples, and anyone just out for a great time, on 5 or 10 K (about 3–6 miles) hike through forest paths and meadows, past occasional old grist mills, castle remains, and always the bratwurst and bier stands.

I always felt like I had walked into the best part of a Grimm's fairy tale.

Signing Up

At Notre Dame High School, I was one of the last people you'd expect to join the Army. The *very* last person was the guy I signed up with, George Mattalock. We both were hanging out with our drinking buddies in the woods by the railroad tracks one June night, sitting on old trashed chairs and couches we had rounded up from the curbs, in front of our usual fire pit. We'd just heard about a new program the Army started. With Vietnam winding down, they cut the draft and were trying to lure recruits into their new VOLAR (Volunteer Army). So they upped the pay scale and even made it possible for you to choose your specialty, your location—about anywhere in the world—and had a "buddy-program." You'd be guaranteed to go through Basic training and AIT (Advanced Individual Training) and then be stationed with a friend of your choice. They also pretty much said there'd be next to no chance of being sent to Viet Nam since they were working on drawing down the troops over there. But if I ever had to go there, a medic seemed a good job.

George and I were both kind of sick of school and didn't have any money to pay for college anyway. The G.I. Bill they were offering would pick up tuition when we got out. In the meantime, we could hang out in Europe for about three years. All interesting entice-ments. And besides that, we probably had a few too many cans of Pabst Blue Ribbon.

Our friends were amazed that we were even thinking about it. "Why not?" I asked Mark Carney, who always had interesting takes on things. "Why not? Because they call you 'boy' and you call them 'sir,'" was all he said. I felt I could play that game if I had to—as I thought of Europe and the G.I. Bill cash. So crossing the ocean starting looking good to me.

Back to Bamberg, Germany

After writing my first-ever diary entry, I decided that I needed to go back and spend some time reading and searching the New Testament in order to somehow find that power I was looking for.

Certainly, it wasn't a matter of knowing *what* do—I had whole Bible to tell me that. Blessed are the meek. Blessed are the pure in heart. Sometimes I'd try being one of those. It was easy enough when I was alone, but most of my friends wouldn't put up very long with some guy doing a Bing Crosby impression, playing Father Fla-nagan of Boys Town.

And there were a lot harder things in the Bible, things I knew I could never do on my own but which I knew I couldn't just skip because they were hard. "He that findeth his life shall lose it and that loseth his life for my sake shall find it." I'd never gotten far with that one. Yet, it was the hardest commandments that I felt were the most important ones to keep. Take up your cross and follow me. Except ye be converted and become as little children, ye shall not enter into the kingdom of God. Except ye eat of the flesh of the Son of Man, and drink His blood, ye have no life in you. Thou shalt love the Lord they God with all thy heart, and with all thy soul, and with all they mind, and with all thy strength. How? How?

I knew somehow what Christ wanted—He wanted me to make His will the most important thing in my life—more important that my own. He wanted me to put everything else aside and just follow him. I was willing to do that. I just didn't know how. There just seemed to be too many distractions. And the distractions would always be there.

And so I just figured that really following him—like they did when he was on the earth—was no longer an option. I guess they had their distractions back then, too. But they also had him right there with them. That had to have made the difference, I figured. But now we were left on our own. After all, he took off after His resurrection, didn't he? And I didn't blame him at all. Maybe he wanted to see how we would do on our own. Not too good. Though there were some who seemed to have a better idea than others. My Mom did better at it than anyone. The most Christian person I ever knew—easy. And more Catholic than the Pope. 6:30 Mass every morning of her life—except Sunday when she ushered us to 9:30 Mass. And I couldn't ask Christ to treat me or anybody else much better than Mom did.

The part that I think I really never got about Jesus was His death. I believed he died a horrible death—as Catholics that horror was ingrained in us. The crucifix was omnipresent. In Our Lady of Lourdes Church the most prominent feature of the huge church was a huge fresco—right behind the altar, from floor to ceiling—of Christ on the cross, with that crown of thorns on His head. I just didn't see why that death was supposed to make a difference in my life. Other people, I would think to myself, died horrible deaths, too. Other people were crucified—even at the same time Christ was killed. It was awful that they would kill the most innocent man who ever lived—but I just didn't see how that was supposed to make my life—or anyone's—much different. But even though that didn't make sense to me, it always did make sense that the most important decision in life was to follow Him as best we could. And the older I got, the harder that seemed to get.

I'd always heard, in Mass and catechism classes, Christ's promises—"ask and ye shall receive, seek and ye shall find, knock and it shall be opened to you." I had the idea that you were supposed to keep your requests vague and not expect any direct answers. Those were called miracles and were reserved by God for special occasions and special people, like at Fatima and Lourdes. It never happened in Utica, New York, and I had no reason to expect it would happen in Bamberg, Germany. Still, I was always tempted to take a dare. And there was this weird sense of optimism and adventure coming from some place in me that said, "Give it a chance; you never know." Anyway, the words kept coming back to me as the only possible solution to the challenge I faced. I couldn't shake them. So I decided to actually ask and actually expect an answer.

I knew three prayers—I'd had them memorized since around Kindergarten. The Our Father, the Hail Mary, and the "Gloria" ["Glory be to the Father, to the Son, and to Holy Ghost, worlds without end, Amen."] The first part of the "Hail Mary" was just a repeat of the words the angel Gabriel spoke when he announced Mary's future role as the mother of Jesus: "Hail Mary, full of grace, the Lord is with thee. Blessed art thou among women, and blessed is the fruit of thy womb, Jesus." The second part is where a prayer is offered to Mary: "Holy Mary, Mother of God, prayer for us sinners, now, and at the hour of our death, amen."

The "Our Father" was just the same prayer the Lord gave as an example in the New Testament. When Jesus said "After this manner, therefore, pray ye," Catholics were just a bit more obedient and precise than most, I guess.

For whatever reason, these prayers never had much effect in my life, but they were the only way I knew how to knock on God's door. I decided to focus on the "Our Father," occasionally reciting a rosary, as I drove my 40-ton armored personnel carrier through the farms and fields of Bavaria. I'd concentrate on each word until it meant something to me.

I just hoped that the Lord was listening.

Bob's Story

Unknown to me, another one of my brothers, Bobby, was on his own personal search and rescue mission right at about this same time. Here is his story in his words.

All my life I felt different. I was not content with the life I was leading from late grade school on up. Sometimes I asked if I really fit. When I began to be honest with myself, I started a change within me—a change that didn't stop until I found the truth.

With the friends I made in high school, peer pressure developed. I felt I was being molded to fit these standards. I knew this but allowed it to occur. At last, in my senior year at Notre Dame High, I tried to become became a new person, to be more in control. My faith in God and in Jesus was always strong, but because my friends had their doubts I also began to have mine. The need to break away from the Utica environment became ever increasing.

So I went to college in Virginia—as a member of the Virginia Polytechnic Institute Corp of Cadets. People were different here, but still the same kind of attitude existed—Eat, Drink, and Be Merry. After about one month, I was invited to a Navigators for Christ meeting. which I agreed to go to. This was the turning point of my life. I at last found the way that led to the straight and narrow road to the Kingdom of God.

At the first meeting , we discussed the Book of Revelation and the Last Days. The topic instantly caught my curiosity and I was eager to learn more. That night this Study Group opened up my eyes further than they were ever opened. I never thought I was in the Latter Days but from this point on I felt the urge to tell everyone that we actually lived in the Last Days and that we needed to prepare themselves for the most important event since the Resurrection of Christ.

When I went home for Thanksgiving and Christmas Holidays, that's all I talked about with my family and my friends—anybody I could get an ear to listen. I would tell them that we should prepare to meet God and not follow after worldly pleasures. I continued this "preaching" for months—at home, school, and later when I joined the Army. I talked to many, many, people. Some called it ridiculous. Others would listen and were changed. But in the summer of 1974, I began to feel uneasy. A friend of mine and I decided to travel to Houston, TX to visit his uncle who worked for the Union Pacific Railroad. En route we met several religious groups that happened to be at the stops along the way. The Jehovah Witness's were one group but we also talked to Baptists, Methodists, and others. I asked them to tell me about their beliefs. These discussions motivated me to keep searching for answers to my religious questions. After arriving in Houston, TX, my friend and I found jobs but we quickly became bored and wanted to return home to New York.

When I returned to New York I decided that to join the Army. That November I enlisted for three years and attended boot camp at Ft Knox and Advanced training at Ft Rucker. At Ft Rucker I began to realized that some of the things I told people were of men and not of God—and so were not always trustworthy. Therefore, I prayed to God that I would teach the truth and not falsehoods.

This was my situation when I joined the Army. I came to a dead end and did not know what else to tell people. I wanted the truth. So I searched. And prayed. While going through Advanced Individual Training (AIT), knowing my baptism was not "good" in God's eyes, I wanted to be baptized right. I made a promise to myself to get baptized by somebody, as long as it was by immersion. Then something happened.

Because I was a holdover until I received my travel orders to Germany, I was given a lot of different details. One night I was assigned as a CQ (Command of Quarters) runner (a twenty-four hour duty of screening those entering the barracks—and doing errands for the company commander). While I was on duty about 11 PM, a guy walked into the office in tears. I told him to "come in and let's talk about the problem." So we talked into the night for about five hours. We discussed religion all that time and he forgot about his problem. He told me about the Church of Jesus Christ of Latter-day Saints. Everything he said fit the impression I had built up of what the true church should be. The next day as he was getting ready to go home on emergency leave I told him I was pleased to be able to meet him and that when I got to Germany I would look up the Mormons. He said to me: "Although I am not an active Mormon, I know it is the only true church." His words really impressed me.

So from this point on, I decided to investigate the Mormon Church. I also wanted to read the Book of Mormon. I looked for one but didn't find one. Then when I go Bad Kreuznach in April and my search ended. After I had been there a month, I noticed that someone had placed a box of books in the break room. On top of the stack was a Book of Mormon. Somebody else saw the book and picked it up before I could. That night I found the guy and asked if I could read it. He said I could have it. After reading the first pages I knew it was inspired. When I got to page one hundred, I knew without a shadow of doubt it was the word of God. One day, while walking in the Mess Hall with the Book of Mormon, another soldier, Norm Paulsen, came up to me and asked if I was a Mormon. I said "no." Norman asked if I wanted to go to Church. I said "yes, that would be great." The Church meeting just happened to be next door to my barracks. I met the missionaries and was very excited to learn more. After several discussions I asked myself if I was worthy to be baptized because

I was not perfect. I had several questions about the Atonement and the repentance process. The elders reassured me that nobody is perfect and all need to repent. I agreed to be baptized. On July 5, 1975 I was baptized at the Kaisernslautern Servicemen's Stake Center and into the only true Church on the face of the earth.

Sometime in July Bobby got in an old BMW and headed down to for a visit to his brother at Lake Chiemsee—in Bavaria.

Transfer to Lake Chiemsee and a Visit from Bob

After almost two years in the Infantry Unit in Bamberg, I read in the Army's Newspaper, the "Stars and Stripes," that applications were being accepted for the position of a "Water Safety Instructor and Recreation Assistant" at Lake Chiemsee in southern Bavaria. I asked my Platoon Leader, Staff Sergeant Dunn, if I could send off an application. "Sure, Gorton. Send it off. But don't count on it. Nobody leaves the 54th Infantry." It turns out that before the Army I was trained as a Lifeguard and Water Safety Instructor. And I figured my training as a medic wouldn't hurt my chances. Two months later, an envelope arrived with one sweet sentence on the top of a transfer order: "You have been reassigned on Temporary Duty Status, from May through October, 1975, as a Recreational Assistant and Safety Patrol at Lake Chiemsee, Germany." I. was. a. happy. boy.

I was transferred to one of the most spectacularly beautiful areas on the planet.

After I had been about four months in Chiemsee, my brother pulled up in an old BMW. I hadn't seen Bob in about three years. He got out of the car, shook my hand, and said: "Terry, I'm no longer Catholic. The Catholic Church is not the true church of Christ. There was an apostasy after all of the original apostles were killed and the Lord's true Church was taken from the earth. In the year 1820, The Lord spoke again to a modern prophet named Joseph Smith and brought His true Church back to the earth. Since that time there has been a living prophet and twelve living apostles on the earth—just like in Christ's original Church."

Interesting greeting, I thought. At the same time, the world seemed to stop spinning for a bit while he spoke. Nothing else seemed very important. It looked like my brother had gotten caught up in some cult or movement and was an enthusiastic recruiter. I think I was about to become the biggest challenge to his confidence so far.

"Bob, you say the Catholic Church is not the true church. But who is the most Christ-like person on the earth you know?" His answer was inevitable: "Mom."

"That's right, and if there's a heaven, Mom will be the first person in line. Well, she's Catholic."

Hard logic to refute.

I wasn't trying to create any conflict between us, but this was a new Bobby I was seeing and I was trying to come to grips with the changes.

"Well, Bob," I said, "you seem pretty wrapped up in all this right now. But, you know, you've been that way your whole life, haven't you? Big enthusiasm for something in the beginning, all kinds of activity and then you just let it drop. Like how you wanted to play the drums and got Mom to buy you a set of drums. That lasted about a month I think. The same with Judo and Boy Scouts, and a bunch of other things. This sounds like just more of the same."

It looked like I was having some effect. He kind of looked down at his feet, as if to check his footing. But then he looked back up, and said: "Yeah, Terry, I know I've had a lot of hobbies and interests that didn't last. But this isn't one of them. I know that The Church of Jesus Christ of Latter-day Saints is the Lord's true church, and no matter what else happens, I will stay true to this church."

He gave me a pamphlet with some guy holding a book up in the air: "The Testimony of Joseph Smith." As I read, it all seemed too good to possibly be true. Christ returning to bring back his original Church to the earth? How far-fetched could you get? But the remote possibility somehow kept creating a spark in me—like an old exposed wire deep down somewhere. I couldn't even imagine a more exciting thought.

My Visit to Bob in Bad Kreuznach

My tour of duty in Chiemsee ended in late October—about the

same time as Bob's birthday. So I decided to detour through Bob's post on my way back to Bamberg.

While I was driving, a certain scripture kept coming to my mind (I had a fairly good acquaintance with a lot of the New Testament from weekly religion classes and from the Mass, where parts of the New Testament were recited each Sunday and were quoted in the priests' sermons or homilies). The warning "Beware of false prophets," echoed as I drove. Was Joseph Smith one more of those who keeps cropping up? I also remembered the test the Lord gave us: "By their fruits ye shall know them." I decided that I would be able to figure out pretty quickly—once I saw a group of these Mormons together—whether they were members of Christ's true church or not. I figured that if these people really were members of Christ's true church, they should act like it. And I should recognize it right away.

Bob was on the second floor of his barracks at the end of the hallway. On his door, someone had crossed out the title "Spec 4" preceding his name and replaced it with "Reverend." The first thing I noticed on Bob's side of the room was a large poster on the back of his locker of a big building with the words: "Why Mormons build temples." On his wall was another large poster full of planets, orbs, arrows, stars, and such things. It looked like something out of the occult and scared me a bit to think Bob was into such things. He offered me a seat in front of this poster and started with the first orb, something he called the "pre-mortal existence," a place where we lived before we came down to earth. Such a thought had never once entered my mind—but I liked the idea immediately. "We made the choice there to come to this earth to receive a body," Bob said, "and go through some kind of test. Some of those at that time rebelled against the plan and became the devil and his companions." I thought, *yeah, that all makes a lot of sense*. And a very pleasant thought also came to me. I thought that since I was here on earth, at some important point in my existence (if all this stuff Bob was talking about was true, and I thought that the possibility, at least, was interesting) I made the right decision.

Bob traced the arrow to the next orb, the earth. He explained why we were here, and then followed the arrows to three different orbs—where we would end up, depending on how we lived this life. A nice plan, I thought. Made a lot of sense, and filled in a lot of the missing parts of the puzzle. So simple. Seemed so obvious when you finally heard it. How else could it be? Strange that I had never conceived of such things before.

The next day was Sunday and so Bob invited me to Church. "By their fruits ye shall know them." All right, I said to myself, as I entered their small meeting place, these people should be different from any group of people I had ever seen or met. We'll see, I thought. After the meeting, a lot of people came up to introduce themselves. A lot of families. I sensed real love, Christ-like love, between husbands and wives, and between parents and kids. I liked what I saw and felt. A lot.

As I was packing to leave, Bob kept finding more Church pamphlets to give me. Along with a Book of Mormon.

The more I saw the more I wanted it to be true. But I just didn't know. And I didn't know how I would ever know for sure. In the meantime, as I was trying to figure things out, I decided on an interesting plan. I would consider the possibility that it was true. I asked myself: if this is true, what kind of changes would I have to make in my life? With that question in mind, on the trip back to my base in Bamberg I stopped at a rest stop on the autobahn, and threw away all those things that apparently Bob had abstained from since his baptism.

Defining a Strange Word

When I got back to my unit in Bamberg, I looked up a medic who seemed to have the same symptoms as my brother. Wes Oliver was also hyper-happy and also spent a lot of time with those nameplate guys in dark suits. And he didn't smoke or drink. "Wes," I asked him in the hallway, "are you a Mormon?"

"Yes, I am." He looked intrigued by the question.

"My brother Bobby became a Mormon and I told him I'd investigate the Church. Is there a representative I can talk to?" Wes was only too glad to hook me up. Soon after, a couple of dark suits and name plates arrived—both named Elder, which they said they preferred to their first names I kept trying to pry out of them.

We went to a member's house for our first discussion. As they taught me, I never let them know how I felt. "Kept my cards close to the vest." But I had read all of the pamphlets Bobby had given me, so I knew a lot of the material. Inside, I indulged myself a bit by opening the door a crack to the remote, strange, possibility that this all just somehow might be true. You could not plant a more exciting thought in my brain than the idea that Christ's true Church, the same one He established when He was on the earth, again was on the earth. And that He was still active as the Savior and leader of His true Church. Wow, did I like that thought. But, at the same time I just didn't know if such a preposterous possibility could pan out. I'd been excited before by possibilities that just didn't materialize. So I'd learned to be skeptical about hope.

But I was feeling those same feelings at the members' house and with the missionaries that I had felt when I went to church with Bobby. And I liked those feelings. They were new.

As I played with the possibilities, I kept coming back to a word the missionaries were using in a strange way—a word that I felt was a key during my investigations. The word was "testimony." The Elders used the word a lot but never let me in on what exactly they meant when they used it. They would teach some principle, like the fact of modern prophets on the earth today, or of the truth of the Book of Mormon, or of the appearance of the Father and the Son to Joseph Smith, and then they might explain that they "have a testimony" that this was true.

Since they didn't explain it, I just tried to assemble its meaning in my mind. I decided three things about a testimony. First, I figured a testimony was a personal knowledge from God directly to an individual. Someone God communicated one-on-one with a person when they got a testimony. I thought that was powerful. God never spoke to Catholics that way, I thought. Secondly, I decided that a testimony was kind of a rite-of-passage or an initiation into the Mormon Church. To be a true Mormon, a person had to go through a testimony experience. Lastly, I figured a testimony had to be memorized—because of the way the missionaries shared their testimonies—it seemed as though they probably used the exact same words over and over again and couldn't change the words once they got their testimony.

Entering the Temple of Mormon

After the second discussion—on the Plan of Salvation—my homework assignment was from the Book of Alma, chapters 11, 12, 40 and 42—all about the Atonement. As I said before, when I was younger, I believed everything I read or heard from the Bible about Jesus Christ. I believed that Jesus Christ was just who he said he was, the Son of God and the Savior of all men. It just never made sense to me why His death should make such a difference to me. It was sad that he was killed. But it was sad when anyone was killed. His death was certainly awful, but so were a lot of deaths. I just didn't understand why one more death was supposed to change anything. Also, I, as most Catholics and most other people period, found confusing the relationship between God's justice and God's mercy. How much of God's mercy and how much of God's justice tipped the scales in the end? What determines that balance? What makes it fair? And these chapters were all about the Atonement. And about the balance of justice and mercy. And why Christ's death mattered.

Something very important was happening as I read. I had a little test I decided to use as I read: was this book making me feel the same way about Jesus Christ as the Bible did, or did it make me feel different about him? Did it bring me closer to Jesus as I read—the way the Bible did; or didn't it? If this book didn't pass that test, it was of no worth to me.

As I read, a few things were happening. First, the book was passing the test. It amazed me that this book seemed to have the exact same "spirit" in it that the Bible did. And I was sure no human being could manufacture or counterfeit that spirit. Second, it became clear that no matter what I read for the rest of my life, no matter what knowledge I gained, no knowledge would or could be as important as the words on these pages. And finally, it became obvious that I was incapable of understanding the words on these pages. Reading them was like trying to catch smoke. I'd think I had the meaning, and I got excited, and then I'd open my hands and it'd be gone. Very frustrating.

In the first discussion, the missionaries had taught me how to pray. Not just memorized prayers, but how to really talk with God.

And they gave me a little card, outlining the four steps to prayer. I took out the card. Why not? I knelt down. Took a look at the card. "Address Him as 'Father in Heaven," it said. So I did. It was kind of "If you are listening, and if you are really my Father in Heaven . . ." Step two: "Thank Him for your blessings." I thanked Him for sending the missionaries to teach me, for the things the Savior did for me that I was reading about. I opened my eyes to see the next step. "Ask Him for whatever things you need."

"Well, I'd like to know about this Book of Mormon. Is it true? Does it come from you—just like the Bible? I think it is. I think it makes me feel about Jesus Christ the same way the Bible does. If these words I've been reading are true, could you help me understand the Atonement?"

Around this point in my prayer, I made a deal that Heavenly Father can't resist. I told Him that if he would let me know for certain that these things are true, and that this church I've been investigating really is His true Church brought back to the earth, I would dedicate my life to living its principles; I would keep all of the teachings—as long as I knew for sure they truly came from God.

Then the answers came.

We have been cautioned to be careful about sharing sacred things too casually. Some things, in any case, can't really be put very well into words. Suffice it to say that even with my eyes closed, I could feel that the room filled with light. Everything in me that was dark, or worldly, or unclean, seemed to be lifted from me in the same way that a sheet is removed from a statue, leaving it as it was originally intended. The words joy and peace and love took on new meanings for me. I realized that I was feeling the love and the spiritual presence in that room of the person about whom I had just been reading—Jesus Christ. He was a real person. I knew the love that I was feeling from Him made it possible for Him to go through that process I had been reading about—the Atonement. And it was that Atonement that made it possible for me to feel all that I was feeling right then—most especially a sense of newness, a sense of cleanness. It became perfectly clear to me that, yes, indeed, the Book of Mormon is, like the Bible, a true witness of Christ, written by those who knew Him as the Savior. And Joseph Smith really was ordained by the Savior to help bring back the original Church of Jesus Christ. Christ's true Church—with living prophets and apostles—was now restored to the earth. And the greatest thought I could ever conceive just became true—I could now become a disciple of Jesus Christ, a member of His true Church.

After that conversation with Heavenly Father, I sat down—a bit overwhelmed. The thought then occurred to me: "I wonder if I just got a testimony." Well, I just received personal knowledge directly from God of the truth of the restoration of the gospel and of the reality of the Atonement. I now knew with the certainty of the Spirit that the Book of Mormon is the word of God and Joseph Smith a prophet just as Moses or Peter, James, and John were prophets. I felt like I had been "initiated." I then got out a pen and some paper to write down my testimony—of what God had made known to me—so that I could memorize it.

The next day I met with the missionaries for the next discussion. We shook hands. "You know, you guys are always sharing your testimonies with me," I said. "I've been wondering what a testimony was. I read those chapters from the Book of Mormon last night. And I used the prayer card you gave me. I think I got a testimony." I was a little nervous, so paused a bit. They looked at each other, a little confused, as if to say "this is not on the script." "I was wondering," I continued, "if I could share my testimony with you guys."

I took out my piece of paper since I hadn't memorized it yet. And I said that God personally revealed these things to me after I read the chapters they had given me in the Book of Mormon, and as I prayed—so I knew they were true. Then I read what I had written: "I know that God is a God of Justice. And that God is a God of Mercy. Because of the mercy of God, Jesus Christ did die for our sins." We then began the next discussion—about continuing revelation. I was baptized in the Nuremburg chapel a few weeks later.

APPENDIX A
The Tracker

In this book I've been suggesting that the Book of Mormon not only fulfills the role of a temple but actually and literally becomes a great latter-day temple for us. When we open the *Book* of Mormon we enter the *temple* of Mormon. And through our sacred experiences there we are better able to meet the two great challenges of life: knowing what is right, and then doing what is right.

People learn in different ways. I'd now like to use a narrative to help explain how the Book of Mormon fulfills its role as a "scriptural temple," making the Messiah manifest and invites us to follow Him and partake of sacred covenants.

THE TRACKER I

The evening call of the loon told him it was time to start packing. One more shot should do. He collected and cradled the rusting milk cans in the tails of his shirt, set them up once more on the table. He looked back—just in time to see the eyes of an old friend peer out from beneath a red and brown tail—from the "cheap seats" down by the stream. Had a kit with her this time. "I'm guess I'm the only show in town right now," he said to himself.

"One more time, buddy?" he asked, looking at his friend.

He'd been stretching out his arm each time during the wind-up—to keep his pitch consistent and to get the maximum velocity and torque he'd need. "Eyes on the prize," he said aloud as he stared the row down, took his long wind-up. The cans went flying. All of them.

That was a month ago, and he was knocking down all ten nearly half the time now.

Unknown to his friends or family, he'd been practicing in a field behind an old barn—after rounding up cans from a Salvation Army store. He'd heard all about how tough it was to scatter all ten milk cans with a single pitch. No one he knew, not even the high school pitchers and quarterback, had been able to do that. So certainly no one would expect *him* to knock them all down—on one throw. But he didn't miss many days out there in the field, behind that rotting barn—with four rows of bottles he could set up and knock down. Still not a sure thing. But more and more they were all falling. He could picture everybody congratulating him. That would be a change. And he could see the barker point to the top shelf, telling him he could pick from those grand prizes. He knew what he would pick. He was ready.

Maybe it was time for him to make some friends. His mom thought he spent too much time alone, hiking, tracking deer, lynx, bobcats, "and whatever else." He told her that she was partly to blame. It started out in one of those mystery letters she'd given him, addressed from some forsaken spot on the planet—with some basic instructions about tracking wild animals. Then in one of those scout classes she'd forced him to go to—they learned how to tell each animal's tracks by small details. He found out a lot more on his own; got some worthwhile books from Sam at the library, even found a book by some guy who'd spent a lot of time in those woods—who insisted there were still cougars roaming those mountains. You just had to know how to track them—and spot them, two very different skills. In the woods, he felt he was welcome, he belonged. But he kind of knew that he was putting more distance between him and the kids at school—and everyone else. Fine.

And there was another way he'd recently found to escape. A way that worried him a lot more. It started as a resource to find out more about tracking and habitats. But one search led him somewhere he hadn't expected. The first time he felt his face flush and he knew he had come across something he needed to just run away from. And he hit the backspace quickly. But he couldn't let those images go. And though he knew better, and though something clearly steered him away, almost a voice inside him saying "Don't click the next click," he did click. And clicked again. And after spending time there, he always felt like he needed to get out into the woods—to clear his head. Once out there, he decided to stay away from those other places for good. And he knew he would.

But then he got back, turned on the computer—for some more tracking information—and found himself straying. "Don't click the next click." But he did. "Why not? I'm no kid. Why shouldn't I know what's going on?" Those words worried him. Because they weren't his. But he was a lot more worried about what he was feeling. They weren't what he'd call his feelings either. No matter how bad things got with school or home, he'd always prided himself on trusting his feelings. His instincts. On blazing his own trail. But now he knew he was being led down some path somehow by something that was messing him up bad. And he was *letting* himself be led. And for the first time in his life he didn't know if he could get off this path. Again, he made up his mind that he wouldn't go back there. And he hoped he would listen.

He thought about all those things as he continued hiking up and down hills, into patches of woods, through wide meadows cut with slashes of deep, narrow streams. He'd been looking for a particular track for a few summers. He'd followed some faded ones for a full afternoon last summer. Now, after a few hot Spring days had melted the last of the snow—leaving damp soil behind—these new tracks looked clear and fresh. He heard a high pitched whistle sound and looked up at a couple of familiar-looking eagles that always seemed curious about this two-legged interloper in these woods.

He felt Houdini—that was the name he gave his target—knew he was being followed and tried to lose him. Almost did a couple of times—at a stream once, and over a wide gulley that must have taken a huge leap to straddle. He didn't find just tracks this time. Houdini was starting to shed his winter coat and he found little tufts of brown and black fur occasionally on low pine branches.

It was getting later in the afternoon, heading toward twilight; knew he'd have to turn back soon. He was a long way off, and the tracks were getting a lot tougher to follow. Had to keep his eyes peeled to the ground. Should have noticed all the birds and squirrels had disappeared. And the quiet. But he didn't. Until he heard the growl—behind him. Didn't even scare him. Seemed more of a greeting than a warning. He knew he couldn't turn around. Couldn't have been twenty yards away. Heard him taking a drink and imagined Houdini's eyes staring at him the whole time as he crouched and lapped from the stream, then just poised on the edge of the mossy bank, his face still dripping with the cold spring runoff, each seemingly aware of the bond of independence and ease they shared in these woods. He even thought a second about just snapping his little disposable camera in Houdini's direction—without even turning. But he knew that would somehow bend that bond between them. Also might startle him. Then he would have reason to be scared.

He just waited. And then—quiet. Waited longer than he had to. All breezes seemed frozen; the only sound—the water meeting rocks in the stream. Then he saw a chipmunk survey the creek from a log. Turned slowly around. He'd never seen so many colors blended in a sunset—some colors he'd never even imagined before—bright pinks, oranges, and purples rippling out into the fading blue skies like a rock dropped into a huge neon pond. And he loved the different shades of green that twilight always brought to the woods, in the pine and fir trees, the birches, and in the grasses—as he looked toward the escape path Houdini might have taken. "Must have somehow climbed straight up that trap dike," he thought. It looked kind of steep. And with a slow stream coming down the midst of it, he knew it would be slick. He had to give it a try. It looked do-able—somehow.

"No problem, so far," he said as he climbed boulder to boulder, occasionally slipping, but never in any real danger. The sprays of water were a nice relief, he thought as he saw the rock face above him. But he didn't like the looks of it and looked around for an easier route. Nothing. This way or the highway, he said to himself. He reached up for a ledge along a rock face, found a crevice for his foot and then a couple more of each. Looking behind, he didn't like where he'd end up if he slipped. He still had a ways to go. He reached carefully for another ledge, knew he'd have to pull himself up quite a bit so his foot could find another crevice. He pulled on the rock. "Can't do it," he realized. Now he had to find a way to get back down.

Started to panic as he felt that he couldn't return the same way he came. His arm and hand started to burn, and he knew he couldn't hold on much longer. Then he heard the chirp of a chipmunk sitting on a ledge he hadn't seen. When the chipmunk moved on, he moved his hand to that ledge on his left. Found some secure ledges for his hands and feet. After a few yards, he found a route that took him back to the bottom of the trap dike. "Whoa," he said, looking back on the route he just took, and then turned to head home.

"Probably just a bobcat," one of the kids, a long-time hunter, said when he made the mistake of telling someone at school about Houdini. "Or a really big, mean beaver," someone else said, getting a laugh from the others. "Just ain't no lions in those woods. Been decades since the last one was killed. Get over it." You get over it, he thought. But the idea got into his mind. *Could* it have been a lynx? Or a large bob? Maybe he was just finding what he wanted to find instead of what was there. Of course it was a cougar. No doubt. Too many signs all added up. He'd seen those fur traces—but he wasn't about to share those things with them. Though now he kind of wished he'd taken a chance on the snapshot.

Back home, he picked up the ticket on his desk. When he opened the package last Christmas, he was expecting another strange gift. Just another one of those things from being adopted, he would say to himself. He decided a long time ago that he ended up with a lot better deal without his dad around. Some of the kids at school told him his Dad probably took one look at him and decided to get right on the plane.

He figured his dad probably made the right decision to take off. His mom had her story—when he asked to see a photo. "I never met him," she said. "Your step father and I wanted a baby so bad." Then silence for a bit. "The agency told us he was headed overseas on a long tour-of-duty in some rough spot nobody but him and his platoon—and whoever sent them—knew about. He knew there'd be other tours like it even if he did come back. When he lost his wife, he just wanted you raised in a regular family." She looked down. Yeah, Johnny thought, regular for about six months. Until his step-dad stepped out—for good. He knew his mom had gone far enough. "Hey, Mom, no big deal." He knew how much his mom had done for him since then—all on her own. With nobody ever giving her any credit. "We're a team that can't be beat," he said, repeating her regular pep line. She looked up, met his smile with hers and gave him a hug. He couldn't stop wondering, though, about that first dad who left him behind. The older he got, the more he wondered and needed to know. "Look, once and for all, dummy," a kid, safely surrounded by his friends, said at school, "will you just open your eyes and realize there ain't no other dad out there on a secret mission to save the world. You were left in the gutter by some chick who likely had no idea herself who your papa was." He stiffened and walked toward the boy. Then stopped. And walked away. To laughs.

The packages always arrived from some strange place he'd never heard of. The gifts were real winners. Always the odd books, some new ones, but a lot of old ones that must have been popular when his so-called dad was his age, but were just dopey now. "Just wants you to have a fighting chance in this world," his mom would say, as she regularly saw his not-so-hidden disappointment. And those long letters. From you-name-it-land: Middle East, Italy, Greece, then later from some places in Central America—had some hokey Mayan stamp on the envelope.

He began to suspect that his mom actually was sending these things herself, though she always insisted she didn't. And this was one of those times he believed her. No way would his mom give him a carnival ticket. In fact, she was sweating it from the moment they arrived. The letter said he'd read about the carnival on-line and thought I might enjoy it. Finally I'm getting the kinds of gifts my "friends" get. They got real air rifles and knives, real baseball gloves, real skateboards . . . real dads, he couldn't help adding. He just got to read about them. The letter even included some hints about how to knock down all ten milk cans with one shot. That got him out to the barnyard these past weeks.

As he felt for the tickets, they reminded him that he was running late. He had to meet his new-found friends. A few of these had taken him aside a few days ago between classes. They knew his mom worked part-time cleaning classrooms and offices at the high school. "Look, all you need to do is get hold of the key. Make a copy. We'll take it from there." He'd thought a lot about it. He didn't feel great about the idea, but kept finding ways to ignore those feelings. Why not? he finally said to himself. No one is going to know, and who's it going to hurt? He had the copy of the key hidden in his room. And right now he was walking with the group of kids everybody either feared or wished they hung out with.

Brian, a curly-haired kid known as "spark plug" because he'd always start trouble and then let others clean it up, looked around to make sure no one was watching. "Check this out, boys," he said. They gathered around. Some of them had never seen such things. Seemed like they were just peeping through someone's windows. Seemed sneaky. And raunchy. Johnny knew he should look away. But didn't. He stared. What else could he do? He'd seen all this stuff before. And more. He decided again if he would keep himself from clicking to places like this later.

"Hey, kid, share the wealth." Tom, a kid who surprised everyone, including himself, by how big he grew so fast the last year or so, had his arm on the shoulder of a young kid who was picking up a bunch of silver dollars he'd dropped. "You won't be needing all that will you?" The kid was out of his league. "Why don't you send a couple of those my way, and we'll just let you keep moving without any hassle?" Poor kid. Wrong place, wrong time. Just let him go, Johnny thought. Let him go. That's what he thought. That's what he should have said. But he didn't. The boy didn't even look up, just put two, big, shiny dollar coins into Jim's hands. "Good move, kid," Tom said. They all moved on. He looked back and the kid still was looking down.

They could hear the music and the noise already. The first thing they saw was the Ferris wheel. "I'm heading right to the freaks," Paul, the clean-up batter on the baseball team, said. "You won't believe what you see," he said to Johnny. Paul was a veteran of carnivals. "Speaking of freaks," he says, nudging Johnny as they passed right by a guy in a wheelchair. They'd all seen him around town. And heard his attempts at language. The guy started to turn his head, but stopped. "This is the famous drooling man." He didn't join the laughter. He knew Sam. Worked at the library. Always had books ready for Johnny—that he knew he'd like. Most of the time he was right. But now he couldn't look at him. He wanted to say hello, wanted to tell the others that it just wasn't right to treat Sam that way. That's what he wanted to do. What he did was walk away with the others.

Then a group of girls from the school glided up to them. But he only saw Jessie. She probably wondered what he was doing with these guys. Or, more to the point—what these guys were doing with him.

They were headed to the Haunted Mansion. But they had to pass the pitching booth on the way.. "I'm going to give this a try," Johnny awkwardly mentioned to the others. "Sure, we got a minute. We'll watch you throw your money away," Paul said. "But first you'll need a lesson," Paul laughed, stepped in front of Johnny, and winked at Sue, who smiled, blushed a bit, and nudged one of her friends. "Give me one of those silver dollars you ripped off," he told Tom. The barker gave him three balls. "How hard can it be?" Paul said, took a huge windup, and whistled the first ball ten yards to send the very top bottle flying off alone. Two more-accurate flings at the center still left a couple bottles standing. "That's why you're playing the outfield instead of pitching," Brian laughed as he and Tom high-fived, and Paul yelled: "these things are all a rip-off!"

Johnny handed the barker a dollar bill and took the three balls. Put two of them off to the side. Most people thought you should aim right at middle. He knew better. You aim at the middle and one of the two end ones still stood. The key was hitting just right of center on the bottom row—with a slight curve ball. And you don't stand dead-center, but a little off to the side. Johnny gripped the ball with two fingers across the top of the ball's seams. He pulled the ball behind his head, his other arm straight out in front. Just like behind the barn, and just liked he was told in the letter. All ten went flying. Even the barker looked impressed. "Whoa, dude, where'd you learn that?" Paul blurted out before he could stop himself. "We could use a lefty that can do that." They all looked up at the top shelf—and saw the kinds of things Johnny would soon have his hands on. They'd heard all about that first-place grab-bag. "We'll see you tomorrow, buddy. I think our lives are going to get a lot more interesting now. We'll show you some great ways to use that stuff." "I got dibs on those trick glasses for the test on Monday," Brian yelled back at Johnny.

Off to the right, the haunted mansion crowd was filing out. "Hey, guys. Let's get in line." "Johnny, we'll save you a place." Then they all scattered. "Who knew Johnny was cool," Jessie said as she slowly walked away with her friend, Amy, resting her eyes on Johnny's for just a second longer than she needed to—as if she noticed him for the first time. "I did!," Amy's younger sister, Kimberly, beamed as she raised her hand smiling. Johnny looked over and remembered where he'd seen her before. After the two seniors wedged him from either side in the lunch room and his tray went flying, and he was cleaning up, he looked over to find her picking up things too. And when someone handed her that crude drawing of him that was going around the school, she ripped it up on the spot. "Oh, grow up," he was surprised to hear her say to those older girls. But he hardly recognized her now. What a winter can do.

And then he was alone, staring at the top shelf.

"Well, son, you're the first one for a while to do that on one throw. Quite a pitch. Your choice. Any one of the three from the very top shelf." He looked over the prizes, pointed to the biggest one— the grab bag. Inside it were more prizes. "What's this?" "Called a Whoopee Cushion." He described the other items for Johnny. The marked card deck. "Nobody will know," it said on the cover. Hand-zapper. Charles Atlas strength program. Showed a picture of a muscle man kicking sand into a scrawny guy's face at the beach, the girls laughing along. Could help with my batting, Johnny thought— and pitching. Glasses. He put them on. He could see things three feet to his right and left.

The next option was sports equipment—basketball, football, and a glove. He asked to try it on. Leather already felt supple; no cheap padding in the palm. Great, tight webbing. Just molded on to his hand.

"What's on the other shelf?" he asked. "The grand prize for girls." Some of the same things. Some different. Looked at the pictures on the outside. "Glow-in-the-dark lipstick," "Hot pink bikini," "Dance with Britney" DVD.

"What's the third option you were talking about?"

"Ah, the third option," the man paused and looked into Johnny's eyes, as if gauging something the eyes might reveal. "Hardly anyone ever takes that." He picked it up—kind of carefully.

"Just a book?" Johnny asked, a little confused. Just for a moment, the man looked disappointed, but recovered quickly. "Not just a book," he said, sweeping his hand across its cover, and pausing. No, not just a book at all."

"What's so special about it?"

"Quite a bit," the man said. "Quite a bit." He opened the book and seemed a bit lost as he scanned a page. He turned again to Johnny, cradling the book as he talked.

"Ever wish you could just sort some things out—what's really the right path? What isn't?"

Quite a bit lately, Johnny thought.

"Ever wished you could just stop doing some things but just can't seem to get the gumption?"

Where'd those words come from? Johnny thought, a bit shocked. He recalled those web sites. And his walk to the carnival today.

"Ever think you're just being led somewhere you don't really want to go, but just haven't figured out how to escape yet?"

Is this guy following me around? Johnny thought, as he tried to cover his tracks by looking away.

"This book will explain those kinds of things," the man said, looking down again at the book in his hands. Then his eyes met Johnny's. "Show you a different path. A better one. Show you how to walk it. Give you what it takes to walk it."

But it's just a book, Johnny thought.

"How's it gonna do all that?" Johnny tried to use a casual voice, but wasn't feeling very casual for some reason.

"Now that's a question that would take a lot more time to answer that you and I have right now, young man," the barker said, as he took a token from a father who handed a ball to his son, giving him some hints. "But the short answer is: *It's* not going to do it. *He's* going to do it. When you open the book, you'll know what I mean by that."

Johnny just kind of stood there. This was not supposed to be a tough decision. "I'll tell you what," the man said. "I'll keep these aside. You think about it. And then come back anytime today. They'll all be waiting for you. Whatever you choose."

He started toward the haunted mansion, still thinking about things and feeling things that were new to him. Then he looked over on the slate bench—just a bunch of flat rocks piled on top of each other, edged up against some building's wall. It was the boy, the one who dropped his money. He looked around; the group was busy talking and laughing. "Hey, kid, look I'm sorry. Where's all your friends?" He pointed toward the Ferris wheel, but didn't look up. Johnny took out four crisp dollar bills. "Look, I owe you. We all owe you. It won't happen again—at least I'll make sure to say something next time. I'm . . . I'm sorry." The kid looked surprised to hear those words. Johnny put the bucks in his hand. "Sometimes older kids can be jerks," he said and managed some kind of half-smile. "Hurry, go catch up with your friends." The kid paused a second, like he just figured out something important. He ran toward the Ferris wheel.

It'd already been a long day. Too many things going on at once. Too much to handle. He just sat and watched all of his friends filing into the Haunted Mansion. And he noticed the fluffy, dark gray and white clouds in the sky above them. That's the ride he'd really like to take right now—just float along on one of those white puffs—without any hassle. His eye caught hold of the tent next to the mansion. How had he missed that before? Beautiful pastel oranges and purple fabrics just kind of flapping in the breeze like a sail on a ship. Must be the entrance to the "Arabian world" show he'd heard about, with real camels and cobra charmers. Most of his friends who had been there said it ended up being a big disappointment, though. Too slow.

"Last chance for the Haunted Mansion. Two Spaces left. Come one, come all." He got ready to run toward the line where his friends were all laughing and getting ready to enter.

But just then the breeze snapped a drape in the silken tent. He looked toward it again. "Don't blow it this time," he thought, and headed toward the Mansion. Then he heard someone by the tent—in an Arabian wrapped robe. "Come. Come see the greatest show on earth." Same old lines, he thought. Doesn't anybody have an original sales pitch around here? But this guy's pitch did sound different somehow. Sure, *this'll* finally be the one truly greatest show on earth. Right. Now the Arabian had parted the opening flap to the tent, and was inviting Johnny in. Some of those newer feelings came over him again. He walked over and passed through tent opening.

Inside, he could see what his friends meant by slow—and

quiet. He was alone. He could just hear the breeze against the tent. But then he realized he was standing above a huge pit, a dungeon. And a man, attached with cords to a harness across his waist and shoulders, was being lowered to the bottom. "This pest won't bother us anymore," he heard a voice say from within a group at the top edge of the pit. "I'm glad we found a good use for that yoke the fool's been hauling around." Laughs echoed in the chamber. He looked down at the man, now mired up to his knees. The man looked back at him, with the same eyes he'd been looking at all day—from the barker at the milk-bottle pitch, from Sam, and from the kid.

"We've got a new problem," he heard. "My cousin has gotten bit by the same bug in a big way. Thinks we all need to straighten out our lives. You know . . . the usual. Too much success. Too much comfort. Too much . . . life. Can't have that, can we? And not enough handouts to the vermin that infect this city. Makin' a big fuss. We'll have to deal with *him* now." Another voice responded: "We won't need a pit for him."

He got scared and walked through the drapes and climbed a few steps to the next room. A lot noisier. Lots of voices screaming at someone. But when the man spoke, his voice rose above the noise.

The Messiah is calling you right now—to come unto him, to follow him.

Did he tell you this personally? They all laughed.

I prayed . . . for you all, and then . . . I saw . . .

Yes, you saw . . . go on.

A pillar of fire upon a rock. A warning to us all. Our families . . . our wives, our children. I am so afraid for them. You, too, would shake if you saw and heard what I saw.

I'm shaking and trembling right now . . . and all I see and hear is you.

But there is more, much more . . .

More than a pillar of fire? Can't wait until the next act . . . Earthquakes, volcanoes? Don't keep us in suspense.

A vision . . . from God. The heavens opened before me.

Wow, better than earthquakes. Right to the heavens opening bit. Does it get any more dramatic?

I . . . thought . . . I saw God . . . upon his throne . . . surrounded by angels.

You *thought* you saw God? Didn't He introduce Himself to such a close friend?

There's more. Much more. Please . . . listen. There is still time . . . we can all escape the things I saw. Our families. Please.

Okay, dreamer, we've got other things to do. We all know what's coming next. What did this mystery man you *thought* was God have to say to you? Cough it up—then go away.

He didn't talk to me.

Now that's unfortunate. Well, thanks for the entertainment. Next dream, try to get some kind of message, would you? That's how this prophet stuff works, remember?

I do have a message, a message that can save you all. Listen.

I do have a message, I don't have a message, I do have a message. This is all getting tedious.

One descended out of the midst of heaven and came down, as bright as the sun, and then twelve others following him, brighter than the brightest stars.

This is very crowded dream, indeed. Okay, so finally the messenger arrives in a cloud of light. Drum roll please. Go ahead, tell us what he had to say . . . (And then we'll share our own message—for anyone else who bothers us like this guy)

He didn't talk to me.

Enough of this nonsense! This is worse than those traveling bards who delay the ending until they have a big enough crowd to buy their wares. We've had enough!

Wait. A book! He gave me a book!

What does God have against you? Can't talk to you directly, like other prophets, like Moses and Abraham? He has to have *a book* do the talking? Do you have any idea how idiotic you sound?

Not just any book. As I read, I was filled with the Spirit of the Lord.

Let's get this straight. You see God, and a bunch of other shiny, tongue-tied people coming and going in and out of heaven. But that's not good enough for your dreams. You start reading a book in your private little song and dance show from heaven.

Just then a bright flash of lightning lit up the sky. Thunder pounded in their ears . . . and silenced their mocking.

I read this in the book: Wo, wo, unto Jerusalem . . . I have seen thine abominations.

This great city . . . its inhabitants . . . will be destroyed. By the sword. Many carried away unto Babylon. Your families. You must listen. Listen. There is a way, our families can still . . . be protected . . . be saved. All of us. The Lord is more powerful than all swords and all armies. He has a plan for us. For our eternal life. For our safety right now. We can turn to . . . him. Isaiah, Jeremiah told us about him. The book . . .

The book again . . .

Another clap of thunder.

A Messiah . . . God gave us a Messiah . . . His Son . . . to redeem us.

Of course, always back to the Messiah. Okay, point the way.

The book, in my vision, the book manifested plainly of the coming of the Messiah . . . and of the redemption of the world. Go home and read; you, too, have the book. Open it and you, too, will see what I saw; you'll hear what I heard. You'll know. You'll know. And . . . and, you'll find the way, the power to follow him.

Look, we gave you a chance to point us to the Messiah. And you can't get past that book.

Johnny saw some gathering stones . . .

Wait, we can do this easier tomorrow, others said quietly.

Johnny ran up the stairs through the next drapes. Things got quieter again. He saw a younger man, his foot against the tensed, curved center of a bow, tightening the thick string across the ends. And talking to a woman.

"Look, why did he have to leave them with me? He knew that I didn't think about them the same way he did."

"It just seemed to your dad like the right thing to do. He prayed . . ."

"Yeah, he prayed . . . that's how he always got things done, right? Always his nose in a book, and always those revelations about who knows what? Maybe *he* did, but he sure didn't make a lot of friends, did he? Too much gold, too big houses, too fancy clothes. And in my case, too much hunting, too much time wasted in the woods. Well, that's where I'm headed right now."

"That wasn't all he wanted you—us all—to know. This life, this world, this isn't our home, our real home. He knew there was only one way to find real . . . real happiness . . . now and forever. He wanted you to find that path—for yourself. To see the signs around you—in the lives of saints—and to follow the Spirit that won't ever lead you wrong. The Spirit, the path, it will lead you to that tree, to that spring of water that will . . ."

"Yeah, the tree, the spring, the next life. All that."

Now here's a guy after my own heart, Johnny thought.

He watched the hunter get ready. The water flask, arrows, slingshot. And then he paused, thought for a moment, picked up a small rolled parchment and added it to his pack. Maybe a map.

He could learn a lot about hunting from this guy. Watched him check out branches, he seemed to just sense which path an animal would prefer. He walked nearly soundlessly and effortlessly over boulders, up steep inclines, jumped across a gulley almost as far as Houdini had crossed the stream. He'd never read about anything like this.

He saw him walk right up to a deer—and then just waited until the deer turned to see him and watch it bound away.

Then, the hunter stopped for a drink, leaned down and cupped the water in his hands, took a drink, paused, looked around him. Off in the distance, there were occasional flashes of lightning and distant claps of thunder. "Looks like it's headed off to the west," he said out loud. "Shouldn't bother me." But he kept staring at the far lighting and clouds. He stayed still for a long time, then got up slowly and walked with a whole different pace. He stopped checking the tracks and signs on the ground and in the bushes; kept moving up a steep rock face, pulling himself up effortlessly from boulder to boulder. Just above the tree line, he paused and just looked down at the ground.

Johnny seemed able to hear aloud the thoughts going through the hunter's mind. "Take these plates, my son. Take these plates. Please promise me you'll keep them, protect them. And read from them, read those plates. I don't know how to tell you this. But when you open those plates . . . he'll make himself known to you, appear . . . more than that . . . he will . . . make himself known to you also . . . with the same power . . . to our descendants, to many others, to the next generation, and to generations far into the future, with that same power—through these plates."

He opened his backpack and took out the small, rolled parchment. "Okay, they're safe. I read them—like you asked me. I read the same words on the plates that you taught everyone . . . that you taught me. I know how important those things were to you. I just don't know how to make them as important to me. I just don't know how to do that."

Then he unrolled the parchment, sat on a flat, raised rock wedged between two boulders. And read. Johnny could hear the words as the hunter read. "I speak unto you again; for I am desirous for the welfare of your souls. Yea, mine anxiety is great for you; and ye yourselves know that it ever has been." The Hunter looked up, seemed to be listening. Looked down again. "I speak unto you these things that ye may rejoice. . . . And thou shalt know that I am the Lord."

But how? How can I know that? How can I know . . . him? the hunter said aloud as he looked up again. How?

He read more. "For this cause the prophet has written these things."

"These things," the hunter repeated. And read more.

Johnny heard another distant rumble of thunder, getting closer now.

"The Lord God hath opened mine ear, and I was not rebellious, neither turned away back."

He did not look down for a long time. When he turned back to the parchment, he read: "The Lord is near."

Johnny then saw the hunter look up—for a long time. And then rise and kneel, his arms upon the flat rock. He watched the day pass by—just as it had when he tracked Houdini, into the afternoon, and twilight. Occasionally he overheard the words of the hunter. "You said you saw Him face-to-face. You saw angels. They came down and ministered to you. And your brother saw Him and saw angels. And so did grandfather." He then looked up and seemed to pause for a long time—as if for a response from someone, somehow. "Why not me? Why should I be kept in the dark? Where are the angels now? Where is this . . . Messiah?"

The hunter stayed on his knees as twilight turned to night, lightened by one of the fullest moons Johnny had ever seen. And then when the birds signaled dawn, he saw the hunter arise, take again the parchment, and just hold it in front of him. He didn't move at all for a long time, then finally looked up. He bowed his head again for a long time. Once more he looked up—this time wiping his eyes. "My Lord and my God," he heard in a low whisper. And then: "Lord, how is it done? How?"

Another voice, a voice unlike any voice he'd heard, seemed to be talking from inside and outside him at the same time: "Because of thy faith in Christ, whom thou hast never before heard nor seen. And many years pass away before he shall manifest Himself in the flesh . . ." The Hunter then smiled, and looked up, whispering again, responding to the other voice . . . "but who is made clearly manifest unto all through the words alone of my father—the words on the plates."

"Go to," the other voice said, "Thy faith hath made thee whole."

He bent his head again—for a long while. "Others need to know what I now know," he said. "They need to know, too." The voice again responded: "I will grant unto thee according to thy desires." The hunter seemed to take strength in this promise: "Please preserve these plates, Lord, please let whoever survives this war, have these plates. I know now why these plates are so important. Now I know. Through these plates, they'll know, too. They'll know and feel what I know and feel. Through these plates."

The voice again: "It shall be done—in my time and in my way. Thy fathers have also required of me this thing." The hunter then seemed finally at ease. "The plates." His body relaxed, he lay down, and fell off to sleep.

Johnny awoke to a loud snap of the thunder. "How long have I been asleep? Looks like rain is on the way." He looked at the Haunted Mansion, ran for the barker.

"I'll take the book."

The man already had it wrapped and waiting. "Thought maybe you would, son."

He took the book, turned around and saw a few of his friends coming toward him. Tom, Paul . . . and Jessie. Then he saw a man a bit further away—in a wheelchair struggling to get out of a deep rut in the path. He started walking toward Sam.

"Hey, Johnny," Jessie said as he passed, "Let's check out that grab bag." This was the first time she had ever spoken to him. He'd dreamed of this moment for a long time. He didn't stop walking. "I didn't get the grab bag," he said as he passed, still looking forward.

He bent down on one knee in front of the wheelchair—in the mud—while his friends stood and just stared. "Look, Sam, I . . . I'm . . ."

Sam just patted him on the shoulder. "I know perfectly well what you are, Johnny. Known that for a long time. You don't think I was ever sixteen years old?" Sam then looked into his eyes and smiled. He knew he could put it all behind him.

"Thanks, Sam. I need to do some quick growing up. Let me give you a push."

"Yeah, looks like I bottomed out here."

Then Johnny looked back at his friends—at Jessie—and started to say something. Before he could, he watched them turn around and walk the other way. "But . . ." he said, and quickly realized he didn't really have anything to say they wanted to hear.

"Like I've always said," Sam turned to him, "I'm glad we only have to be sixteen once." They smiled. "Thanks, again, Sam . . . for everything." And he turned to walk home.

"Hey, kid," he heard Sam call after him. When he turned, Sam just made a gesture with one finger toward his other cradled arm. "Nice choice," he said.

Johnny lifted his package he was cradling toward Sam and just nodded. And waved.

THE TRACKER II

Johnny put his new book in the backpack, started walking toward the computer. Who—what—am I becoming? he thought. Halfway across the room, he made a quick decision, grabbed his backpack and jacket, and left a note—to let his mom know he'd be on a weekender in the mountains. "I need to know some things," he wrote. "For sure."

He took out his topo map and the pattern he'd penciled in years ago—after one of those letters arrived from who-knows-where-land. He never told his Mom about this letter. Or the map. "One day, this may come in handy, son," the letter began. "This is a place I went as a kid. Not many know about it. Not easy to get to. I've included some milestones, but you'll have to search for them carefully." Okay, Johnny thought, "let's just see if these letters actually come from someone. Let's see if this map takes me anywhere." He continued. "Here's a list of some things to watch out for on the trail. Most animals won't hurt you. But some may target you as prey as soon as they scent your trail. Just remember—these animals are natural cowards and will only strike when they sense some weakness. They also can sense strength—and will back off. But others—not the animals—worry me more. People. Who also prey on those they think are weak and whom they can use or hurt. Not in most parts of these woods, though—at least you should be away from that danger while you're there."

"Yeah," Johnny thought, "that's always been good news."

"Finally," the letter ended, "there's another danger. Someone you can't see, just feel. He will always be on your trail, and always try to steer you his way, to make do his bidding. Be careful. Since you've come this far, you've already made an enemy." That sounds ominous, Johnny thought. "But trust those other feelings inside you. The good ones. You know what I'm talking about. You can always trust them to lead you right."

At first the path was pretty familiar. This was where Houdini had taken him. It was good to be back on this trail. Then he finally came to the granite rock face. And the trap dike. He stopped. Looked at the map. "Yep, that's the way," he said to himself. "Not sure I want to go through that again. . . especially just on a hunch."

On the other hand, he didn't like letting that trap-dyke get the last word. "Ah well, no guts, no glory," he said as he began the ascent. Like before, he got up the first part of the way with no trouble. Then he stopped. Looked behind him. "Not going to do anything stupid," he said to himself. "I'll stop this time before I get myself in a fix." He plotted out a slightly different route in his mind. One that he felt he could back up on if he ran into trouble. He reached for the first ledge. After four more reaches and steps, he looked above him and saw what it would take to lift him to the next ledge. He looked back. Knew he wouldn't have much of a fall. If he was slipping, he could easily jump away from the rock and land safe. He had to give it a try. He grabbed the ledge and pulled. No way, he said to himself. "Well, did you write this letter or didn't you," he said mostly to himself. "Do you want me to follow this trail you sent me on or not?" Then he tried once more, pulled himself to the next ridge. And then he climbed a lot more easily over some more ridges and faces that normally might have given him reason to give up. About an hour later, at the top of the trap dike, he looked down over the canyons he'd crossed all that morning, at the lakes and streams he'd passed. He saw what looked like a familiar eagle crossing one of those streams—getting ready to swoop for fish, it looked like. He enjoyed the breeze pushing up from the rock face he'd just climbed—and the combined smells of balsam fir, spring water, and wild mint leaves.

As soon as he turned back around he noticed some faint familiar tracks. "Back on your trail," Johnny thought.

It was not easy following the trail. He found he had to keep checking with the map. But he found it usually set him straight whenever things got a bit unclear. He discovered some new lakes and canyon paths he knew he'd have to take more time investigating on another trip. He turned one corner and saw a cow with two calves lunching on water plants in a shallow pond. They finally heard him approaching; the calves didn't even stop chomping—just stared at the new curiosity in town. Mom had other ideas and quickly whisked them into the woods. While crossing a meadow he was enjoying discovering some new wildflowers and the flight of a turkey buzzard so much that he forgot for a moment that he was still alone in the wild—where inattention could cost you dearly. Jumping off one boulder, he heard the clear warning in mid-air and then saw the yellow brown and grey coils unraveling as he descended—all too late to retreat to safety. He landed between two of them and froze. He'd seen a lot of snakes but these were the first timber rattlers he'd ever seen in these mountains. Looked over six feet each. No jerky movements now. They were a whole lot quicker than he was. Their rattlers were on full throttle and their broad diamond shaped heads were both maneuvering for position. It'd been a long time since he felt so out of control in the woods—and subject to the whims of other forces. His next thought came out of nowhere and surprised him: "If you're the one who got me here, you better figure a way to keep me going." He didn't hear it or see it coming—it was so quick. Somehow the huge eagle grabbed one of the diamond heads while the other retreated into the brush.

"Stay alert to stay alive," he said to himself and took a big gulp form his canteen.

About an hour later, he saw a dense stretch of woods up ahead. He checked the map again to make sure. Yep, he said, and found a faint trail into the woods. He enjoyed the flashes of sunlight breaking through the openings in the pine, aspen, and white birch canopy as he walked. As the canopy thickened, though, the trail got tougher to read. But he saw no need to slacken his pace.

Then, while he walked, he missed one of the gnarled roots that were always appearing from out of nowhere. This one was at the top of a decline—and it sent him tumbling down into a narrow, steep path. "What am I doing out here, anyway?" he said as he picked himself up. Some strange map from some strange dude that is taking me on some strange trail. And for what? That's the question. For what?" He picked up his backpack. "For nothing at all. That's what." And turned around. "People at school got me all figured out, I'd say. Some freak. Once a goof, always a goof." He threw the map on the trail as he started walking back the way he'd come.

He came to a rock on the side of the path and sat down for a drink. When he opened his back pack, the book fell out on the ground. As he bent down to pick it up, he felt drawn to the book and started reading from the opened page—about some Nephi kid out hunting food for the family. Cool. Bow breaks. Gets back to the tent and everybody finds someone to rag on and blame for all their problems. Not Nephi. Even though he's everybody's favorite punching bag. Instead he goes out and builds a new bow and arrow. Heads right back up into the mountains again. And just like that—dinner's on the table. Something about that guy, he thought. Didn't let things get in the way of what was most important.

Okay, Nephi. I'll take you up on that. He packed up the book and turned back on the path, found the map back up the trail and tried to figure out his next move. But after just a few more steps he heard something in the woods off to his left. Just a shuffling sound—but it kept getting louder—and seemed to change directions when he looked for it. Then the sun seemed to go behind some cloud—and it got a lot darker a lot quicker. More shuffling, from more than one direction this time. He'd never been this kind of afraid in these woods before.. He started to walk fast up the trail—but now whatever direction he moved, something in those woods found a way to shuffle to the woods beside him and behind him. Seemed like more than one of whatever it was. Seemed like the woods were closing in around him.

Then he heard a familiar growl—only a lot louder this time, a lot more menacing. He knew it wasn't directed at him. He heard a lot of shuffling in the woods again—real quick ones. This time the sounds just kept fading deeper into the woods. Whatever it was, it was leaving in a hurry.

It got real quiet. He could only hear himself breathe, surprised by how much he'd been sweating. Then he saw a flash of light break through the far canopy up ahead, some kind of clearing maybe. He walked in that direction. And then looked out over one of the most peaceful meadows he'd ever seen. He had arrived.

He walked up to a waterfall that seemed to be fed by some spring emerging from the wall of granite behind it. It fell into a deep pool of blue green water. He followed a stream until it seemed to merge again under a rock face. As he looked further, at the opposite end of his entrance to this meadow, he saw that the dense woods continued. He would have to investigate where that path led some other trip. Right now, he found a place on a hillside to set up camp—behind a bunch of rocks piled on each other—for a convenient barrier that he could use to look out at anything that might show up for a drink as twilight approached. He then looked out across the small lake. He knew the key to "seeing" animals in the wild. You have to "envision" them before you look. You don't just sweep your eyes across the landscape and wait for something to show up. You "see" the otter, beaver, or bobcat—and *then* you look.

He looked through his binoculars. Nothing. Put them down. It had been a long hike. He chomped on a piece of jerky. Soon he would have a fire going, cook some egg noodles and pour chili over them. His favorite camp meal. He loved this time of day—when the late afternoon shadows added new shades to the greens and browns of the woods. The lake looked like an epoxy covering he could walk across. He leaned on the rock pile and just felt amazed that such a place was still available in this messy world. And all his—he thought. Until he heard some rustling coming from that opposite entrance to the woods. He ducked behind the rocks—and looked through a space in the middle.

The rustling got louder—but he somehow knew he had no reason to be afraid this time. "Must be a bunch of whitetail coming through," he thought. But these weren't whitetail at all. People. Three men walked out of the woods and surveyed his side of the lake. "I think this'll work just fine," one said. The others nodded. They all seemed relieved. Two left and the third walked out further toward the shore. He then stopped, closed his eyes, knelt. His words, though not loud, echoed from the granite rock face. "Thank you. Thank you." He didn't get up for a while, then walked to the stream flowing into the lake, crouched down and cupped his hands for a taste of the water. And drank more, looked up, his eyes glistening. He filled a leather pouch strapped to his side with the water.

The others arrived. More men at first, then kids and women, and more men again. The men were dressed in kind of tunics, carrying bows and swords by their sides.

"I saw this place in my dream," the first one, the kneeler, said. "A place of clear water, and streams, and falls, inside a forest where we could find refuge."

More people kept arriving.

"I know this place," another one said. "My father described it to me. It is called Mormon." Like my book, Johnny thought. "Named after the great King." They all seemed to know this king. "Yes, we'll be safe here. For now. And the waters from these falls are said to have special healing properties. Cure all kinds of ailments. You have not yet been refreshed, my father would say, until you have drunk from the waters of Mormon."

"I can confirm the truth of your father's testimony, Jacob" the kneeler, returning from the woods, said. "We at last can understand how the thirst of the children of Israel was quenched in the desert." And he handed the still-wet pouch to Jacob. "Enjoy, my friend."

"Ah, Alma," Jacob turned to greet and embrace his friend, "Joseph tells us we have stumbled upon the forests of Mormon."

"Stumbled, indeed," Alma smiled and put his arm around Jacob, walking over to the others. They all sat down on the soft, dry, sod sloping up toward the forest. Some built fires, others took out nets and poles and went off to the streams and pools below one of the falls. Others found another pool and walked in fully clothed, wading underneath a veil of water, mouths opened. Still others, with bows and arrows, went back into the woods.

Soon they all returned to the slope, gathering around the subdued flames, the coals radiating warmth, drying their clothes as they arranged rocks and tree trunks close to the orange and blue glow.

Hunters came through the woods, carrying slain deer on stretchers they had built.

All settled and became quiet. All knelt. A faun was taken by several of the men, who were now dressed in some new robes. Some kind of ceremony—and more prayers.

Upon spits above the larger fires, the meat and fish were cooked, with what looked like corn and potatoes. And bread. A group of younger men and boys passed out food to all. And drinks—until all had eaten and were filled.

"We can rest here," Jacob said, looking up to the group, speaking from the edge of the lake. He was an older man, a grandfather type. "Each of you knows what happened to Abinadi." He paused. "We are . . . so much in debt to that servant of the Lord. He gave His life so that we could be here right now." He surveyed the entire group. "Alma was there. As were a few of you. We now have Abinadi's words. Alma has taught some of them to each of you. After teaching me and Joseph and others, Alma sent us to teach these words to many of you. And you were invited to start your lives over again. To follow the Messiah . . . made manifest by Abinadi—and by Isaiah. I know that many of you still wonder and want to learn more, about that Messiah—how to receive that redemption and eternal life that Alma and Abinadi spoke of. Here, in the forest of Mormon, we have that chance. Here at last, by the waters of Mormon, we can receive the full message of that redemption." Jacob then beckoned with his hand toward Alma, standing beside him, and sat down.

Alma then turned to teach the people. Johnny must have fallen asleep for a while, because when he next saw Alma and the people, the lake reflected the bright orange and pink clouds pushing against the setting sun.

The faces of the people also seemed to reflect that sun. They all seemed to bask in that soft light. All was quiet for several minutes.

"How beautiful," Alma then spoke softly, only the sound of the stream adding to his words, "as the prophet Abinadi taught us, how beautiful upon the mountains are the feet of him that bringeth good tidings, that is the founder of peace, yea, even the Lord, who had redeemed his people; yea, him who has granted salvation unto his people."

Then Alma opened his arms, motioning to one side and then the other, at the amazing spectacle unfolding around them. "And how beautiful is this, the land of Mormon, and the waters of Mormon, in this the forest of Mormon, the place of Mormon; yea, how beautiful are these waters and forests to the eyes of them who here have come to the knowledge of their Redeemer; yea, how blessed are they, for they shall sing to his praise forever."

Johnny thought of the book in his backpack. He moved and broke a branch.

"Hear that?" Alma said to Jacob, as they both looked out across the water. "A loon. Beautiful bird. Great way to start a new day"

Johnny then awoke and looked out on the lake. Two loons were skimming the surface. The second responded with her own call. How long have I been asleep? he wondered. The mist was just lifting from the water. Still a bit overcast, but he could see a bright sliver of sun ready to push through some gray puffy clouds.

He got up and stretched.

He opened his back pack, retrieved the book, and turned to the first page.

"Let's see if I can figure out what that barker was trying to tell me," the thought. And maybe see where this map's lead me. And who sent it. He opened the leather book, then read from the first page. "I, Nephi, having been born of goodly parents . . ."

A surge of warmth filled him. *Where'd that come from?* he wondered.

It's just a book, he thought. *Just a book.* "No, not just a book at all."

He knew somehow that he was starting down a path that would change everything.

He then heard a rustling sound in the aspen and birch grove behind him. Didn't need to look. Didn't need his camera.

"You and me, Houdini," he said aloud, feeling a strange sort of hope he'd never quite felt before—that he could get off the trail those others voices had been taking him, and find the right trail. He liked that idea—always liked the idea of a new trail. "You and me," he said out loud again, his voice cracking a bit, not thinking of Houdini this time, as he looked down on the page, wiping his eyes, recalling the barker's words. "You and me."

QUESTIONS TO CONTEMPLATE

- In what ways is our encounter with the Book of Mormon like the efforts of the Tracker in this story? How can we "track down" and "discover" that power of the Book of Mormon?

- Are you prepared to actually enter and explore the precincts of one of the holiest places in all this world?

- What are some of the ways we can prepare ourselves for such a journey of sacred discovery?

APPENDIX B

Charts and Tables

Table 1.6.1: The Links—with Scriptural Citations

Truths we would have to believe about ourselves and our situation in this life in order to come unto Jesus Christ ("how great the importance")	Associated Untruths (i.e., lies) the adversary and the world would have us believe about ourselves and our situation in life (2 Nephi 28:20)
We are in eternal danger and therefore need salvation (1 Nephi 10:6; 2 Nephi 9:8, 5–17, 2:5; Helaman 14:16–18; Alma 34:9, 42:9, 12:16–18; 3 Nephi 27:19; Mosiah 2:33, 4:30, 16:4; Moses 6:57; Romans 3:23, 6:23)	All is well; no need to worry about our actions or destiny (Alma 1:4; 30:27; 2 Nephi 28:21; Helaman 13:26, 6; 14:18–19); Your only danger is missing out on life's immediate opportunities
There was a law given and we broke it (2 Nephi 2:5, 13, 9:25; Alma 42:16–18, 45:16; Doctrine & Covenants 130:20–21, 132:5; Isaiah 59:1–2; Romans 3:23)	All life is random and unaccountable; Commandments and prohibitions are designed by institutions to keep us in submission (as the anti-Christs put it) (Alma 30:23)
We had sufficient knowledge about the law before we broke it. We all have an innate sense of good and evil and can distinguish between the two. (Moroni 7:16; Moses 4:3, 7:32; Doctrine & Covenants 93:30–31; Alma 5:41–42)	You cannot understand such things; meaning and language continuously deconstruct themselves and leave only confusion; every statement can be re-interpreted into its contradiction. Morality is just relative to our culture and society. One person's sin is another's virtue. You can't judge or condemn someone else's morality—or trust your own (Alma 10:24; Mosiah 12:13–14).
We had sufficient agency or freedom to make the decision to break the law (2 Nephi 2:16, 27, 10:23; Mosiah 2:21; Helaman 14:30; Moses 6:56, 7:32, 3:17; Doctrine & Covenants 101:78, 58:27–28; Mosiah 2:21; Alma 12:31)	We aren't free; our actions are completely determined by such things as our culture, our genetics, our sexual or economic urges, our astrological signs, our prejudices, etc. (Alma 30:24, 27).

We devise the idea of divine sanctions and punishments because of societal pressures and psychological repressions—from which we must liberate ourselves as we mature and become emotionally healthy (Alma 30:17; Jacob 1:4; Helaman 16:21; Alma 42:1)	There were clear consequences or punishments attached to that decision to break the law (1 Nephi 15:33; 2 Nephi 9:16, 28:23; Mosiah 2:33, 3:25; Jacob 6:10; Alma 7:21; 11:40–41, 34:16, 42:16–18, 41:3–4, 29:5; Helaman 14:31; Mormon 9:14; Doctrine & Covenants 88:34; Genesis 4:7; Deuteronomy 11:26–28; Galatians 6:7; James 4:17)
Everything is confusion and chaos, so just follow your vibes or your karma or wherever your emotions and desires take you. Punishments or sanctions are just institutional impositions to keep us in line (Alma 30:17; 2 Nephi 28:8).	A clear punishment for breaking the law was eternal separation from the presence of God and from the blessings of becoming like God—including eternal family-hood (2 Nephi 9:8, 9, 26:10; Alma 5:41–42, 42:14, 10:23, 42:14)
Through such tools as psycho-therapy, drugs, meditation, improved relationships, money, imagination, reason, self-actualization, bio-feedback, motivational seminars, will power, nature, gurus, government, or education we can transcend any difficulties we face and reach our ultimate potential (Mosiah 13:15; Alma 30:17)	We, by ourselves, are incapable of resolving our danger or transcending the temptations or sins that beset us—we need the Savior to intervene on our behalf (1 Nephi 10:6; Alma 2 Nephi 2:8, 10:24–25, 11:6, 25:23; Mosiah 15:8–9; Alma 13:28, 15:17, 22:14, 34:9, 39, 42:11–12, 15; 3 Nephi 18:18, 27:19; Moroni 6:4; Doctrine & Covenants 3:20)
It all ends when you die, and only oblivion awaits you, so why bother? (Alma 30:18)	We are eternal beings, made in God's image and likeness, who will continue to live after this life (Genesis 1:26–27; Mosiah 7:27; Alma 18:34, 42:16; Ether 3:15; Abraham 4:26–27; Moses 1:39, 2:26–27)
Your life was just randomly begun as a result of exclusively chemical and biological—not divine—processes (Alma 30:17)	We lived as children of God before this life—when we chose to be tested here (1 Nephi 17:36; 3 Nephi 12:48; Alma 13:3; Abraham 3:23–26, 4:27–28; Doctrine & Covenants 76:24; Acts 17:28–9; Hebrew 12:9;)

We are worthy and capable of being forgiven and receiving eternal happiness and salvation (See Enos; Mosiah 3:19; Mosiah 4; Alma 36; King Lamoni: Alma 19:12–13; Zeezrom: Alma 15:6–12; Anti-Nephi-Lehies: Alma 24:15; 2 Nephi 2; 2 Nephi 9, etc.)	You are not even worthy of being forgiven, so give up. It is no longer an option. Your anxieties, weaknesses, or predilections doom you to unhappiness and despair (Alma 30:16)
Adam and Eve were our first earthly parents and their decision in the garden brought about the fallen condition in which we now live—and gives us a chance to choose to follow Christ and thereby reach our divine potential (2 Nephi 2:25–26; Alma 42:2–8; Doctrine & Covenants 29:39–43; Moses 5:4–12)	We are all just naturally part of the animal environment; man is just naturally wicked and selfish and beastly; the account of the fall is just a fantasy (Alma 30:25, 17)
Truths we would have to believe about God the Father in order to come unto Jesus Christ	Associated Untruths the adversary and the world would have us believe about God the Father
He lives and is our Eternal Father; All things testify of Him (Alma 30:44; 2 Nephi 2; Helaman 8:24; Moses 6:63; Doctrine & Covenants 88:47–50; Moroni 7:16; Psalm 19:1; Hebrews 12:9; John 20:17)	There is no God—the urge to believe in God is just a genetic, evolutionary, trait acquired for survival; or a societal myth; or a ritualistic survival mechanism; or a way to devise supernatural explanations for natural processes; or a self-deceptive crutch to provide naive and childish comfort; or a sham foisted upon the masses by those in power to control and subdue them. The idea of God is unscientific (if you can't prove his existence empirically, he doesn't exist), irrational, illogical, anti-social, divisive, exclusionary, self-delusionary, ethnocentric, and ultimately harmful to yourself and others (Alma 30:28, 15; Helaman 16:18, 20–21; 1 Nephi 17:17)

He is both perfectly just and perfectly merciful, as is His plan for our Salvation (Alma 42:13–15, 34:15–16)	He is either a harsh, capricious being who already has decided who will be saved, or else one who plans to save everyone in the end—no matter what they do, or else one who offers salvation based on simple declarations of belief rather than actions (Alma 31:16–17)
He gives everyone an equal chance at salvation, even in the next life if necessary (Alma 42:27; 2 Nephi 26:27–28; Helaman 3:28–29; 1 Timothy 2:4; 2 Peter 3:9)	Some will be given more of a chance than others—it's all a shell game (Alma 31:16)
He instituted a plan for our eternal happiness and salvation (Alma 42:15; Moses 1:39)	There was no plan—we are making this all up as we go (Alma 30:28; Jacob 1:7, 9)
His plan is based on perfect love (1 Nephi 11:17; 2 Nephi 26:24; John 3:16)	He is just playing games with us—and looks at us as pawns or else as despicable, worthless beings
He possesses eternal power and knowledge (i.e., He is omnipotent and omniscient) (1 Nephi 9:6; 2 Nephi 9:20; Moroni 7:22; 1 Nephi 17:50–51)	He has various limitations of power and knowledge, and therefore His plan is not entirely reliable or dependable; so our faith in Him must also be malleable (2 Nephi 30:13; Alma 30:24; 21:8; Jacob 7:7)
He desires that we know and successfully live His plan—and therefore has given us the priesthood, prophets, and scriptures (John 3:16; 1 Nephi 11:14–22; Moroni 7:22–25, 36; Alma 12:28–33; Moses 5:58), all of which reveal him—via faith	He just leaves us here to stumble through life on our own; those records and those prophets are just to keep us in submission and ignorance (2 Nephi 30:23, 28); If he existed and wanted us to believe in him, he would let us see him with our physical eyes (Helaman 16:18–20; Alma 30:15; Ether 12:5); Why should we accept or trust a man's word (and the priesthood) for these things? We want more (Alma 9:2, 6; 1 Nephi 17:18–20; 2 Nephi 28:5–6; JS–H 1:21)

Truths we would have to know and believe about Jesus Christ in order to come unto Him to be saved	Associated untruths the adversary and the world would have us believe about Jesus Christ
The creation, our birth upon the earth, our talents, bodies, and hopes are all gifts from Him (Moroni 10:8, 18; Acts 17:28–29)	We, the earth, our talents, and everything about us just emerged naturally and randomly (Alma 30:17) OR: We accrue our gifts from our own efforts and genius
We will one day have to stand before Him and the Savior to account for our actions—with eternal consequences (2 Nephi 9:15, 2:5–10; Alma 42:23, 12:14, 5:15; 2 Corinthians 5:10; Revelation 20:12; Helaman 14:15–17)	Everyone ends up in the same place in the end, and is treated the same way (Alma 1:4; 21:6; 2 Nephi 28:7–8; Alma 21:6)
He is capable of saving us (2 Nephi 2:8–9; Doctrine & Covenants 18:11; Hebrews 2:10; Mosiah 3:17; Alma 38:9, 7:14)	He was just a another teacher, elevated to divine status by tradition (Helaman 16:20)
He rose from the dead and lives today (3 Nephi 11; Doctrine & Covenants 76:22–23; JS–H 1:17; Luke 24:36–40; Acts 2:22–24)	His resurrection is just a myth or metaphor. Only children or the foolish accept it literally (1 Corinthians 1:23)
He is willing and desirous to make Himself manifest to us through the process of prayer, the scriptures, and revelation (as he does in our day through the Restoration of his Church and the Book of Mormon) (1 Nephi 14:1; Moroni 7:31–32)	We can't and won't ever find Him (Jacob 7:7, 9). Even if he did live at some point, we are on our own now, and attempts to "find" him just sap valuable resources and time from our responsibilities here in this life.
He loves us and wants to save us (3 Nephi 22:8, 10; Alma 5:33–34; Doctrine & Covenants 19:16, 18:13, 34:3, 138:1–4; Matthew 11:28; John 3:16, 15:13; 1 John 4:7–10)	He doesn't love us or care about us. If he did, why are so many people so miserable, and why do so many innocent people suffer? John 11:37

He was chosen and sent by the Father to save us (3 Nephi 11:10–11, 32–33, 27:13–14, 19; Mosiah 4:6–7, 15:7; Alma 34:9; Ether 3:14; Moses 4:2, 7:47; Doctrine & Covenants 19:16–19, 93:21; John 14:6, 11:25; 1 Timothy 2:5; Revelation 13:8; Acts 4:12)	He is just another man, chosen by political and social forces who designated him a God (Matthew 27:62–65)
During his earthly ministry, he was the only person who was both God and mortal and set a perfect example for us to follow (1 Nephi 11:18–21; Mosiah 3:8; 2 Nephi 31:7; Alma 7:10–12, 3 Nephi 18:16, 27:21, 27; 1 Peter 2:21)	Just a historical figure, and no more a God than anyone else; or: "there were a lot of other great teachers like him, some in each religion" (John 10:20)
He lived a perfect, sinless life and therefore overcame both sin and death (2 Nephi 2:8; Doctrine & Covenants 45:4, 20:22, 3 Nephi 12:48; Hebrews 4:15, 7:26)	Just a man, like us all, mythologically raised to the status of a God; his supposed resurrection is just a metaphor for the idea that his teachings continue
His Atonement is more powerful than the consequences of sin (Mosiah 24:15; Alma 7:14; Helaman 5:11–12; Alma 11:40–43; 34:8–10; 36:13–19; 22:15–18; 14:15–18; Doctrine & Covenants 18:11; 19:16; John 16:33; 1 Corinthians 15:19–23	Sin and evil are ultimately more powerful and will triumph; in any case, you can't get past your sinful nature—it is too ingrained and inevitable. Or: "that may be the case for others' sins, but not for mine"
His love and light are more powerful than the hate and darkness of the adversary (Romans 8:35–40; 2 Nephi 1:15; 2 Nephi 24; Helaman 5:12)	Darkness and hate are more powerful in this world and will give us more success in the end. In this life, look out for # 1; others are worthless and get in your way.
He successfully endured the penalties of all our transgressions and therefore is authorized to mediate on our behalf and expiate our penalties (Alma 7:11–12; Moroni 10:32–33; Doctrine & Covenants 18:11;19:15–19; 45:4–5; Isaiah 53:4–5; Luke 22:44)	All creatures succeed only by their own strength, and must not rely on others—as children and cowards do (Helaman 16:15); or: "my particular sins are so heinous that they are not covered by the sacrifice of the Savior"

Justification (settling the demands of eternal law) and sanctification (making possible for us to become like God) are available to us through the Atonement and grace of Christ (Alma 42: 22–24; Moses 6; 1 Nephi 11:33; Helaman 5:10–11; 3 Nephi 27:13–16; Mosiah 4:2)	We cannot escape the grasp of natural law and genetic predisposition. Any sin we commit mars us forever and places us on an unalterable road to submission to our animal natures. The search for Holiness or Virtue is always hypocritical and self-righteous, and even the appearance of such must always be avoided
Truths we would have to know and believe about the adversary (Satan, Lucifer, etc.) (See Doctrine & Covenants 29, 76, Moses 1, 4; JS–H; 2 Nephi 28)	Associated untruths the adversary and the world attempt to make us believe about the adversary
He is a real being whose goal is to make us miserable and keep us from receiving our potential (1 Peter 5:8; Ephesians 6:11–12; 2 Nephi 2:18, 27; Alma 30:42, 53, 60; 3 Nephi 18:18; 1 Nephi 14:7; 3 Nephi 9:2; Doctrine & Covenants 10:22, 26–27)	There is no devil—he is just a silly construct devised to explain our own weaknesses (2 Nephi 28:22; 2 Nephi 2:27)
He works by tempting us to disobey and disbelieve the words and laws of God, and therefore is an enemy to all truth, light, life, and righteousness (Mosiah 4:14 Alma 30: 53; Moroni 7:12; 2 Nephi 28:20, 22; 9:28; Ether 8:25; Helaman 6:30; 3 Nephi 6:15; Doctrine & Covenants 10:20, 24–25; Matthew 13:19, 38–39; 24:24; John 8:44)	Those are not temptations you are experiencing; they are psychological mechanisms and repressive tendencies. Just let yourself go and follow your vibes (2 Nephi 28:20; see all of 2 Nephi 28:19–23; 2 Nephi 29:3)
He cannot force us to do things that we do not agree to do; through the Savior, we can overcome the temptations of the adversary (1 Nephi 15:24; 2 Nephi 2:26–27; Alma 13:28; Helaman 3:29–30; 5:12; 14:30; 3 Nephi 18:15; Doctrine & Covenants 10:5; John 8:36; Moroni 7:16–19; John 7:17; 16:13)	"The devil made me do it": Each of us is inevitably subject to various carnal and sensual forces in this life (such as lust, greed, hate, pride) that have been inculcated in us genetically or socially. Repressing such "natural" tendencies is perverse and unhealthy

The devil and evil are stronger than God and goodness; so I am joining the adversary's team.	There are limits set to his power, which he cannot exceed (Nephi 28:39; Doctrine & Covenants 29:47; Genesis 3:15; Job 1:10–12; Romans 16:20; 1 Corinthians 10:13; James 4:7)
I cannot get back to God; the adversary and sin have too great a hold on me. My character has become so ingrained that any major change is impossible	His power will always be less than the power of God (1 Nephi 22:26; 11:36; 2 Nephi 27:31; Helaman 3:29; 5:12; Ether 8:26; Doctrine & Covenants 19:3; 33:1; 88:114–115; Moses 1:18–22; Mark 5:2–13; Matthew 26:53; 2 Chronicles 20; 2 Kings 6:16–17; Psalm 27:1; 23:4; Ephesians 6:14–17; Revelation 12:7; 19:20; 12:9–10; 20:1–3, 10; Moses 7:13)
The pursuit of carnality and unrestrained pleasure is our goal in life and we should free ourselves to enjoy these things; restraint about such things equals repression (Alma 30:18, 27; 2 Nephi 28:7–8)	What he sets forth as fun, pleasure, and happiness ultimately leads to misery (Alma 41:10; Helaman 13:38; 2 Nephi 15:20; 2 Corinthians 11:14)

Chart 2.3.1: Summary for Chart 1, Columns 1–4

The Lord's prophet within this Scriptural Temple made the Messiah Powerfully Manifest, and the Covenants Available ...	... while located within this Actual Temple (or substitute temple, such as a mountain, hill, or forest), after having referenced or having quoted a manifestation of Messiah from ...	... a prophet within this other Scriptural Temple from a previous record or dispensation,...	... which was accompanied by this manifestation of the Messiah within this other Scriptural Temple from a previous record or dispensation
The Immediate or Primary Manifestation of the Messiah: Within the Book (or Temple) of Mormon		The Referenced or Secondary (or instrumental) Manifestation of the Messiah: Within the Brass Plates (or much of what is contained within our Old Testament)	
Book of Mormon 2 Nephi 25-33: Nephi's wonderful manifestation of the Messiah, his atonement, and his covenants	Temple Built by Nephi (2 Nephi 5) (Occurred right after we read of this temple being built by Nephi, which seems a reasonable place for Nephi to 1) store and access the sacred brass plates; as well as his own sacred plates; and 2) receive important revelations)	The Book of Isaiah, from the Brass Plates Isaiah 2-14 (qtd. by Nephi in 2 Nephi 12-24)	Isaiah's vision of the Lord, his atonement, and his covenants See especially: 2 Ne. 16; Isaiah 6 2 Ne. 18; Isaiah 8 2 Ne. 19; Isaiah 9 2 Ne. 21; Isaiah 11 2 Ne. 22; Isaiah 12

The Lord's prophet within this Scriptural Temple made the Messiah Powerfully Manifest, and the Covenants Available …	… while located within this Actual Temple (or substitute temple, such as a mountain, hill, or forest), after having referenced or having quoted a manifestation of Messiah from …	… a prophet within this other Scriptural Temple from a previous record or dispensation, …	… which was accompanied by this manifestation of the Messiah within this other Scriptural Temple from a previous record or dispensation
Book of Mormon 2 Ne 9-10: Jacob's great manifestation of the Messiah, his atonement, and his covenants	Temple Built by Nephi (Occurred right after we read of this temple being built by Nephi, which seems a reasonable place to suppose Jacob taught the "brethren," since he explicitly announces this location for his teaching of the "brethren" later (Jacob2:2))	The Book of Isaiah, from the Brass Plates Isaiah 49:22-23, 24-26 (qtd. by Jacob in 2 Ne. 6:6-7, 16-18); Isaiah 50; 51:1-2 (qtd. by Jacob in 2 Ne.7 & 8)	"thou shalt know that I AM the Lord" (Isaiah 49:23; 2 Nephi 6:7) "Isaiah speaks Messianically" (Ch. Heading for Isaiah 50)
Book of Mormon Mosiah 15-16: Abinadi's powerful manifestation of the Messiah, his atonement, & his covenants	Temple Built by Nephi (?), Now occupied by Noah and his priests (Mosiah 11:10-11) as they question Abinadi	The Book of Isaiah, from the Brass Plates Isaiah 53 (qtd. by Abinadi in Mosiah 14)	Perhaps the greatest Messianic manifestation of the Old Testament: Isaiah 53 (see also Isaiah 54-57, 61-62)

The Lord's prophet within this Scriptural Temple made the Messiah Powerfully Manifest, and the Covenants Available . . .	. . . while located within this Actual Temple (or substitute temple, such as a mountain, hill, or forest), after having referenced or having quoted a manifestation of Messiah from . . .	. . . a prophet within this other Scriptural Temple from a previous record or dispensation, . . .	. . . which was accompanied by this manifestation of the Messiah within this other Scriptural Temple from a previous record or dispensation
Book of Mormon Alma 33: 22-23; 34:8-16; 30-37: Alma and Amulek testify to Zoramites of the Atonement	"Upon the hill Onidah": 32:4 (mounts or hills used as temples when other temples not available—as they were not to the poor Zoramites)	The words of Zenos, Zenock, and Moses, from the Brass Plates (qtd. in Alma 33:3-14; 15-17; 18-21)	The words of Zenos, Zenock, and Moses quoted by Alma bore powerful manifestation and witness of the Savior and his atonement (see Alma 33:12-14; 34:6-7)
Book of Mormon (Helaman 8:13-24): Nephi testifies to his people	"Nephi had bowed himself upon the tower which was in his garden": Hel. 7:10 (a substitute temple, perhaps as was the city wall upon which Samuel later manifested the Messiah)	The words of Moses, especially (8: 13-15); also Abraham, Zenos, Zenock, Ezias, Isaiah, Jeremiah (8:16-20) from the Brass Plates; previously quoted often by his grandfather, Alma. (Note that Lehi, Nephi, et al also noted)	See also the words of Zenos, Zenock, and Moses as quoted by Alma, which bore powerful manifestation and witness of the Savior and his atonement (see Alma 33:12-14; 34:6-7)

The Lord's prophet within this Scriptural Temple made the Messiah Powerfully Manifest, and the Covenants Available . . .	. . . while located within this Actual Temple (or substitute temple, such as a mountain, hill, or forest), after having referenced or having quoted a manifestation of Messiah from . . .	. . . a prophet within this other Scriptural Temple from a previous record or dispensation, . . .	. . . which was accompanied by this manifestation of the Messiah within this other Scriptural Temple from a previous record or dispensation
Book of Mormon 2 Nephi 2: Lehi's climactic manifestation of the role of--and our need for--the Redeemer	Outside of the tent of Lehi (the tent serving perhaps as a type of tabernacle perhaps, where Lehi and his family earlier offered sacrifices and burnt offerings unto [the Lord]"(1Ne 7:22; 5:9)	Lehi had just listened to his son, Nephi, quoting liberally from the Brass Plates, especially from Isaiah (1 Ne. 19:22-24; 1 Ne. 20-21; 2 Ne. 1:1)	"I AM he; I AM the first, and I AM also the last. Mine hand hath also laid the foundation of the earth....Come ye near unto me" (1Ne. 20:12-13, 16; 21:7-16)

Chart 2.3.2: Temples within Temples within Temples

Book or temple of
Mormon

Within the book (or temple) of Mormon, the Prophet Nephi
makes the Messiah manifest in 2 Nephi 12–33 while located
(likely) in...

... the temple
built by Nephi

(2 Nephi 5:16) as he makes the Messiah manifest to us
through his own quoting and commentary from the

Scriptural
temple of Isaiah

... which acts as a scriptural temple within both the
temple of Nephi and the temple of Mormon—by making the Messiah manifest to Nephi, while located in...

A temple
within the book
of Isaiah (16:1)

as Isaiah begins his great manifestation of the
Messiah with his vision of a latter-day Temple,
and then enters another temple and sees the
Lord (Isaiah 12:2; 16:1)

APPENDIX B

Chart 2.4.1: Summary of (Scriptural and Physical) Temples for Chart 3 (now interlaced with the earlier manifestations from chart 2)

The Immediate or Primary Manifestation of the Messiah: Within the Book (or Temple) of Mormon		Earlier manifestations from the Plates of Nephi (what we now call parts of the Book of Mormon) now become the instrumental or referenced manifestations for the later or primary manifestations (in first column)—now assuming the former role that was served previously by the Brass Plates	... which Words and Manifestation occurred within this Actual Temple (or substitute temple, or envisioned temple of Isaiah).	... which was accompanied by this manifestation of the Messiah within this other Scriptural Temple from a Previous Record or Dispensation
The Lord's prophet within this Scriptural Temple made the Messiah Powerfully Manifest, and the Covenants Available	... while located within this Actual Temple (or substitute temple, such as a mountain, hill, or forest), after having referenced or having quoted a manifestation of Messiah from ...	... a prophet within this other Scriptural Temple from a previous record or Dispensation, ...		
Enos "Lord, how is it done?" "Because of thy faith in Christ [as manifested by the words of your father, in which you exercised faith], whom thou hast never before heard nor seen [physically]"	"In the forest" It appears that forests, like mountains, may be appropriated by the Lord for places of sacred manifestations or substitute temples, such as The Sacred Grove and Alma's refuge, "the forest of Mormon": "how beautiful are they to the eyes of them who there came to the knowledge of their Redeemer" (Mosiah 18:30)	The Words of Jacob: "The words [of] my father [Jacob] sunk deep into my heart" (i.e., Enos' received his manifestation of the Savior by exercising faith in the manifestations of the Savior he obtained from his father (which manifestations we know of as the Book of Jacob and the Books of Nephi—within in the Book of Mormon).	The Temple of Nephi (see entry above for Jacob (2 Ne. 9-10)	See 2 Nephi 9-10 (see entry above for Jacob in 2 Ne. 9-10)

Book of Mormon Alma the Elder Mosiah 18:1-2, 7-22, 30	"Forest of Mormon" (see entry above): "how beautiful are they to the eyes of them who there came to the knowledge of their Redeemer" (Mosiah 18:30)	"The Words of Abinadi—concerning ... the redemption of the people ... through the power, and sufferings, and death of Christ" (18:1-2)	The Temple of Nephi (Mosiah 11:10-11) (See entry above for Abinadi, Mosiah 15-16 above)	See Mosiah 15-16 (See entry above for Abinadi)
Alma the Elder Mosiah 26:14-33 (Although he was converted while listening to Abinadi, and though he baptized others in the Forest of Mormon, this is his great manifestation to us of the Messiah)	A Temple in Zarahemla? (It seems likely that Alma, the presiding high priest and President of the Church in all of the land of Zarahemla would go to one of the multiple temples in the land of Zarahemla to receive this important guidance and revelation from the Lord)	The Words of Abinadi ("Thou art blessed because of thy exceeding faith in the words alone of my servant Abinadi" (Mosiah 26:15)) "on what condition [is he] saved?" ... did not my father Alma believe in the words which were delivered by the mouth of Abinadi?" (Alma 5:10-11)	The Temple of Nephi now occupied by Noah and his priests (Mosiah 11:10-11) as they question Abinadi (See entry above for Abinadi)	See Mosiah 15-16 in the left column above for Abinadi

Book of Mormon Alma the Younger (Mosiah 27:24-31; Alma 36:12-21)	From the clouds ([the angel of the Lord "descended as it were in a cloud" Mosiah 27:11). Clouds are, of course, consistent places where the Lord manifests himself and his power (see Exodus 19:9, 16)	Words of Alma the Elder: "I remembered also to have heard my father prophecy (which prophecies we have recorded in the Book of Alma) unto the people concerning a Son of God, to atone for the sins of the world" (Alma 36:17). I.e., it was that which is contained in the Book of Mormon that manifested the Messiah so that he could then come unto Him and be saved.	Temple in Zarahemla? (See Entries above for Alma the Elder in Mosiah 26:14-33 above)	See Entries above for Alma the Elder in Mosiah 26:14-33 above
Alma the Younger (See especially Alma 5:21, 27, 34, 38, 48-58) to the people of Zarahemla	Temple of Zarahemla (Seems likely—since he spoke directly "to the people in the church which was established in the city of Zarahemla," and the pattern of gathering large groups to the temple when available had already been established (Jacob, Benjamin, Limhi Mosiah 7:17)	Emphasizes the words of Abinadi and their power to manifest the power of the Savior and bring about "a mighty change" (5:7-13); and "the words of our fathers," the truth of which were "manifest[ed]" unto him (5:21, 44, 47): the words of Lehi about the Tree of Life (5:33-34, 62), Nephi (5:13, 21, 34, 37, 53, 62), Jacob (5:25-26, 33-39, 50-52, 55), and Benjamin (5:18, 26, 38)	Abinadi delivered his manifestation from the Temple of Nephi (see See entry for Mosiah 15-16, above, col. 1) See temple locations for Lehi, Nephi, Jacob, and Benjamin above	See Mosiah 15-16 Above (column 2)—and associated entries See entries above for Lehi, Nephi, Jacob, and Benjamin

Alma the Younger (See especially Alma 7:7–27) to the people of the church which were established in the land of Gideon	Temple of Gideon? Since we know that there were multiple temples build up in the land of Zarahemla (See Alma 16:13), and that Gideon was such a well-established city, it seems likely that there was a temple here. This may or may not suggest why we hear of a "high priest" in Gideon (Alma 30:21).	See Footnotes that show that Alma was quoting liberally from the Brass Plates—especially Isaiah and Psalms—as well as the words of Abinadi and Benjamin	See entry for Abinadi and Benjamin above re: temple locations for the manifestations of the Savior given by Isaiah and Abinadi and Benjamin	See entry for Abinadi and Benjamin above
Alma the Younger and Amulek (Alma 9:26–28; 10:39–45; 12:22–35)	Temple or "sanctuary" of Ammoniah? (See Alma 16:13; 10:2: what temple was Amulek referring to here? Perhaps the temple of his home town of Ammoniah? Since its wickedness posed a great threat to the Nephites, it seems to have been an established city)	Words of Lehi and "the fathers" (see Alma 9:8–17), and of an angel (9:25, 29)	See entry for 2 Nephi 2 above	See entry for 2 Nephi 2 above

Chart 2.5.1: Possible Responses to Chart 3

The Immediate or Primary Place of Manifestation of the Messiah: Within the Book (or Temple) of Mormon	... while located within this Actual Temple (or substitute temple), after having referenced or having quoted a manifestation of Messiah from ...	The Referenced or Secondary Place or Manifestation of the Messiah: ... this prophet (or some other divine messenger) within ...	... this other Scriptural—or extra-scriptural—temple
The Lord's prophet within this Scriptural Temple made the Messiah Powerfully Manifest, and the Covenants Available ...			
Book of Mormon Nephi (1Ne 11-12)	"an exceedingly high mountain" (11:1)	Words delivered by an angel from the presence of God (although we learn that Nephi's faith was in direct response to his acceptance of the words of his father: 1 Ne.10:17; 11:4-5)	The actual dwelling of the Lord in the heavens

Book of Mormon King Benjamin (Mosiah 3)	Temple of Zarahemla	Words delivered directly by an angel from the presence of God (Mos. 3:2) (although we learn that before he gives his great manifestation of the Messiah, Benjamin has spent time teaching his sons from "the records which were engraven on the plates of brass" and greatly emphasizes the importance of studying and heeding the words of both the previous Book of Mormon prophets as well as the Brass Plate prophets (see Mosiah 1:3-7; 2:34-41)	The actual dwelling of the Lord in the heavens
Book of Mormon Samuel (Hel 13-15)	From the high walls of the city	Words delivered directly by an angel from the presence of God and as spoken into his heart (Hel. 13:3-5, 7)	The actual dwelling of the Lord in the heavens
Book of Mormon 3 Nephi 9-30	Temple of Bountiful	Delivered by Savior himself, though he also quotes much from the prophets of the Brass Plates (3 Ne 11:10; 15:3-10; Chptrs. 16, 22-25)	The Savior's physical presence
Brother of Jared (Ether 2-4)	Mountain of "exceeding height" (Ether 3:1)	Appearance by Savior himself	The Savior's physical presence

Chart 2.5.2: Final Chart: Summary of Charts 1–3

	The Immediate or Primary Manifestation of the Messiah: Within the Book (or Temple) of Mormon		The Referenced or Secondary (or instrumental) Manifestation of Messiah: Within the Brass Plates (or much of what is contained within our Old Testament)		
	The Lord's prophet within this Scriptural Temple made the Messiah Powerfully Manifest, and the Covenants Available …	… while located within this Actual Temple (or substitute temple, such as a mountain, hill, or forest), after having referenced or having quoted a manifestation of Messiah from …	… a prophet within this other Scriptural Temple from a previous record or Dispensation, …	… which Words and Manifestation occurred within this Actual Temple (or substitute temple, or envisioned temple of Isaiah).	… which was accompanied by this manifestation of the Messiah within this other Scriptural Temple from a Previous Record or Dispensation
2 Nephi 25–33:	Temple Built by Nephi	The Book of Isaiah,	2 Ne. 12:1–3; Isaiah 2;	Isaiah's vision
2 Ne 9–10:	Temple Built by Nephi	The Book of Isaiah,	"standard"	"Isaiah speaks Messianically"
Mosiah 15–16:	Temple Built by Nephi,	The Book of Isaiah,	Latter-day Temple seen in vision by Isaiah	Perhaps the greatest Messianic manifestation of the Old Testament:
Alma 33: 12–23; 34:8–16; 30–37:	"Upon the hill Onidah": 32:4	The words of Zenos, Zenock, and Moses,	The brass serpent raised up by Moses was an explicit type of Christ	The words of Zenos, Zenock, and Moses (see Alma 33:12–14; 34:6–7)
(Helaman 8:13–24):	Nephi's garden tower	The words of Moses	The brass serpent raised up by Moses (8:14–15)	The words of Zenos, Zenock, and Moses

2 Nephi 2:	The tent of Lehi	Brass Plates	"…, my standard"	"I AM he; I AM the first, and … the last."
The Immediate or Primary Manifestation of the Messiah: Within the Book (or Temple) of Mormon		Earlier manifestations from the Plates of Nephi (what we now call parts of the Book of Mormon) now become the instrumental or referenced manifestations for the later or primary manifestations (in first column)—now assuming the former role that was served previously by the Brass Plates		
Enos	"In the forest"	The Words of Jacob:	The Temple of Nephi	See 2 Nephi 9-10
Alma the Elder	"Forest of Mormon"	"The Words of Abinadi—	The Temple of Nephi	See Mosiah 15-16
Alma the Elder	A Temple in Zarahemla?	The Words of Abinadi	The Temple of Nephi	See Mosiah 15-16
Alma the Younger	From the clouds	Words of Alma the Elder:	Temple in Zarahemla?	See Mosiah 26:14-33 above
Alma the Younger	Temple of Zarahemla?	Emphasizes the words of Abinadi	from the Temple of Nephi	See Mosiah 15-16
Alma the Younger	Temple of Gideon?	Isaiah and Psalms—as well as the Abinadi & Benjamin	See entry for Abinadi and Benjamin above	See entry for Abinadi and Benjamin above
Alma the Younger and Amulek	Temple or "sanctuary" of Ammoniah?	Words of Lehi and "the fathers" (see Alma 9:8-17), and of an angel (9:25, 29)	See entry for 2 Nephi 2 above	See entry for 2 Nephi 2 above

	The Immediate or Primary Place of Manifestation of the Messiah: Within the Book (or Temple) of Mormon	The Referenced or Secondary Place or Manifestation of the Messiah: God's Throne	
Book of Mormon Nephi (1Ne 11-14)	High Mountain	Words delivered by an angel from God's presence (after hearing Lehi's words)	The actual dwelling of the Lord in the heavens
Book of Mormon King Benjamin (Mosiah 3)	Temple of Zarahemla	Words delivered directly by an angel from the presence of God (as well as having read and taught from Brass Plates and Plates of Nephi)	The actual dwelling of the Lord in the heavens
Book of Mormon Samuel the Lamanite (Hel 13-15)	From the walls of the city	Words delivered directly by an angel from the presence of God	The actual dwelling of the Lord in the heavens
Book of Mormon 3 Nephi 9-30	Temple of Bountiful	Delivered by Savior himself, while also pointing us to previous manifestations of his atoning mission as given by "Brass Plate" prophets	The Savior's physical presence
Brother of Jared (Ether 2-4)	Mountain	By Savior himself	Savior's Personal Pre-Mortal Presence

Chart 2.6.1

The Lord's prophet within this Scriptural Temple made the Messiah Powerfully Manifest	Statement of PURPOSE/ Call to Repentance	Statement of Priesthood Authority	Bearing of a Personal Witness	INVITATION to follow Christ	Statement of CONSEQUENCE/ JUDGMENT of accepting or reject. message
2 Nephi 25-30: Nephi's manifestation of the Messiah,					
2 Ne 9-10: Jacob's manifestation of the Messiah,					
Mosiah 15-16: Abinadi's powerful manifestation of the Messiah					
Alma 33: 22-23; 34:8-16; 30-37: Alma and Amulek testify to Zoramites of the Atonement					

The Lord's prophet within this Scriptural Temple made the Messiah Powerfully Manifest	Statement of PURPOSE/ Call to Repentance	Statement of Priesthood Authority	Bearing of a Personal Witness	INVITATION to follow Christ	Statement of CONSEQUENCE/ JUDGMENT of accepting or reject. message
Book of Mormon (Helaman 8:13–24): Nephi testifies to his people					
2 Ne. 2: Lehi's manifestation of the Redeemer					
Enos					
Alma the Elder: at the Waters of Mormon Mosiah 18:1-2, 7-22, 30					
Alma the Elder: as Judge Mosiah 26:14-33					

The Lord's prophet within this Scriptural Temple made the Messiah Powerfully Manifest	Statement of PURPOSE/ Call to Repentance	Statement of Priesthood Authority	Bearing of a Personal Witness	INVITATION to follow Christ	Statement of CONSEQUENCE/ JUDGMENT of accepting or reject. message
Alma the Younger: to his son, Helaman (Mosiah 27:24-31; Alma 36:12-21)					
Alma the Younger to Zarahemla (See Alma 5:21, 27, 34, 38, 48-58)					
Alma the Younger to the people of Gideon (See especially Alma 7:7-27)					
Alma the Younger and Amulek (Alma 9:26-28; 10:39-45; 12:22-35)					

The Lord's prophet within this Scriptural Temple made the Messiah Powerfully Manifest	Statement of PURPOSE/ Call to Repentance	Statement of Priesthood Authority	Bearing of a Personal Witness	INVITATION to follow Christ	Statement of CONSEQUENCE/ JUDGMENT of accepting or reject. message
Nephi (1Ne 11-14)					
King Benjamin (Mosiah 3)					
Samuel the Lamanite (Hel 13-15)					
3 Nephi 9-30					
Brother of Jared (Ether 2-4)					

Chart 2.6.2: Possible Responses to Chaart 2.6.1

	Statement of PURPOSE/ Call to Repentance	Statement of Priesthood Authority	Bearing of a Personal Witness	INVITATION to follow Christ	Statement of CONSEQUENCE/ JUDGMENT of accepting or reject. message
2 Nephi 25-30: Nephi's manifestation of the Messiah,	2 N 11:3-7; 25:8 25:3, 16-18, 21, 23, 26-27; 30:4-8; 31:17	2 N 11:3; 25:11, 28; 28:1; 33:4-5, 10-15	1 Ne. 14:30; 2 N 11:3; 25:20; 31:16, 31; 33:4-5, 10	2 N 25:29; 26:13, 33; 28:32; 30:2; 31:5, 10-11-13; 32:3-4, 9	2 N 25:18, 22, 28 26:8 (8-11); 28:16, 26-32; 31:14; 33:2, 9, 11, 14-15
2 Ne 9-10: Jacob's manifestation of the Messiah,	2 N6:4; 9:1, 3	2N6:2; 9:40,48	2 N9:40	2 N9:41, 45-46, 50-51; 10:23-25	2 N 9:14-18; 31-32, 42-44, 46; 10:23-25
Mosiah 15-16: Abinadi's powerful manifestation of the Messiah	Mos. 11:20; 12:1; 13:4, 11	Mos. 11:20; 12:1; 13:4,6,26	Mos.12:30;	Mos. 11:21, 23, 25; 15:11-12,22, 28-31	Mos. 11:21-23; 15:11-12.21-27; 16:5-6, 10-13
Alma 33:22-23; 34:8-16; 30-37: Alma and Amulek testify to Zoramites of the Atonement	Alma 31:34-35	Alma 31:26, 36	Alma 34:8,30	Alma 31:34; 32:15-16, 23, 40; 33:22-23; 34:17-18, 27, 30-33, 37-8	Alma 32:15-16, 40-42; 34:16, 33-36, 39

The Lord's prophet within this Scriptural Temple made the Messiah Powerfully Manifest	Statement of PURPOSE/ Call to Repentance	Statement of Priesthood Authority	Bearing of a Personal Witness	INVITATION to follow Christ	Statement of CONSEQUENCE/ JUDGMENT of accepting or reject. message
Book of Mormon (Helaman 8:13-24): Nephi testifies to his people	Hel. 7:15, 17-18	Hel. 7:29; 8:12-13; 9:36; 10:4-7, 16	Hel. 7:29; 8:24	Hel. 7:17	Hel. 8:25; 10:11
2 Ne. 2: Lehi's manifestation of the Redeemer	2 N 1:13, 16; 2:3-8, 30	2 N 1:6, 15	2 N 1:4	2 N 1:21, 23; 2:28	2 N 2:28-29
Enos	Enos 1:2, 13	Jacob 7:27; Enos 1:5, 18, 26	Enos 1:6	Enos 1:13	Enos 1:10
Alma the Elder: at the Waters of Mormon Mosiah 18:1-2, 7-22, 30	Mos. 18:2, 7	Mos. 18:12-13, 18, 29	Mos. 23:9-10	Mos. 18:8-11	Mos. 18:30; 26:16, 18
Alma the Elder: as Judge Mosiah 26:14-33	Mos. 26:33	Mos. 26:20	Mos. 23:9-10	Mos. 26:21-22	Mos. 26:22, 28

The Lord's prophet within this Scriptural Temple made the Messiah Powerfully Manifest	Statement of PURPOSE/ Call to Repentance	Statement of Priesthood Authority	Bearing of a Personal Witness	INVITATION to follow Christ	Statement of CONSEQUENCE/ JUDGMENT of accepting or reject. message
Alma the Younger: to his son, Helaman (Mosiah 27:24-31; Alma 36:12-21)	Alma 36:24, 26; 37:32-33	Alma 36:26 (See also: Alma 5:3,43-4; 8:4,23-4	Alma 36:4-5, 28; (See also: 5:45-48)	Mosiah 27:25; Alma 36:24, 26; 37:9-10, 19	Alma 36:30 (See also: Mos. 27:31, 25-26)
Alma the Younger to Zarahemla (See Alma 5:21, 27, 34, 38, 48-58)	Alma 5:19-20, 40	Alma 5:3, 43-44, 49 (See also Alma 8:4, 23-4)	Alma 5:45-48	Alma 5:33-35, 38, 50, 57, 60-62	Alma 5:36-37, 39,51-53,56,58; Alma 6:2-3
Alma the Younger to the people of Gideon (See especially Alma 7:7-27)	Alma 7:22	Alma 7:26 (See Alma 8:4,23-24)	Alma 7:13,8,5	Alma 7:9, 14-15	Alma 7:16, 21
Alma the Younger and Amulek (Alma 9:26-28; 10:39-45; 12:22-35)	Alma 8:16; 9:25	Alma 8:4,23-25, 30-32; 9: 1; 10:7, 9	Alma 10:10	Alma 9:27-30; 12:21-22, 27, 30	Alma 9:28; 12:10-11, 14-18, 33-37

The Lord's prophet within this Scriptural Temple made the Messiah Powerfully Manifest	Statement of PURPOSE/ Call to Repentance	Statement of Priesthood Authority	Bearing of a Personal Witness	INVITATION to follow Christ	Statement of CONSEQUENCE/ JUDGMENT of accepting or reject. message
Nephi (1 Ne 11-14)	1 N 6:4	1 N 9:3, 5; 10:22; 11:1	1 N 14:29-30	1 N 15:14-15, 25	1 N 15:24, 30-36
King Benjamin (Mosiah 3)	Mos. 3:4	Mos. 3:2	Mos. 3:23; 5:2	Mos. 3:13	Mos. 3:18, 22, 24-27
Samuel the Lamanite (Hel 13-15)	Hel.13:2; 14:11-12	Hel. 13:3, 5; 14:9-10	14:10, 26	Hel. 13:13; 14:8, 13, 21, 31	Hel. 14:16-19, 29
3 Nephi 9-30					
Brother of Jared (Ether 2-4)	Ether 4:4, 7; 5:6	Ether 3:22, 27; 4:5, 10	Ether 3:2, 4-5, 12	Ether 2:14; 4:13-15, 18	Ether 4:8, 11, 18-19; 5:4-5

Chart 2.6.3

The Lord's prophet within this Scriptural Temple made the Messiah Powerfully Manifest	Manifestations and Covenants How does each manifestation of the Messiah below also include invitations and exhortations to keep covenants of Obedience, Sacrifice, and Consecration?

2 Nephi 25-33: Nephi's manifestation of the Messiah,

Obedience:

"There is none other name given under heaven save it be this Jesus Christ, of which I [Nephi] have spoken, whereby man can be saved. Wherefore, for this cause hath the Lord God promised unto me that these things which I write shall be kept and preserved" (2 Nephi 25:20-21); see also 2 Nephi 25:26

And now ... hearken unto these words and believe in Christ ... And if ye shall believe in Christ ye will believe in these words, for they are the words of Christ, and he hath given them unto me"; "And you that will not partake of the goodness of God, and respect ... my words ... I bid you and everlasting farewell" (2 Nephi 33:10, 14)

(See also: 2 Ne. 28:26; 30:3, 5, 6; 31:12; 31:17-18

Sacrifice:

Counter-Doctrine: "And there shall be many which shall say: Eat, drink, and be merry, for tomorrow we die; and it shall be well with us" 2 Nephi 28:7

"O the wise, and the learned, and the rich, that are puffed up in the pride of their hearts, and all those who preach false doctrines, and all those who commit whoredoms ... wo unto them" (2 Nephi 28:15)

See also: 2 Nephi 31:13, 16

Consecration:

"Ye must pray always and not faint ... ye must not perform any thing unto the Lord save in the first place ye shall pray unto the Father in the name of Christ, that he will consecrate thy performance unto thee" (32:9)

"Ye must press forward with a steadfastness in Christ. ... having a love of God and of all men" ... "relying wholly upon the merits of him who is might to save" (2 Nephi 31:20, 19)

See also: 2 Ne. 32:1

The Lord's prophet within this Scriptural Temple made the Messiah Powerfully Manifest	Manifestations and Covenants How does each manifestation of the Messiah below also include invitations and exhortations to keep covenants of Obedience, Sacrifice, and Consecration?

2 Nephi 9-10: Jacob's manifestation of the Messiah,

"How great the covenants of the Lord" (2 Nephi 9:53; 10:15, 17)

Obedience:
"O, my beloved brethren, give ear to my words ... Do not say that I have spoken hard things against you; for if ye do, ye will revile against the truth; for I have spoken the words of your Maker (2 Nephi 9:40, 44, 48);
"Hearken diligently unto me, and remember the words which I have spoken; and come unto the Holy One of Israel" (2 Nephi 9:50)
See also: 2 Ne. 9:23

Sacrifice:
"wo unto the rich, who are rich as to things of the world [and] despise the poor, and they persecute the meek, and their hearts are upon their treasures; wherefore their treasure is their god" "and they ... who are puffed up ... they are they whom he despiseth; and save they shall cast these things away, and consider themselves fools before God, and come down into the depths of humility, he will not open unto them" for "To be carnally-minded is death, and to be spiritually-minded is life eternal" (2 Ne. 9:30, 42, 39)
"Wherefore ... reconcile yourselves to the will of God, and not to the will of the devil and the flesh" (2 Nephi 10:24)

Consecration
"Remember the greatness of the Holy One of Israel" (2 Nephi 9:40, 10, 13, 19-20);
"remember the words of your God; pray unto him continually by day, and give thanks unto his holy name by night" (9:52);
See also: 2 Nephi 10:24

The Lord's prophet within this Scriptural Temple made the Messiah Powerfully Manifest	Manifestations and Covenants How does each manifestation of the Messiah below also include invitations and exhortations to keep covenants of Obedience, Sacrifice, and Consecration?

Mosiah 15-18 & 26: Abinadi's powerful manifestation of the Messiah— and Alma's response

Obedience

"Who shall be his seed. . . . whosoever has heard the words of the prophets, yea all the holy prophets who have prophesied concerning the coming of the Lord—I say unto you, that all those who have hearkened to their words, and believed that the Lord would redeem his people" (Mosiah 15:10-11); See also: 15: 28-30; 17:9-10; "Who is Abinadi, that I and my people should be judged of him" (Mosiah 11:27)

"Blessed art thou, Alma, and blessed are they who were baptized in the waters of Mormon. Thou art blessed because of thy exceeding faith in the words alone of my servant Abinadi. And blessed are they because of their exceeding faith in the words alone which thou hast spoken unto them" Mosiah 26:15-16

See also: Mosiah 13:4; 18:4, 6, 7, 10; 17:2, 4, 18:1; 18:10

Sacrifice:

"Willing to bear one another's burdens.... And are willing to mourn with those that mourn; yea, and comfort those that stand in need of comfort, and to stand as a witness of God at all times and in all things, and in all places ye may be in, even until death" (18:11)

"they should impart of their substance.... of their own free will and good desires toward God ... unto every needy, naked soul" (Mosiah 18:28)

Consecration:

"I will not recall the words which I have spoken ... for they are true; and that ye may know of their surety I have suffered myself that I have fallen into your hands. Yea, and I will suffer even unto death, and I will not recall my words" (Mosiah 17:9-10)

"And he commanded them that they should observe the Sabbath day, and keep it holy, and also every day they should give thanks to the Lord their God" (Mosiah 18:23)

See also: Mosiah 18:18-22, 26

The Lord's prophet within this Scriptural Temple made the Messiah Powerfully Manifest	Manifestations and Covenants How does each manifestation of the Messiah below also include invitations and exhortations to keep covenants of Obedience, Sacrifice, and Consecration?

Alma 31-34: Alma and Amulek testify to Zoramites of the Atonement

Obedience:
"And ye also behold that my brother has proved unto you, in many instances, that the word is in Christ unto salvation" (Alma 34:6-8)
"But, behold, if ye will awake and arouse your faculties, even to an experiment upon my words..." (Alma 33:27)
See also: Alma 33:14; 34:30; 34:38

Sacrifice:
Lack of: "Behold, O my God, their costly apparel, and their ringlets, and their bracelets, and their ornaments of gold, and all their precious things which they are ornamented with; and behold, their hearts are set upon them, and yet they cry unto thee and say—We thank thee, O God, for we are a chosen people unto thee, while others shall perish" (Alma 31:28)
"If ye turn away the needy... and impart not of your substance ... behold, your prayer is in vain" (Alma 34:28-29)

Consecration:
"... that ye may humble yourselves even to the dust, and worship God, in whatsoever place ye may be in, in spirit and truth; and live in thanksgiving daily, for the many mercies and blessings which he doth bestow upon you. Yea, and I also exhort you, my brethren, that ye be watchful unto prayer continually (Alma 34:38-39)
"let your hearts be full, drawn out in prayer unto him continually for your welfare, and also for the welfare of those who are around you" (Alma 34:27)
See also: Alma 31:30, 34-35, 38

The Lord's prophet within this Scriptural Temple made the Messiah Powerfully Manifest	Manifestations and Covenants How does each manifestation of the Messiah below also include invitations and exhortations to keep covenants of Obedience, Sacrifice, and Consecration?

(Helaman 8:13-24): Nephi testifies to his people

These people had received "great knowledge" already (7:24):—and were rebelling against it. Therefore, Nephi condemns them for forsaking their covenants of Obedience, Sacrifice, and Consecration. So here we will find examples of anti-covenant keeping, or anti-obedience, anti-sacrifice, and anti-consecration

(Lack of —or opposite of) Obedience (to the Savior as he is made manifest by the prophets and the scriptures)

"Have ye not read that God gave power to one man; even Moses.... And now behold, if God gave unto this man such power, then why should ye dispute among yourselves, and say that he hath given unto me no power.... But, behold, ye not only deny my words, but ye also deny all the words which have been spoken by our fathers, and also the words which were spoken by this man, Moses ... yea, the words which he hath spoken concerning the coming of the Messiah.... But behold, ye have rejected the truth, and rebelled against your holy God" (Helaman 8:11-13, 25)

They have also denied the words of Abraham, Zenos, Zenock, Ezias, Isaiah, Jeremiah, Lehi, and Nephi (8:18-22); see also Helaman 10:15; 11:16, 18

(Lack of—or opposite of) Sacrifice:

"But behold [the reason for your wickedness] is to get gain, to be praised of men, yea, and that ye might get gold and silver. And ye have set your heart upon riches and the vain things of the world" (7:21)

"Yea, wo shall come upon you because of that great pride [the opposite of self-sacrifice] which ye have suffered to enter your hearts, which has lifted you up beyond that which is good because of your exceedingly great riches!" (7:26)

(Lack of—or opposite of) Consecration:

"O, How could you have forgotten your God in the very day that he has delivered you?" (7:20)

"Yea, at the very time when he doth prosper his people.... Yea, then is the time that they do harden their hearts, and do forget the Lord their God, and do trample under their feet the Holy One" (Helaman 12:2)

One of the greatest statements of anti-consecration, the opposite of grati-tude and humble reliance on the Lord and prayerful supplication for his grace:

"How quick to hearken unto the words of the evil one, and to set their hearts upon the vain things of the world! Yea, how quick to be lifted up in pride; yea, how quick to boast ... and how slow to remember the Lord their God, and give ear to his counsels.... Behold, they do not desire that the Lord their God, who hath created them, should rule and reign over them; notwithstanding his great goodness and his mercy towards them ... they will not that he should be their guide" (12:4-5)

And all those anti-covenant behaviors are in stark contrast to Nephi's definitive example of obedience, sacrifice, and consecration:

"Blessed art thou, Nephi, for those things which thou hast done; for I have beheld how thou hast with unwearyingness declared the word.... And thou hast not feared them, and hast not sought thine own life, but hast sought my will, and to keep my commandments" (Helaman 10:4)

The Lord's prophet within this Scriptural Temple made the Messiah Powerfully Manifest	Manifestations and Covenants How does each manifestation of the Messiah below also include invitations and exhortations to keep covenants of Obedience, Sacrifice, and Consecration?
Enos Obedience (to the words of a prophet—his father) "and the words which I had often heard my father speak concerning eternal life, and the joy of the saints, sunk deep into my heart" Sacrifice (Forgetting of self in service of others) "Now, it came to pass that when I had heard these words [his personal forgiveness] I began to feel a desire for the welfare of my brethren, the Nephites.... My faith became unshaken in the Lord; and I prayed unto him with many long stugglings for my brethren" (1:9, 11) Consecration "And I have declared it in all my days, and have rejoiced in it above that of the world" (1:26)	

The Lord's prophet within this Scriptural Temple made the Messiah Powerfully Manifest	Manifestations and Covenants How does each manifestation of the Messiah below also include invitations and exhortations to keep covenants of Obedience, Sacrifice, and Consecration?

Alma the Younger: to his son, Helaman (Mosiah 27:24-31; Alma 36:12-21)

Obedience (to manifestations and witnesses of Christ via the words of the prophets and scriptures)

His previous lack of obedience to the prophets is contrasted with his later faith in the words of his father:

"I rejected my Redeemer, and denied that which had been spoken by our fathers" (Mosiah 27:30)

Vs.

"I remembered also to have heard my father prophesy unto the people concerning the coming of one Jesus Christ, a Son of God, to atone for the sins of the world [and with faith on those words of my father], I cried within my heart: O Jesus, thou Son of God, have mercy on me" (Alma 36:17-18)

Sacrifice and Consecration

"Marvel not that all mankind, yea, men and women, all nations, kindreds, tongues and people, must be born again; yea, born of God, changed from their carnal and fallen state, to a state of righteousness, being redeemed of God, becoming his sons and daughters; and thus they become new creatures" (Mosiah 27:25)

"Yea, and from that time even until now, I have labored without ceasing, that I might bring souls unto repentance; that I might bring them to taste of the exceeding joy of which I did taste; that they might also be born of God, and be filled with the Holy Ghost" (Alma 36:24)

"And now it came to pass that Alma [and the sons of Mosiah] began from this time forward to teach the people ... preaching the word of God in much tribulation, being greatly persecuted by those who were unbelievers, being smitten by many of them" (Mosiah 27:32)

The Lord's prophet within this Scriptural Temple made the Messiah Powerfully Manifest	Manifestations and Covenants How does each manifestation of the Messiah below also include invitations and exhortations to keep covenants of Obedience, Sacrifice, and Consecration?

Alma 5:21, 27, 34, 38, 48-58: Alma the Younger to Zarahemla

Obedience
"Behold, he changed their hearts; yea, he awakened them out of a deep sleep, and they awoke unto God.... And now I ask of you on what condition are they saved? Yea, what grounds had they to hope for salvation? .... Behold, I can tell you—did not my father Alma Believe in the words which were delivered by the mouth of Abinadi? And was he not a holy prophet" Did he not speak the words of God, and my father Alma believe them? And according to his faith [in those words of a Book of Mormon prophet, words which we have preserved and can likewise read] there was a might change wrought in his heart.... And behold, he preached the word unto your fathers, and a might change was also wrought in their hearts, and they humbled themselves and put their trust in the true and living God" (Alma 5:7, 10-13)

"And now I, Alma, do command you in the language of him who hath commanded me, that ye observe ot do the words which I have spoken unto you" (Alma 5: 61)

See also: Alma 5, 43-44, 45-52

Sacrifice
"Are ye stripped of pride.... of envy.... Is there one among you that doth make a mock of his brother, or that heapeth upon him persecutions?" (Alma 5:28-30)

"Can ye be puffed up in the pride of your hearts; yea, will he still persist in the wearing of costly apparel and setting your hearts upon the vain things of the world, upon your riches? Will ye persist in supposing that ye are better one than another.... And will you persist in turning your backs on the poor, and the needy, and in withholding your substance from them? (Alma 5:53-55)

See also: Alma 5:57

Consecration

The Lord's prophet within this Scriptural Temple made the Messiah Powerfully Manifest	Manifestations and Covenants How does each manifestation of the Messiah below also include invitations and exhortations to keep covenants of Obedience, Sacrifice, and Consecration?

Alma 7:7-27: Alma the Younger to the people of Gideon

Obedience
"And now my beloved brethren, I have spoken these words unto you according to the Spirit which testifieth in me; and my soul doth exceedingly rejoice, because of the exceeding diligence and heed which ye have given unto my word. And now, may the peace of God rest upon you ... " (Alma 7:26-27)

Sacrifice
"I trust that ye are not lifted up in the pride of your hearts; yea, I trust that ye have not set your hearts upon the riches and the vain things of the world; yea, I trust that you do not worship idols, but that ye do worship the true and living God, and ye look forward for the remission of your sins, with an everlasting faith, which is to come" (Alma 7:6)

Consecration
"And I would that ye should be humble, and be submissive and gentle; easy to be entreated; full of patience and long-suffering; being temperate in all things; being diligent in keeping the commandments of God at all times; asking for whatsoever things ye stand in need, both spiritual and temporal; always returning thanks unto God for whatsoever ye do receive" (Alma 7:23)

The Lord's prophet within this Scriptural Temple made the Messiah Powerfully Manifest	Manifestations and Covenants How does each manifestation of the Messiah below also include invitations and exhortations to keep covenants of Obedience, Sacrifice, and Consecration?
Mosiah 3-4: King Benjamin **Obedience** "The Spirit of the Lord came upon them ... because of the exceeding faith which they had in Jesus Christ who should come, according to the words which kind Benjamin had spoken unto them" (Mosiah 4:3) "Yea, we believe all the words which thou hast spoken unto us; and also, we know of their surety and truth, because of the Spirit of the Lord Omnipotent, which has wrought a might change in us. . . . And it is the faith which we have had on the things which our king has spoken unto us that has brought us to this great knowledge, whereby we do rejoice with such exceedingly great joy. And we are willing to enter into a covenant with our God to do his will, and to be obedient to his commandments" (Mosiah 5:1-5) See also: Mosiah 5:7-8 **Sacrifice** "And they had viewed themselves in their own carnal state, even less than the dust of the earth" (Mosiah 4:2) "And also, ye yourselves will succor those that stand in need of succor; ye will administer your substance unto him that standeth in need ... for are we not all beggars?" (Mosiah 4:16, 19; see also 4:20-26)	

Consecration

"I would that ye should remember, and always retain in remembrance, the greatness of God, and your own nothingness, and his goodness and long-suffering towards you, unworthy creatures, and humble yourselves even in the depth of humility, calling on the name of the Lord daily, and standing steadfastly in the faith of that which is to come, which was spoken by the mouth of an angel.

And behold, I say unto you that if ye do this, ye shall always rejoice, and be filled with the love of God, and always retain a remission of your sins; and ye shall grow in the knowledge of him that crated you, or in the knowledge of that which is just and true. (Mosiah 4:11-12)

And ye will not have a mind to injure one another, but to live peaceably,,,, And ye will not suffer your children that they go hungry or naked; neither will ye suffer that they transgress the laws of God, and fight and quarrel one with another.... But ye will teach them to walk in the ways of truth and soberness; ye will teach them to love one another, and to serve one another" (Mosiah 4:13-15)

The Lord's prophet within this Scriptural Temple made the Messiah Powerfully Manifest	Manifestations and Covenants How does each manifestation of the Messiah below also include invitations and exhortations to keep covenants of Obedience, Sacrifice, and Consecration?
Ether 2-4: Mahonri	

Obedience

"He that believeth not my words believeth not my disciples; and if so be that I do not speak, judge ye; for ye shall know that it is I that speaketh, at the last day. But he that believeth these things which I have spoken [through my disciples], him will I visit with the manifestations of my Spirit, and he shall know and bear record.... He that will not believe my words [as spoken by my servants the prophets in these scriptures you are now reading] will not believe me—that I am" (Ether 4:10-12)

"Therefore, when ye shall receive this record ye may know that the work of the Father has commenced upon all the face of the land. Therefore, repent all ye ends of the earth, and come unto me, and believe in my gospel, and be baptized in my name" (Ether 4:17-18)

See also: Ether 4:8

Sacrifice

"Behold, when ye shall rend that veil of unbelief which doth cause you to remain in your awful state of wickedness, and hardness of heart, and blindness of mind ... yea, when ye shall call upon the Father in my name, with a broken heart and a contrite spirit, then shall ye know that the Father hath remembered the covenant which he made unto your fathers, O house of Israel" (Ether 4:15)

Consecration

"O, Lord ... do not be angry with thy servant because of his weakness before thee; for we know that thou art holy and dwellest in the heavens, and that we are unworthy creatures before thee; because of the fall our natures have become evil continually; nevertheless, O Lord, thou hast given us a commandment that we must call upon thee.... O Lord, look down upon me in pity, and turn away thine anger from this thy people.... And I know, O Lord, that thou hast all power, and can do whatsoever thou wilt for the benefit of man" (Eth. 3:2-4)

"And in that day that they shall exercise faith in my, saith the Lord, even as the brother of Jared did, that they may become sanctified in me, then will I manifest unto them the things which the brother of Jared saw, even to the unfolding unto them all my revelations, saith Jesus Christ, the Son of God" (Ether 4:7)

The Lord's prophet within this Scriptural Temple made the Messiah Powerfully Manifest	Manifestations and Covenants How does each manifestation of the Messiah below also include invitations and exhortations to keep covenants of Obedience, Sacrifice, and Consecration?

Helaman 13-15: Samuel the Lamanite

Obedience
Lack of: "Wo unto this people...you do cast out the prophets, and do mock them, and cast stones at them, and do slay them, and do all manner of iniquity unto them" (Helaman 13:24)

"And now, it came to pass that there were many who heard the words of Samuel, the Lamanite, which he spake upon the walls of the city. And as many as believed on his word went forth and sought for Nephi; and when they had come forth and found him they confessed unto him their sins and denied not, desiring that they might be baptized unto the Lord" (Helaman 16:1)

See also: Helaman 13:39

Sacrifice
Lack of: "for behold, he saith that ye are cursed because of your riches, and also are your riches cursed because ye have set your hearts upon them, and have not hearkened unto the words of him who gave them unto you. Ye do not remember the Lord your God in the things with which he hath blessed you, but ye do always remember your riches, not to thank the Lord your God for them; yea, your hearts are not drawn out unto the Lord, but they do swell with great pride, unto boasting, and unto great swelling, envyings, strifes, malice, persecutions, and murders, and all manner of iniquities" (Helaman 13:21-22)

Consecration
"And now, because I am a Lamanite, and have spoken unto you the words which the Lord hath commanded me, and because it was hard against you, ye are angry with me and do seek to destroy me, and have cast me out from among you. And ye shall hear my words, for, for this intent have I come up upon the walls of this city, that ye might hear and know of the judgments of God which do await you because of your iniquities, and also that ye might know the conditions of repentance; And also that ye might know of the coming of Jesus Christ, the Son of God, the Father of heaven and of earth, the Creator of all things from the beginning; and that ye might know of the signs of his coming, to the intent that ye might believe on his name." (Helaman 14:10-12)

Chart 2.7.1: Summary Chart 2

	This great Manifestation of the Messiah was made in the Temple known as the New Testament (or the temples of Matthew, Mark, Luke, and John) . . .	. . . while located within this Actual Temple (or substitute temple, such as a mountain or hill) . . .
Luke 1:8-9, 16 John's mission to manifest the Messiah & his mission revealed	"And many of the children of Israel shall he turn to the Lord their God" 1:16	"he went in unto the temple of the Lord" Luke 1:8-9
Luke 1: 68, 70, 72-73, 76 At John's circumcision Zacharias prophecies of his mission as Elias	Blessed be the Lord God of Israel; for he hath visited and redeemed his people. . . . As he spake by the mouth of all the holy prophets. . . . To perform the mercy promised to our fathers, and to remember his holy covenant; the oath which he sware to our father Abraham. . .	"Hill Country of Judea" Luke 1:39 The home of John's parents
Luke 1:39-55 Mary visits Elisabeth and both receive revelation of Jesus's messianic mission	"his mercy is on them that fear him from generation to generation" 1:50. He hath holpen his servant Israel, in remembrance of his mercy; As he spake to our fathers, to Abraham, and to his seed for ever" 1:54-55	"Hill Country of Judea" Luke 1:39 Quotes from Psalms and Isaiah (see footnotes)
Luke 2:4, 6-18 Manifestation of Birth of Messiah to Shepherds at Bethlehem	"unto you is born this day . . . a Savior, which is Christ the Lord" 2:11	The heights of Bethlehem (That happens to be perched in the Judean hills, rising just above Jerusalem)

Luke 2:27-32: Simeon testifies of the Messiah's mission	Lord, now lettest thou thy servant depart in peace, according to thy word: For mine eyes have seen thy salvation, Which thou hast prepared before the face of all people; A light to lighten the Gentiles and the glory of thy people Israel (Lk. 2:27-32).	"And he came by the Spirit into the temple"/ Quotes from Psalms and Isaiah (see footnotes)
Luke 2:36-38): Anna testifies of the Messiah	"spake of him to all them that looked for redemption in Jerusalem" (Luke 2:37-38).	"Departed not from the temple, but served God . . . night and day" Luke 2:37
Jn 8:1-2, 12, 18, 24, 28-29, 42, 44, 58-59 Feast of Tabernacles	"I am the light of the world," he proclaimed, and "the Father that sent me beareth witness of me" / "Before Abraham was, I am"	"these words spake Jesus in the treasury, as he taught in the temple" (John 8:20).
John 10:23-25, 27-38 During the Feast of the Dedication	"How long dost thou make us to doubt? If thou be the Christ, tell us plainly" (10:24). "I and my Father are one" (10:30).	the Savior again testified plainly of his redemptive role, while he "walked in the temple in Solomon's porch" (Jn 10:23)
John 5 Feast of the Passover	The entire chapter is a direct statement of the Lord of his atoning mission	"Jesus findeth him in the temple" (5:14)
John 6	I am the Bread of Life	Synagogue at Capernaum

Matthew 17:1–2, 5 The Transfiguration	This is my beloved Son, in whom I am well pleased; hear ye him. (Mt. 17:5)	"After 6 days Jesus taketh Peter, James, and John . . . and bringeth them up into an high mountain apart"
Luke 22:39, 41–42, 44 Atonement in Gethsemane	And being in agony, he prayed more earnestly: and his sweat was as it were great drops of blood falling down to the ground. (Luke 22: 44)	And he came out, and went, as he was wont, to the mount of Olives
John 4:10, 14, 20–26: To the Woman of Samaria	When "the Messias cometh, which is called Christ . . . he will tell us all things." "I that speak unto thee am he" (John 4:25–26).	"Our fathers worshipped in this mountain . . ." John 4:20–21
Luke 22:19–20 The Last Supper (The Passover Meal)	"This cup is the new testament in my blood, which is shed for you" (Luke 22:20)	"a large upper room" (Luke 22:12)

Chart 3.3.1

Qualities of Sacred Covenants / Specific Covenant	An Undeviating Standard or Template to measure the rightness of our attitudes and actions: the same standard for each person who receives it (Teaches us: "How to Know What is Right")	A Just Standard for Judgment—since each person's faithfulness is measured by the exact same standard	Always Accompanied by the gift of power and grace to enable those who receive it to keep it (Empowers us: "To Do What is Right")	Immediate Reward for Faithful Acceptance: A Manifestation of the Savior (which also empowers the receiver to Know and Do What is Right and therefore, to keep the covenant)	Eternal Reward for Faithful Dedication to the Covenant:
Sacrament (and Baptism) Covenant					
Priesthood Covenant					
Abrahamic Covenant					
Temple Covenants					
The Savior (The Mediator of the New Covenant)					
The Book of Mormon: The New & Everlasting Covenant					

Chart 3.3.2: Shared Qualities and Blessings among Sacred Covenants

Qualities of Sacred Covenants / Specific Covenant	An Undeviating Standard or Template to measure the rightness of our attitudes and actions: the same standard for each person who receives it (Teaches us: "How to Know What is Right")	A Just Standard for Judgment—since each person's faithfulness is measured by the exact same standard	Always Accompanied by the gift of power and grace to enable those who receive it to keep it (Empowers us: "To Do What is Right")	Immediate Reward for Faithful Acceptance: A Manifestation of the Savior (which also empowers the receiver to Know and Do What is Right and therefore, to keep the covenant)	Eternal Reward for Faithful Dedication to the Covenant:
Sacrament (and Baptism) Covenant	Each and every person has the exact same standard: the words of sacrament prayer DC 20:77-79; Moroni 4 & 5; 3 Ne.18:6	Must be spoken exactly so that each person is held to same standard; 3 Ne. 18:13; 2 Ne.31:14-16	Accompanied by Power and Grace of the Lord's Spirit—to keep the covenant 3 Ne. 18:12	The Presence of the Spirit of the Lord: "that they may always have His spirit to with them" See also 3 Ne.20:8	"thus saith the Father: ye shall have eternal life" 2 Nephi 31:13-15, 20 3 Ne. 20:8;
Priesthood Covenant	"Without beginning of days or end of years" DC 84:17-18, 33, 35; Alma 13:7	"Whoso is faithful ..." ""All those who receive this Priesthood" DC 84:33, 35, 40-42, 46-48; Alma 13:5	"Sanctified by the Spirit unto the renewing of their bodies" "I have given the heavenly hosts and mine angels charge concerning you'" DC39:11-12; 84:33, 42, 88	"Key of the knowledge of God," that through the priesthood "the power of godliness is manifest" DC 84:19, 35	"all that my Father hath shall be given unto him" DC 84:38

Qualities of Sacred Covenants / Specific Covenant	An Undeviating Standard or Template to measure the rightness of our attitudes and actions: the same standard for each person who receives it (Teaches us: "How to Know What is Right")	A Just Standard for Judgment—since each person's faithfulness is measured by the exact same standard	Always Accompanied by the gift of power and grace to enable those who receive it to keep it (Empowers us: "To Do What is Right")	Immediate Reward for Faithful Acceptance: A Manifestation of the Savior (which also empowers the receiver to Know and Do What is Right and therefore, to keep the covenant)	Eternal Reward for Faithful Dedication to the Covenant:
Abrahamic Covenant	Renewed (DC 84:48) Everlasting (DC 1:22); Alma 13:22-23, 26	"the Father teaches...of the covenant which he has renewed and confirmed upon you" DC 84:35-42, 48	"and my power shall be over thee" Abr. 1:18	"Through thy ministry, my name shall be made known [or manifested] in the earth" Abr. 1:19	Eternal Life: Abraham 2:11
Temple Covenants	Temple = Template = Sacred Standard of Truth & Righteousness	Each person is held to the very same standard	"armed with thy power" DC 109:13, 22, 35, 38, 15	"that the Son of Man my have a place to manifest himself" DC 109:5, 12, 13; 110:7	Eternal Life: DC 109:75-76

Qualities of Sacred Covenants / Specific Covenant	An Undeviating Standard or Template to measure the rightness of our attitudes and actions: the same standard for each person who receives it (Teaches us: "How to Know What is Right")	A Just Standard for Judgment—since each person's faithfulness is measured by the exact same standard	Always Accompanied by the gift of power and grace to enable those who receive it to keep it (Empowers us: "To Do What is Right")	Immediate Reward for Faithful Acceptance: A Manifestation of the Savior (which also empowers the receiver to Know and Do What is Right and therefore, to keep the covenant)	Eternal Reward for Faithful Dedication to the Covenant:
The Savior (The Mediator of the New Covenant)	The same from all eternity to all eternity 3 Nephi 27:21, 27; 3 Ne.12:48; 18:6, 16, 24; Jn. 13:15; 14:6	2 Ne. 31:16-17; John 15:6; Alma 12:33; DC 93:31; DC 84:50-53	"If ye will have faith in me, ye shall have power" Moroni 7:33, 48; 10:32-33; 3 Ne. 9:17; Eth. 12:27; 2 Ne.12, 13, 18, Jn. 15:4-5	"I will sup with him" Rev. 3:20; DC 88:63; DC 93:1, 20	Eternal Life: 3 Ne. 9:17
The Book of Mormon: The New & Everlasting Covenant	"I speak the same words unto one nation like unto another" 2 Nephi 32:3; 33:10; 31:17; 1 Ne. 13:41; 2 Nephi 29:8, 2	"shall judge them at the last day" 2 Nephi 25:18, 22, 28; 29:11; 33:14, 15; DC 84:57; 20:13-15	"by the power of the Lord [The Book of Mormon] shall bring my people unto salvation" 2 Ne. 3:12; 3 Ne. 21:6; 1 Ne.14:1	"Jesus Christ, who hath been manifest by the things which we have written" Eth. 2:12; 1Ne. 13:40; 14:1; 15:13-15	Eternal Life: DC 20:14; 2 Ne. 33:4

Chart 3.5.1: 2 Nephi 25–33: Nephi's Second Vision

In this Chapter of the Book of Mormon…	…The Manifestation of the Messiah (or of the anti-Messiah) and the Covenants are Offered to this group…	…through the instrumentality of:
2 Nephi 25	Nephi prophesies of the manifestation of the Messiah and his Covenants to which group in this chapter (25:12-14)? Though they rejected the Messiah and crucified him (see 2 Ne.25:10-13), what will again be offered this group in the latter days (25:11, 16-18)?	What does Nephi say will be the instrument used to accomplish these things (25:16-18, 21-23, 26-28)? How is that instrument being used right now to fulfill Nephi's prophecy—even as we now read? In other words, how is the Messiah made clearly manifest in this very chapter as we read (see 25:13, 19-29). What effect are Nephi's words having on you right now? What difference will they make in your life?
2 Nephi 26	Nephi at first prophesies of the manifestation of the Messiah and his Covenants (and their rejection) to which group in this chapter (26:1-10)? Though they rejected the Messiah, what will again be offered this group in the latter days (26:14-19)?	What does Nephi say will be the instrument used to accomplish these things (26:14-17)? How is that instrument being used right now to fulfill Nephi's prophecy—ever- as we now read? In other words, how is the Messiah (and his Messianic qualities) made clearly manifest in this very chapter as we now read (see esp. 26: 3-11, 23-28, 33)? What effect are Nephi's words having on you right now? What difference will they make in your life?
2 Nephi 27	Nephi prophesies of the manifestation of the Messiah and his Covenants to which groups in this chapter (27:1, 5)? What does Nephi say will be the instrument used to accomplish these things (27:6-11, 13-14, 26-35)?	What distinguishes those who respect and receive "the book" spoken of in this chapter from those who don't (see esp. 2 Nephi 27:16, 23-26, 30-32)? Which of the two groups will you join? Why? How are you doing that right now?

2 Nephi 28	Whose efforts and tactics is Nephi now clearly making manifest in this chapter? In what way are these efforts meant to abrogate the need for a Messiah (28:7-9, 21-22)? In what ways will the adversary seek to undermine faith in the latter days (28:4-6, 9, 11-15, 26) How will you resist these attempts?	What does Nephi say will be the primary focus of the adversary in the latter days—to keep people from receiving the Messiah and the Covenants, as well as to deny the Lord's power and continued ministry in the latter days (28:26-31, 16, 20, 32)? Why would the adversary focus on this target or instrument? How will you resist such tactics of the adversary? How are you right now responding to his tactics? How does this focus of the adversary teach us that the Book of Mormon is the manifestation of the Messiah?
2 Nephi 29	In what way does the Lord tell us he chooses to make himself manifest and to fulfill his covenants with Abraham and Israel in the latter days (29:1-2, 7-14)? What does this teach us about the purpose of the Book of Mormon? How does this chapter continue to make manifest the efforts of the adversary to keep us from receiving the Messiah and his covenants?	To keep us from the Messiah and his covenants, what will the adversary seek to undermine (29:3-6)? Why would the adversary focus on this target or instrument? How will you resist such tactics of the adversary? How are you right now responding to his tactics? How does this focus of the adversary teach us that the Book of Mormon is the manifestation of the Messiah?
2 Nephi 30	In this chapter, the Lord celebrates what events and blessings that shall occur in the latter days (30:2, 6-9, 15-18)? To whom shall these blessings occur (30:1-2, 4)?	What does the Lord make clear will be the instrument for the successful fulfillment of these great events (30:3-8)? What does this teach us about the sacred role of the Book of Mormon? How is that role now being fulfilled for you? What difference will it make?

2 Nephi 31	To whom is Nephi directly speaking to in this chapter? Since we have clearly seen the choices we must make between the plain manifestations and witnesses of the Messiah (as well as the anti-Messiah, or the adversary), what natural choice does Nephi make clear we must now make—if we would now receive and follow the manifested Messiah (31:5-13, 16, 18-20)? What, as always, follows such a choice (31:14, 17-18)? Why (31:16)? So that we can gain the power to do what? How can we continue to exercise that faith (31:20)? How complete and comprehensive is the manifestation and invitation we have just received (31:21)?	In order to follow Nephi's (and the Lord's) invitation, in what (or in whom) must we exercise faith right now (31:2, 12-13, 17, 21)? In what way have we shown our "unshaken faith in [the Savior]" up to this point (31:19)? What responsibility that does place upon us? What does this teach us about how the Book of Mormon contains the fulness of the Gospel? What is the fulness of the Gospel? Can it be anything less than a full and complete manifestation of the Savior? Is the manifestation we are now receiving in any way less than complete or full? What does this teach us about the sacred role of the Book of Mormon?
2 Nephi 32	Now that we currently know what is the right thing to do, what does Nephi tell us we need to do in order to continue to know what is right (32:1-6)? Besides knowing what is right, what second challenge do we still face each day? How does Nephi teach us we can gain and maintain each day the power to continue to do what we know is right (32:8-9)?	According to Nephi, how complete and thorough is the manifestation and doctrine of Christ that he has just given to us in these pages (4, 6-7)? What is the relation between verses three and four in this chapter? What does this teach us about the sacred role of the Book of Mormon? What does this teach you about how you should treat and use the Book of Mormon in your life? What goals should you now make?

Chart 3.5.2: Summary of Chart 3.5.1

In this Chapter of the Book of Mormon . . .	. . . The Manifestation of the Messiah (or of the anti-Messiah) and the Covenants are Offered . . .	. . . through the Book of Mormon
2 Nephi 25	Nephi's witness and manifestation of the Messiah and His Covenants to Judah: though Judah rejected the Messiah and crucified him (see 2 Ne.25:10–13), Redemption once again will be offered Judah in the latter days—	—when Judah accepts the Messiah as the Book of Mormon makes Him manifest (25:16–18, 21): i.e., "until they shall be persuaded to believe in Christ, the Son of God, and the atonement, which is infinite for all mankind . . . and not look forward any more for another Messiah, then at that time . . . it must needs be expedient that they should believe these things" ". . . for this cause hath the Lord God promised unto me that these things which I write shall be kept & preserved." (25:13, 19–29) And that manifestation clearly occurs even as we read this chapter
2 Nephi 26	Nephi's witness and manifestation of the Messiah and His Covenants to his seed, the Nephites and Lamanites as well as to the Gentiles: And though the Nephites ultimately rejected the Messiah and His Covenants (26:3–8, 9–10), both before and after his physical appearance to them, and though the Gentiles will be in a state of unbelief (26:20–22).	. . . the words of the Book of Mormon will whisper from the dust to them as an invitation from the Lord to repent and come unto Him (26:13, 16, 27, 33): ". . . it must needs be that the Gentiles be convinced also that Jesus is the Christ, the Eternal God; and that he manifesteth himself unto all those who believe in him, by the power of the Holy Ghost. . . . when the Lord God shall bring these things forth" "[The Nephites] shall speak unto them out of the ground . . . and their voice shall be as one that hath a familiar spirit . . . and their speech shall whisper out of the dust" This instrument is being used right now to fulfill Nephi's prophecy by manifesting to us some of the Messiah's most salient qualities: his justice (26:3–6, 10–11, 29–32) and mercy (26:8–9); and also his openness: "the Lord God worketh not in darkness" "and he doeth nothing save it be plain unto the children of men"; love: "He doeth not anything save it be for the benefit of the world; for he layeth down his own life that he may draw all men unto him"; equity & fairness: "all men are privileged the one like unto another. . . . Black and white, bond and free, male and female . . . the heathen; and all are alike unto God" (26:23,24, 27–28,33).

2 Nephi 27	Nephi's witness and testimony that the Messiah will make himself (27:23) and His Covenants (27:11,14,29-35) manifest and available to both the apostate and lost Jew and Gentile (27:1, 5) in the latter days—	... through the Book of Mormon (27:6-11, 13, 26, 27-30). "the Lord God shall bring forth the words of a book, and they shall be the words of them which have slumbered.... [and] the words of the faithful should speak as if it were from the dead"
2 Nephi 28	Nephi now clearly makes manifest the efforts and tactics of the adversary to keep people from receiving the Messiah and the Covenants as well as to deny the Lord's power and continued ministry in the latter days. The adversary will attempt to keep people away from the Savior in two ways, which are interrelated: 1) by attempting to deny the power of the Book of Mormon and to turn them away from the Book of Mormon; and 2) by attempting to deny the reality, justice, and power of God as well as the reality and need for the atonement of Christ.,	1) His attempts to keep us from the Book of Mormon or to cause us to undervalue the Book of Mormon (28: 4-6, 14-16, 20, 26-31), through persuading us to: Deny the power of the Holy Ghost to give utterance Deny the current hand and power of God at work among his children Deny the possibility of miracles (such as revelation, tongues, translation) Look upon the things of God as "of no worth" Accept that truth can only be discerned through the tools of mortal, material, natural, man—through man's limited wisdom and learning Agree that we don't need or want further revelations from God 2) His attempts to convince people that they don't need to come unto the Messiah who is made manifest in the Book of Mormon (28:7-9, 21-22) by: Denying the Justice of God Denying the reality of sin and punishment for the consequences of sin Denying the reality of the devil and of evil Putting trust in man instead of God Denying Christ himself

2 Nephi 29	The Lord tells Nephi He will help fulfill his covenants with Abraham and Israel (29:1-2, 7-14) ...	... through the Book of Mormon: "I shall proceed to do a marvelous work ... that I may remember my covenants which I have made unto the children of men.... And that the words of your seed [Nephi] should proceed forth out of my mouth ... unto the ends of the earth, for a standard unto my people" "Wherefore, I speak the same words... and I do this that I may prove that I am the same yesterday, today, and forever.... For out of the books which shall be written I will judge the world, every man according to their works, according to that which is written" In this way, "I will show ... that I am God, and that I covenanted with Abraham that I would remember his seed forever" and of the foolish rejection of these further manifestations of the Lord and his covenants: "And because my words shall hiss forth—many of the Gentiles shall say: A Bible! A Bible! We have got a Bible and there cannot be any more Bible"
2 Nephi 30	Nephi makes clear how the covenants and blessings of the Lord are available to all who repent and accept the manifestations and covenants ...	... made available through the Book of Mormon (30:2-57): "the Lord covenanteth with none save it be with them that repent and believe in his Son.... And now I would prophecy somewhat more... for after the book of which I have spoken shall come forth.... there shall be many which shall believe the words that are written... and the gospel of Jesus Christ shall be declared among them; wherefore, they shall be restored unto the knowledge of their fathers, and also to the knowledge of Jesus Christ... " "And then shall they rejoice; for the shall know that it is a blessing unto them from the hand of God; and their scales of darkness shall begin to fall from their eyes..."
2 Nephi 31	Nephi makes clear the blessings that come to those who accept, exercise faith in the manifestations of the Messiah and His Covenants ...	through the Book of Mormon, which, of course, includes the words that Nephi is now writing (31:2, 17, 21), and therefore repent: their acceptance of these things is certified through the covenant of Baptism, after which they may receive the gift of Holy Ghost.
2 Nephi 32	Nephi tells us what to do next: Look, you just received a plain manifestation of the Messiah.	... through these words I have given you (32:4, 6)—so continue to search these words through the gift of the Holy Ghost and prayer, and you will thereby continue to feel His presence and guidance and power.

ABOUT THE AUTHOR

R aised as a New York Catholic, TERRY GORTON embraced the Lord's restored gospel and Church while serving as a US Army medic in Germany. A life-long love for language, literature, and the Book of Mormon has led him to teach both humanities and Book of Mormon classes at BYU (in Utah and Idaho) and Stony Brook University in New York. It has also led to several shoeboxes full of index card sets each labeled "The Plates of Terry," from which the ideas for this book emerged (though computer files have lately replaced index cards and shoe boxes). Such interests have also motivated him to assemble perhaps the greatest collection of inspired poetry in support of the principles of the gospel—as well as occasionally to compose his own. However, "there is no greater poetry," Terry adds, "than a summer hike in the mountains with Lisa, Carli, and Nikki."